Lost in Transition

Contemporary Hispanic and Lusophone Cultures

Series Editor
L. Elena Delgado, University of Illinois at Urbana-Champaign
Niamh Thornton, University of Liverpool

Series Editorial Board
Jo Labanyi, New York University
Chris Perriam, University of Manchester
Paul Julian Smith, CUNY Graduate Center

This series aims to provide a forum for new research on modern and contemporary hispanic and lusophone cultures and writing. The volumes published in Contemporary Hispanic and Lusophone Cultures reflect a wide variety of critical practices and theoretical approaches, in harmony with the intellectual, cultural and social developments that have taken place over the past few decades. All manifestations of contemporary hispanic and lusophone culture and expression are considered, including literature, cinema, popular culture, theory. The volumes in the series will participate in the wider debate on key aspects of contemporary culture.

Lost in Transition

Constructing Memory in Contemporary Spain

H. ROSI SONG

LIVERPOOL UNIVERSITY PRESS

First published 2016 by
Liverpool University Press
4 Cambridge Street
Liverpool
L69 7ZU

Copyright © 2016 H. Rosi Song

British Library Cataloguing-in-Publication data
A British Library CIP record is available

ISBN 978-1-78138-287-5 cased

Typeset in Borges by
Carnegie Book Production, Lancaster
Printed and bound in Poland by BooksFactory.co.uk

Contents

Acknowledgements

Writing a book, it turns out, takes a global village. It really does. I cannot count the many ways in which I have been helped by colleagues and friends living and working all over the world, who have kept me focused on this project to the end with their support and constant encouragement. My interest in the Spanish *Transición* began many years ago, perhaps explained by the fact that I missed living through my own political transition twice: once in the place where I was born, and again in the place where I grew up. Looking back, all of my scholarly research has been related in one way or another to this period in Spanish politics and culture, attempting to understand what political change means, how it affects individuals and their everyday lives, and, most importantly, what sort of stories are told about those experiences. The past has always haunted my imagination: from my mother's recollections of the Korean War to the many versions of why and how my family ended up moving to South America, I have always been interested in hearing these repeated versions of the past. I have enjoyed these memories not for the truth they contained, but for all of the times they have allowed me to discover unexpected links to my present. Small and seemingly unimportant details have the potential to become powerful memories and unforgettable lessons. I will never look at a blister on my foot without hearing my mother tell me about hers escaping the war and how I learned to treat them despite the pain in order to be able to walk again the following day.

Walking and writing, repeatedly and without pain, has always been possible because of the support of colleagues and friends. I am grateful to María Fernanda Lander, who has consistently been there for me over two decades, as a friend, a colleague, and a trusted reader of my work. To Wadda Ríos-Font for her support and friendship, and for all the fabulous travelling we have done together over the years. I have been lucky to find a supportive group in my field of study, from whom I have learned so much over the years; I am constantly inspired by their thinking and research, our scholarly collaborations, our conference meetings, and friendly digital exchanges. I am deeply thankful to William J. Nichols, Robert Davidson, Francisco Fernández de Alba, Cristina Moreiras-Menor, Malcolm Compitello, Alberto Mira, Elena Luisa Delgado, Joseba Gabilondo, Mary Ann Newman, Paul Julian Smith, Jo Labanyi, James D. Fernández, Benita Sampedro, Leigh Mercer, Jerelyn Johnson, Ofelia Ferrán, Ana Corbalán, Sohyun Lee, and Annabel Martín. Special thanks are in order for Jorge Marí for the fun presentation on the 23-F we put together for the 2015 Cine-Lit. Thanks to José F. Colmeiro for making a cameo appearance during our paper and to Marcela T. Garcés for organising the panel. To Steven Marsh for letting me use his photograph of the 15-M on the cover of this book and to Txetxu Aguado for sending me a copy of his monograph on memory in Spain at the precise moment when I needed it. Finally, I am immensely grateful to Enric Bou, from whose knowledge, wisdom, and support I have benefitted for so many years. Always ready to lend a hand and generous with his time and encouraging words, he brought much joy to my academic wandering with an invitation to join him for a semester in Venice. Having finished the last corrections to the manuscript in this city floating on a magical lagoon, my memories of this book will always be tied to its enchanting landscape. Thank you.

My work and life at Bryn Mawr College would not be as productive or satisfying without the brilliant colleagues I work with and have the privilege of calling friends: Homay King, Bethany Schneider, Kate Thomas, Sharon Ullman, Camilla MacKay, Michelle Mancini, Hoang Tan Nguyen, Elly Truitt, Ignacio Gallup-Díaz, Jennifer Hartford-Vargas, and Shiamin Kwa. Special thanks go to Bethany and Kate once more for all the amazing meals they have prepared for me and for the timely drinks they have offered me over the years. And also to Sharon, without whose companionship every day last summer as my writing partner (and fellow soccer watcher), I would not have finished this book.

I will always be thankful to my departmental colleagues, who have consistently been supportive of my work: María Cristina Quintero, Inés Arribas, Kaylea Mayer, Enrique Sacerio-Garí, and Martín Gaspar, and to my colleagues in the Spanish departments at Haverford and Swarthmore: María Luisa Guardiola, Luciano Martínez, Nanci Buiza, Adrián Gras-Velázquez, Israel Burshatin, Ana López-Sánchez, Roberto Castillo Sandoval, Graciela Michelotti, and Aurelia Gómez Unamuno. My life is constantly enhanced by the wonderful support and caring friendship of Oliva Cardona.

Thanks also for the patience and editing skills of Camilla MacKay, my awesome student Emily McBride, and the magic wand of Caitlin Keenan. To Alex Wescott for his attention to the index of this book. I have been very lucky to work with Anthony Cond, editor at Liverpool University Press, who welcomed my initial proposal and patiently and generously guided me through the process of finishing this project. Thanks too to the external readers for their insightful comments to the early version of the manuscript. To the editorial team at Liverpool University Press and especially to Rachel Adamson from Carnegie Book Production. I am grateful to the Office of the Provost at Bryn Mawr College for providing financial support to cover editing costs; to the Cañada Blanch Centre for Contemporary Spanish Studies and to Paul Preston for hosting me as a visiting scholar during the academic year 2012–13; and to the Dipartimento de Studi Linguistici e Culturali Comparati at Università Ca'Foscari Venezia, where I spent a happy semester as a Visiting Professor in the fall of 2015.

My deepest gratitude goes to Kim, Rosa, and Xènia Coromines-Rizvi, who welcomed me into their family in Barcelona. I am grateful to Montse, Aitor, and Leire Zuloaga-Gil for being part of my social and culinary world when I am in the Catalan capital. Other friends and colleagues in Philadelphia and beyond who have offered friendship and support over the years include, in no particular order, Imke Meyer, Heidi Schlipphacke, Todd Shepard, Juan Arbona, Chris Farr, Anita Bechtholt, Virginia Chang, Marcelo Sánchez, Saïd Gaia, Dredge Kang, Tick Ahearn, Tim McCall, Farid Azfar, Raji Mohan, Nilgün Uygun, and Henry Sias. Thanks to Bob and Fran for letting me be part of their underground kitchen crew. I also thank my brother B. Jerry Song and his family for their continued support.

Finally, I dedicate this book to my parents: to my father, who embarked my family on a wild adventure four decades ago, and to my mother, who lived this craziness with love and unmeasurable generosity to those around her. And my deepest gratitude and love to Duncan Black, who willingly and lovingly became part of my multi-everything world.

Part of the discussion on the Spanish Law of Historical Memory was included in my article 'Visual Fictions of the Spanish Civil War', published in *MLN* 129 (2014): 367–90 © 2014 by Johns Hopkins University Press.

Introduction

History is hysterical: it is constituted only if we consider it,
only if we look at it—and in order to look at it,
we must be excluded from it.
Roland Barthes, *Camera Lucida*, 65

On 23 March 2014, while I was writing this book, Adolfo Suárez died. Afflicted by Alzheimer's, the politician most associated with the political transformation of Spain into a democracy following the death of General Francisco Franco in 1975 lived much of his later life away from the public eye. His death had been expected for a few days and the headlines of the Spanish dailies predictably highlighted his role in the *Transición*. This coverage explicitly identified Suárez's persona with this political process, and the front-page photographs of him, repeatedly juxtaposed with the word *transición*, reinforced this direct association. While this intimate identification had long been made, official recollections of this era, such as that offered by King Juan Carlos on the day of Suárez's death, cemented this connection:

> Pero el dolor no es obstáculo para recordar y valorar uno de los capítulos más brillantes de la Historia de España: la Transición que, protagonizada por el pueblo español, impulsamos Adolfo y yo junto con un excepcional grupo de personas de diferentes ideologías, unidos por una gran generosidad y un alto sentido del patriotismo. Un capítulo que dio paso al período de mayor progreso económico, social y político de nuestro país.[1]

What has become evident in recent years, however, is that this version of the past is no longer sustainable. For many, the king's speech served as another

---

1 The text of this speech can be found in Junqueras (2014).

reminder of how much has been forgotten in Spain. Fuelled by the ongoing financial crisis, grassroots protest movements such as the 15-M of 2011–12 have challenged the memory of the *Transición*. The rise of the populist party Podemos, the demand for a referendum in Catalonia in 2013–14, and the string of political scandals covered in the press all reflect a broader questioning of the triumphant rhetoric surrounding the Spanish transition. The remembered brilliance of this period, along with the economic, social, and political progress recalled in the speech above, seems painfully at odds with the daily coverage of Spanish politics and finance. The struggles reported in the press, involving both the main right-wing and left-wing political parties, have revealed deep-seated problems that go beyond current economic and political challenges to the country's democratic system. The financial crisis that began in 2008 became an ideological struggle that quickly transformed into a critical inquiry into the nation's troubled past.

Ironically, this sense of crisis has also reinforced for some the mythical status of the Spanish *Transición*. As one of *La Vanguardia*'s headlines stated, 'Spain in crisis elevates Adolfo Suárez to the category of myth' ('La España en crisis eleva a Adolfo Suárez a la categoría de mito').[2] Here, the triumphant memory of—or perhaps, the forgetting of the true nature of—Spain's political shift has worked to counter the narratives of the nation's ongoing financial and political crisis. Curiously, what both positions reveal is an intimate connection between the troubled political and financial present and what happened during the period of the *Transición*. Though the narrative of Spain's political transformation has been under scrutiny since the 1980s, it is only now that the foundational pieces of this triumphant story are being challenged directly.[3]

Lost in Transition examines this challenge through a close reading of recent films, television series, and novels that revisit the political period of Spain's transformation from a dictatorship into a democracy. The memories narrated and represented in these works derive from what I call a 'memory project' in which a generation of writers, filmmakers, and TV producers born in the sixties and early seventies obsessively revisit this period in an effort to capture and narrate the experience of political change. I characterise these memories as 'projects' because of the way the *Transición* is perceived: as an open question or a conundrum to be solved individually and collectively.

2 Headline available at http://www.lavanguardia.com/politica/20140324/54404 368641/adolfo-suarez-mito-espana-crisis.html. Accessed 24 March 2014.

3 Case in point: around the time of Suárez's death, the long-time conservative journalist Pilar Urbano published a highly controversial book entitled *La gran desmemoria. Lo que Suárez olvidó y el Rey prefiere no recordar* (2014), in which she suggests that the Spanish king is not exactly a hero of the political transformation in Spain.

In this context, the term 'project' refers to the nature of the undertaking of these memories. The recollections are carefully planned and broken down into details, reflecting a desire to achieve a particular objective. The goal is to recreate conditions that facilitate the possibility of experiencing the past *in the present* through affect, intimate connection, or as an extension of one's self or one's current circumstances. For this reason, the past in these works is often positioned in direct reference to the present, establishing a causal connection between what *has been* and what currently *is*. A relationship of contiguity is also established in which the physicality of the past can be found embodied in objects, places, or gestures. To better understand this relationship, I engage with the period of the *Transición* through a flexible, representational relationship that allows different modes of signification. While such a contextual method of engagement may not always be historically accurate or comprehensive, the meaning of the past depends on its connection to and with the present. The *Transición* has acquired increasing relevance today precisely because of the way it is positioned in relation to current events. As Michel-Rolph Trouillot writes in *Silencing the Past*, the past is only the past because there is a present; 'pastness' is but a position (15). I examine this 'positioning' in two separate ways: first, as a logical continuation of the discussion regarding the suppressed and traumatic memory of the Spanish Civil War and the repression of Franco's dictatorship and, second, as a generational experience that reflects an affective and physical relationship with the past.

The written and visual texts I analyse in this book expose how the years of the political transition, between the end of Franco's dictatorship in 1975 and the victory of the Socialist Party in 1982, represents an unfinished (or not quite understood) chapter in Spanish history. By collecting and blending archival materials, personal recollections, and the cultural events of these years, the texts produce a comprehensive memory of the *Transición* that emphasises the notion of an open-ended task inviting intervention from the present. These memories establish a relationship between history and subjectivity that forces a continuation of the debate about the legacy of the Spanish Civil War, a conflict that took place more than three quarters of a century ago, yet remains closely connected to Spain's ongoing political, historical, and cultural conversation. The recollections I explore also reveal a relationship with history based on affect, where past and present events merge and permeate daily life. In this practice, historical referents are turned into flexible signs that permit an endless renewal of the relationship between present and past.

A couple of months after Suárez's death, King Juan Carlos I announced his abdication from the throne in favour of his son Felipe, who was crowned

Felipe VI on 19 June 2015. His coronation took place amid large protests calling for the return of the republic. The royal family, embroiled in family scandals that ranged from corruption charges to paternity suits, quietly defended its place in the future of Spanish politics. Its claim to the country's destiny and its democratic identity was emphasised and strengthened in numerous newspaper editorials and columns that intimately tied together the result of the *Transición* and the person of King Juan Carlos I. Among those who reinforced this association was novelist Javier Cercas, who went so far as to declare that '[s]in el Rey no habría democracia'.[4] The departure of the king has become part of a final effort to cement the foundational myths of Spain's democracy and its political project after the end of the Franco dictatorship. In both the king's speech and reports in the media, we witness an attempt to put the still-contested memory of this time to rest.

In 1996, Manuel Vázquez Montalbán interviewed King Juan Carlos I on the eve of Spain's general elections—elections that signalled the revival of the conservative Partido Popular (PP) that would, four years later, achieve a ruling majority. The writer's journey to meet the king is cast as a voyage down memory lane, recounting a political adventure that began with the death of Francisco Franco and ended, symbolically, with the failed coup d'état of 1981, later known as '23-F'. When Vázquez Montalbán meets the king, he mentions the subsequent media coverage of the 23-F that connected Juan Carlos I with the events of that day. Listening to Juan Carlos I talk about 23 February, however, Vázquez Montalbán comes to the realisation that kings have no memory (nor, for that matter, do they write memoirs). Unlike the president of a republic, a king cannot openly reveal his own perspective. The writer concludes that perhaps kings are 'condenados a no tener memoria' (Vázquez Montalbán 2006: 446). Almost two decades later, the departure of the king confirmed this absence of memory and signalled the end of a political cycle. The burden of the memory of the *Transición*, once embodied in the political careers of Suárez and Juan Carlos I, now resides elsewhere, but its recollection remains as urgent as ever.

---

4 In his column for *El País*, Cercas explains that '[l]a abdicación es, verosímilmente, el último servicio fundamental que Juan Carlos I va a hacerle a este país'. The novelist reviews the king's three services to the country: his role in bringing democracy to Spain, his intervention to stop the 23-F (a contended version of history, as I shall discuss in this book), and, finally, his abdication. Cercas believes that the state of Spain's democracy is not only the fault of its founding fathers, who have certainly made mistakes, but also of a collective 'we' to which his own generation belongs (Cercas 2014).

CHAPTER ONE

Transitional Memories

*Me quejo de que no hay ningún modelo nuevo y de que los modelos
viejos no sirven, para mí, que siempre me ha gustado cruzar el
charco de las transgresiones. Ahora no me queda espacio para
la transgresión, como antes. Y no somos tan mayores, ¿verdad?*
Manuel Vázquez Montalbán, *Un polaco en la corte del Rey Juan Carlos*, 37

The political period between the death of dictator Francisco Franco in
November 1975 and the victory of the Socialist Party (PSOE) in the
general election of 1982, widely known as the *Transición*, has been held up by
many as a model of successful political transformation from an authoritarian
regime to a democratic government. Yet criticisms of this period abound,
and discussions of the means and ends of this political and cultural
transformation continue. Previous historical, literary, and cultural studies
have emphasised the imperfect nature of the *Transición*'s accomplishments,
and many critics contend that essential political, socioeconomic, and cultural
changes, necessary to transform a post-dictatorial society, were not tackled
directly by the politicians of the time. Indeed, the 1980s are commonly
understood as years of disenchantment, trauma, and melancholy during
which Spaniards struggled with the vestiges of Franco's regime.

More than 30 years after the *Transición*, recollections of this period are
beginning to resurface. The visual and literary texts I examine in this book
are representative of this renewed attention and, while the selection of works
I present is certainly not exhaustive, they share an important generational
imprint. The experiences of their creators, born into the same cohort,
can be traced through their complex cultural representations and critical
discussions of the (memory of the) Spanish Civil War, the dictatorship,
and the transition. These authors and artists are familiar with trauma and
understand the complexities and politics involved in the act of remembering.
Their work exposes the evolution that has taken place in the treatment of

memory, through which Spain's political past has become a flexible referent with multiple connotations with (and to) the present. The persistence of (and the renewed insistence on) this connection to the present in recollections of the past demands a closer look—one that takes into account the specificities of a cohort of Spanish artists who came of age in the late 1970s and the early 1980s. I use the term 'evolution' in this context to indicate the fluidity of memory and to acknowledge the significance of the passage of time to the production and proliferation of a generational experience. Throughout the text, I couch this memory work as a 'project', one that is unfinished and feels in need of completion. The detailed yet repetitive narration of the past is a laborious and fiercely subjective enterprise.

The current relevance of the *Transición* can be characterised without exaggeration as a 'generational moment'. As Germán Labrador observes, the years of political transformation in Spain exposed the tension felt by those born after the war regarding the world to which their parents belonged: 'allí, el franquismo, sus valores, sus estructuras, se sentían viejos, no sólo ideológica sino también demográficamente' (77). Recent recollections of this period have shifted focus from the political to the personal, seeking to narrate the behaviour, values, and belief systems of the Spanish people during the years of the *Transición*. Considering that the impact of Spain's democratisation was felt most keenly by the youth, the men and women of this generational group are particularly well situated to convey the experiences of those years: how Spanish citizens of the time adopted and exercised their freedoms and values even before they were recognised by law (78).[1] The recent work of journalists like Guillem Martínez, in his collection *CT o la Cultura de la Transición* (2012), likewise articulates a generational position. While the identification of a transitional culture bears certain negative connotations (inasmuch as it inherently questions the ability of the intellectuals and artists of that time to truly transform Spanish society), it does articulate the idea that there exists a specific cohort affected by these shortcomings. As it was part of the status quo and defended by the political forces of the time, Spanish culture after the dictatorship was not so vulnerable to change. The young generation of the *Transición* was the group most constrained by the cultural practices of the past.

The Spanish population that came of age during the *Transición* first came into focus as a generational collective through the work of historian

---

1 While it is hard to characterise this generation precisely, it can be described in general terms as belonging to the middle class and as having been college educated in the 1960s and 1970s. Labrador describes how the transition was felt (and lived) within this group through the use of psychoactive drugs (psycopharmacology) (78).

Pablo Sánchez León, himself part of this cohort. This group, he says, 'no se destacaron precisamente por el interés en reabrir al debate público esas parcela de la historia reciente: no habían desde luego vivido los acontecimientos y, como la mayoría de los españoles, atravesaron la transición necesariamente en medio del olvido instituido acerca del tema' (163).[2] Despite having come of age in a society that was working to forget and reject the memory of the Spanish Civil War, the members of this cohort remained connected to the memories of this conflict through their families and the political realities of post-war Spain. Shaped as they were by recollections of the war, an understanding of the experiences of this generation in confronting transition-era narratives can give crucial aid in comprehending the ongoing debate about memory in contemporary Spain. Traditionally, this debate has centred on the need for a more open, inclusive history of the Spanish Civil War and the Franco dictatorship—one that acknowledges the experiences of those who suffered and perished during these years. It is clear now that the *Transición* should be part of this inquiry, and that the official account of the success of this political transformation must be challenged too. The question to be asked is: '¿[h]ubo también otra transición que ha quedado velada para el gran público y que, sin embargo, llevan tal vez en su seno semillas para pensar otro futuro colectivo en España?' (Sánchez León: 164). The authorised version of the *Transición* has, according to Sánchez León, erased the memory of emerging alternative political initiatives. Now that this group has acquired a generational identity and is bringing visibility to their collective experience, the possibility of reclaiming these political experiences arises (165–66).

The memory of this particular cohort is especially significant because of its connection and relevance to the present. The identity of this generation is deeply connected to its memory of the *Transición*, 'merced a la cual actualizamos el valor que damos a unas cosas que creemos propias y constitutivas de nuestra personalidad y nuestras actitudes' and, more importantly, '[s]eguimos viviendo allí, en la transición, nos guste o no' (166–67). Spaniards today are being constantly and consistently 'returned to' the past, to the 'allí' of the *Transición*, through newspaper headlines, political speeches, works of art, and informal conversation. Despite the prominence of these historical and cultural markers, the youth that lived through the *Transición* years have not yet managed, as a group, to establish

---

2 Sánchez León defines the 'generation of the transition' as those born in the mid-1950s and on, aged between 15 and 20 in 1975. They were able to vote during the first democratic election of 1977 and, more representatively, in the second one of 1979 (167–68).

a set of contextualised referents through which to process their 'own' transition (167). Recent recollections of the transitional years by members of this cohort show a newfound interest in the legacy of the Spanish Civil War and the Franco dictatorship, paired with a desire narratively to comprehend the historical and cultural consequences of these experiences in the present.

In the years following Franco's death, historians like Raymond Carr and Juan Pablo Fusi suggested that one consequence of the dictatorship was the creation of a generation of politically inexperienced people (Carr: 135; Fusi: 172). The government's power and control had conditioned a generation of lethargic Spaniards to believe that politics was reserved for a minority (Merino and Song 2005: 14), though this political apathy was felt and practised differently by different age groups. While most of the older generation of Spaniards who lived through the (post-)war period wanted to forget the past and welcomed a democratic Spain with a minimum of upheaval, the younger generation of political activists (those identified with the political opposition, the so-called 'generation of '68') desired a change in the country's political institutions above all else. Caught between these two groups, the youth of the *Transición* had their own separate interests, for which they were often vilified: '[l]a libertad de orientación sexual, el consumo responsable de drogas, la exploración en suma de libertades personales, y sobre todo las manifestaciones públicas de éstas' (Sánchez León: 174). Indeed, even the political left did not know how to respond to these new interests, reacting with a vehemence more typical of the conservative right. Sánchez León picks up on this failure of cross-generational understanding, calling for the rejection of stereotypes like 'pasota' to describe this cohort, and attributing the political misunderstanding of the *Transición* youth to a lack of representation and visibility in the newly 'ordered' society (176). Remedying the invisibility of this generation is essential, he argues, because 'con ellos comenzó una pauta de sociabilidad juvenil en España que continúa esencialmente intacta, en la que se mezclan la falta de reconocimiento y el estereotipo por un lado, y por otro una identidad radical cultural y políticamente en un amplio sector de la juventud española' (178). The recollections of this group have the potential to transform Spain's current political landscape while challenging the official version of the *Transición*; their memories offer 'el nexo más firme para entroncar la cultura política alternativa de nuestro presente con su propio pasado, en el que sólo llegó a quedar larvada' (Sánchez León: 179). It is particularly instructive to note how Sánchez León expresses this need: '[d]esenterrar el olvido instituido a tantos jóvenes de los años setenta es importante si aspiramos a librarnos del encantamiento de los mitos de la transición' (179). In other words, the desire to break free from Spain's transitional past, by giving this period the examination and remembrance it deserves, is in fact an aspiration for a future where a possibility for alternative politics exists.[3]

In one of his early works on the subject of the Spanish *Transición*, historian Paul Preston has remarked that the nature of this transformation, and the crisis-torn politics that accompanied it, could only be properly understood by paying attention to the internal contradictions of the Franco regime during the last six years of the dictator's life (1987: 2–3). Preston argues that the dictatorship's inability to respond to the demands for liberalisation from different sectors of Spanish society was itself a catalyst for the change that Spain experienced after Franco's death. Furthermore, the deliberate continuation of the divisions of the Spanish Civil War during the dictatorship created an environment in which the liberal servants of the regime were driven to engage in dialogue with the political opposition. Summarising this situation, Preston states that '[m]ilitary interventionism, the virulence of the extreme right and the violence of the Basques, obsolete industries and uneven development have all conditioned Spain's political trajectory since 1975' (1987: 3).

Even if the challenges the country faced were predominantly the product of a worldwide recession, they nevertheless proved harder to resolve because of the imbalances left by the dictatorship (Preston 1987: 3). The legacy of the dictatorship takes centre stage in explanations of Spain's trajectory towards constitutional monarchy, and the politics of both the *aperturismo* and the *continuismo* are understood as by-products of the Franco regime. Although desire for change (liberalisation and democratisation) necessarily went toe-to-toe with a desire to maintain the status quo, early readings of the transition as a political process fraught with challenges quickly gave way to an understanding of the past that focused primarily on its ultimate democratic success. The tense living conditions in Spain in the late 1970s and early 1980s—amid the violence of terrorism (both ETA and GRAPO) and a deep economic recession that resulted in continued strikes and demonstrations—were progressively downplayed, to be overwritten by a narrative portraying the Spanish transition as an ideal model for other non-democratic countries desiring political transformation.[4]

3 This examination of the past is, as I argue in this book, significant more for the remembering itself than the actual historical memories that this labour reveals.

4 ETA stands for the Basque separatist group Euskadi Ta Askatasuna (Basque Homeland and Freedom). GRAPO (Grupos de Resistencia Antifascista Primero de Octubre), a splinter group from the Spanish Communist party, began its terrorist activities in August 1975.

During this period of rosy recollection, criticism of the *Transición* mainly focused on its handling of the legacy of the Spanish Civil War and the dictatorship, as well as the creation of autonomous regions in the peninsula, which was regarded simultaneously as a challenge to and a product of a unified vision of the national territory. Despite the government's effort to close this problematic chapter of the country's history, a view of the past as 'unresolved' has persisted. Attempts to equate the pain and loss suffered by both sides of the conflict must be interpreted as an attempt to whitewash the past; the repression experienced by the losing side of a war cannot be overcome when there is no official avenue through which to discuss and to legitimise this collective pain. Ultimately, then, the greatest obstacle to achieving recognition of this suffering is, in fact, the widely accepted view that the Spanish political transition was a democratic triumph.

Almost a quarter of a century after the *Transición*, Gregorio Alonso and Diego Muro published a collection of essays on this political period in which they revisited the idea of the 'Spanish Model of Transition'. They traced the efforts of past scholars to highlight the idyllic characteristics of the process of political transition, the uniqueness of the Spanish case, the moderation and compromises of the elites, the timing of the general elections, the drafting of the Spanish constitution, and the rising levels of social mobilisation. By highlighting these aspects, the authors argue, 'Spain could set an example of how moderation and commitment to democratic rules can lead to a peaceful and gradual political transformation' (1). According to Alonso and Muro, politicians from Eastern Europe, including Hungary, Poland, Romania, and Czechoslovakia, visited Spain and examined its political transition just as did Latin American countries, especially Argentina and Chile (1–2). They contend, however, that this interest in the Spanish model was paradoxical, as 'Spain did not follow a democratic road map' (2). The triggering of the process by an internal crisis (the death of Francisco Franco) and the absence of a key figure capable of leading a political transformation meant that Spain had been obliged to figure out its own political path despite the lack of a stable democratic tradition (2).

Studies of the *Transición* has often emphasised the role of the negotiated reform controlled by the political elite, including both the democratic opposition and members of the Francoist apparatus who were open to change. However, Alonso and Muro point out that this reading of 'pact making' ignores the favourable conditions that allowed the transformation to take place. They reject the imposed dichotomy between the importance of the ruling elite and the role of the masses, arguing that this scenario presents a false dilemma in democratisation theory (4). Political decisions are not made in an historical vacuum and indeed, in Spain, 'the number of terrorist acts, strikes and demonstrations had a considerable impact on the agendas of the political elites' (Alonso and Muro: 4). While the real effect of mass action in the Spanish *Transición* remains to be explored—especially given the lack of influence of trade unions and workers' representations in the Moncloa Pacts of 1977—Alonso and Muro consider their work an opportunity to address new questions about the Spanish transition in new contexts, including the context of memory studies (13).[5]

The politics of memory is intimately tied to societies' need to 'rework the past in a wider cultural arena, both during the transitions and after official transitional policies have been implemented or even forgotten' (Barahona et al.: 1–2). Truth commissions, trials, amnesties, and purges are part of possible government-sponsored efforts, as are policies concerning compensation, restitution, or reparation. This work is typically complemented by a variety of unofficial and private socio-based initiatives promoted by human rights organisations (HROs), churches, political parties, and other civil society organisations (Barahona et al.: 1). Such efforts, which comprise part of the political and ethical question of what a government *does*, should be expected whenever nations with legacies of repression transition from an authoritarian or totalitarian regime to democratic rule. In the case of Spain, the lack of government involvement in these standard measures during the *Transición* seems to expose, for many observers, a will to simply forget the past.[6] Negotiated transitions can have adverse consequences, as 'institutional frameworks designed for periods of change consolidate a way of engaging in politics and avoid open discussion of the most delicate matters that can cause profound cleavages within society' and 'impose serious limits on accountability' (Aguilar 2001: 118). As argued early on by Josep Maria Colomer and later reinforced by Aguilar, 'avoiding retroactive justice because the balance of forces after the death of Franco did not permit it has allowed the political elite to refer abusively to the "legacy" argument and to blame the authoritarian past for behaviour that is unacceptable under a consolidated democracy' (Colomer: 177; Aguilar 2001: 118). More recent studies on the *Transición*, such as Omar G. Encarnación's *Democracy*

5 An examination of the Moncloa Pacts of 1977 in the context of the political changes taking place in Spain that year can be found in Omar Encarnación's *Spanish Politics: Democracy after Dictatorship* (36–39).

6 In Spain, for instance, the Amnesty Law of 1977 worked almost as an act of institutionalised forgetting of the Spanish Civil War and the dictatorship. In fact, what happened in Spain does not mirror at all what happened in the mid-1980s and the 1990s in Latin America, where 'transitional truths' and justice efforts were carried out by 'truth commissions' (it was Latin America that gave rise to them) and parliamentary or government-sponsored commissions (Barahona et al.: 4–5).

without Justice in Spain: The Politics of Forgetting, continue to insist on how '[t]he rise and persistence of the politics of forgetting in Spain pose important questions about how nations settle a "dark" past and the consequences of the policies put in place to deal with that past for the emerging democratic regime' (Encarnación 2014: 4).

The period of Spanish history following the dictatorship has been identified as one of 'collective amnesia'. Analyses of this period have focused on the limitations of the political reforms that took place in the late 1970s, under which the sociocultural structures of the previous authoritarian government were kept largely in place and the repression suffered by those who fought on the Republican side of the Spanish Civil War was largely ignored. Throughout the *Transición*, Spaniards continued to struggle with the memory of the war and the repression and violence suffered under Franco. Even today, the memories of these experiences loom large as Spanish society grapples with the disappearance of older generations who preserved direct recollection and experience from this time. Ironically, the law proposed by the Socialist government of José Luis Rodríguez Zapatero to remedy this situation only served to reveal the structural flaws in the debate over the legacy of the war, including the government's determination to conflate the violence unleashed during the war and the Franco dictatorship as unavoidable outcomes of armed conflicts, equating victims and perpetrators from both sides of the ideological divide.[7]

In *Memory and Amnesia*, Paloma Aguilar highlights the paradoxical nature of the discourse surrounding the issue of memory and the Spanish Civil War. The frequent media commentary on the lack of discussion about the war contrasts oddly with the clear abundance of films and other artistic works on this topic, as Aguilar points out. Indeed, the enduring collective belief in the neglect of this topic signals 'the existence of a traumatic collective memory of the Civil War' (Aguilar 2002: xix). In order to understand this contradiction, Aguilar examines the type of war memories that existed during the dictatorship and how these recollections played a crucial role in the institutional design of the *Transición* (2002: 25). Among the documents she scrutinises are the collection of newsreels and documentaries which were compulsory in all commercial cinemas between 1943 and 1975 (and voluntarily between 1976 and 1981), the NO-DO (Noticiarios y Documentales, the State-controlled cinema newsreels), and the textbooks that were used well into the years of the political transition. The memories of the war

---

7 I discuss the 2007 'Law of Historical Memory' in detail in the next chapter.

captured in these sources were, at least from the early 1960s onwards, set against images and discourses of political stability, social peace, national unity and harmony, and, especially, economic progress and rising standards of living. This view of the past, promoted by the Francoist regime, was used as a peace-making ploy to guarantee the dictatorship's authority and posterity. Aguilar argues that this use of war memories resulted in the development of a collective trauma about the past:

> Throughout this period the régime strove to legitimise both its founding myth and its own survival; first, through a black-and-white narration of the war in which it sought to justify the 'need' for the Uprising and, second, by associating, over time, this memory of the war with peace and progress, legitimising the regime further by appealing to the results of its administration (performance-based legitimacy) rather than its origins (origin-based legitimacy), although without losing sight of the latter for an instant. Finally, Francoism instilled a ferocious, obsessive and omnipresent fear of any repetition of the Civil War, justifying the survival of the regime by alluding to the alleged dangers that a liberal democracy could hold for Spain, thus taking refuge behind a traumatic memory on which the 'never again' consensus was already built. It is also true that other factors were involved in this process, such as the very passing of time, factors which helped to facilitate both forgiveness and an ability to forget. (2002: 25–26)

In other words, when we consider the existence and propagation of war memories under Franco, we must do so with a conscious awareness of the ways in which those memories were evoked and in what context; for our purposes, such a critical examination is doubly important because the Francoist attitudes towards the war reflect a particular mnemonic style that persisted in the press during the *Transición* (Aguilar 2002: 27). The presence of this style of memory is detectable in the documentation from the Cortes, parliamentary debates, legislation, the press, history books, memoirs, and autobiographies, all of which paint a clear picture of how Spanish society understood its past.

Aguilar's work reveals how the collective memory of the Spanish Civil War referenced during the years of the *Transición* was an ideological product of Francoism. As such, this 'socialised memory'—to use Aguilar's term— influenced the way the past was negotiated during Spain's transition to democracy. The trauma connected to this memory served as a basis for consensus-building after Franco's death: negotiation about the past boiled down to the idea of 'never again' (Aguilar 2002: 26). Neither side of the government—the heirs of the Francoist regime and their political opponents now shaping Spanish politics for the first time—ever differed significantly in their relationship with the past. The persistence of this socialised memory, crafted under the dictatorship, explains why the Law of Amnesty of 1977 was able to homogenise the past, equating victims and perpetrators from both sides of the ideological divide.[8]

The Spanish people's traumatic relationship with the Civil War has subsequently functioned as a point of origin for other traumas, endlessly complicating Spain's relationship with the past. The trauma manufactured under Francoism was embraced (or perhaps, more precisely, inherited) by the politicians of the *Transición* who, in turn, inflicted more trauma. The enduring pain created by this process became apparent when the political left, after decades of political struggle and persecution under the dictatorship, proved itself incapable of delivering on promised social changes during the years of political transition. The politics of consensus based on the idea of 'never again' meant the continued silencing of the losing side of the war; Spaniards were limited to mourning the lost opportunities of this time.

Ironically, the narrative that grew out of this forced compromise was one of success, in which the democratic transformation of Spain was hailed as a political model for other nations. Given the troubled nature of this change, however, it is no wonder that despite the triumphant rhetoric of the *Transición*, the 1980s saw the emergence of a new discourse critical of this political transformation.

The disillusionment or 'desencanto' that followed the euphoria of political change was perfectly captured by Pedro Almodóvar in his film *¿Qué he hecho yo para merecer esto?* (1984). The story of Gloria (Carmen Maura), who struggles to get ahead cleaning buildings in Madrid while addicted to amphetamines, reflected clearly the stark reality of many Spaniards whose lives remain unchanged despite the political and cultural transformation taking place at this time. Gloria's abusive husband, her openly gay teenage son whom she gives up for adoption to a paedophile dentist, her older son addicted to cocaine, and her crazy mother-in-law (Chus Lampreave) offer snapshots of the hardships suffered by the Spanish people. While the social circumstances in which these characters live seem to reflect a different era, opportunities or possibilities for change never seem to come to fruition. Gloria's newfound independence, for instance, is threatened by

8 A reading of this amnesty law from 1977 in relation to Spain's current politics is offered in Helen Graham's *The War and its Shadow* (147–49).

her conservative and violent husband. The new availability of recreational drugs and open sexuality in post-Franco Spain only brings to light the continued asymmetry of power dynamics and does little to alleviate Gloria's pain. Even when, at the film's end, she overcomes her husband's repression by accidentally killing him and her mother-in-law leaves the city with one of her sons, Gloria's future remains uncertain at best.

Almodóvar's early critical view of the transition, reflected in this film, has again become relevant in the recent revisiting of this period by a younger generation of Spaniards. What the writers and filmmakers I discuss in this book rediscover and recreate is a time of uncertainty, fear, and violence erased by the rhetoric of political success. Their work allows us to re-examine the endurance of this critical perspective and the way these experiences are recovered through personal and intimate connections with the present.

Critics of contemporary Spanish culture over the years have remarked on the country's complicated relationship with the past. Their works often analyse the tendency towards wilful silence (or amnesia) in contemporary fiction, visual arts, and film. Drawing on concepts like melancholia, trauma, and violence in their theorising, critics have argued for a reading of the *Transición* as a symptomatic period during which the suppressed memories of the past (of both the Spanish Civil War and the dictatorship) were seeking means of expression. This work, as a body, reveals that the most significant legacy of the Franco dictatorship was its dysfunctional relationship with the past. Through censorship, oppression, triumphalist rhetoric, propaganda, and violence, the Francoist regime turned the past into a taboo for generations of Spaniards. Normalising Spain's collective relationship to the past should have been part of the process of democratisation, but the government failed to address this need. The political transformation thus came to be better known as a 'pacto del olvido', a compromise based on forgetting, crystallised by the passing of the 1977 amnesty law that effectively forbade any historical discussion under the guise of governmental legitimacy.

Within this context of silence, Alberto Medina reflects on the emptiness that surrounds the Valle de los Caídos (Valley of the Fallen), a symbol of Francoism and a mausoleum for both the dictator and the martyr of the Falangist cause, José Antonio. He ponders the Spanish 'ejercicio de olvido' and the vacuum that surrounds this symbolic space, asking whether '¿[e]s esa invisibilidad la mera afirmación de un olvido real o quizá el indicio de una autoimpuesta disciplina?' (14). Medina highlights the systematic, symbolic elimination of representations of the dictator as pointing to a clear desire to control and even exterminate the memory of Franco (14–15).[9]

---

9 For Medina, this process of forgetting responds to a process in which 'El

He draws a parallel with the apparent amnesia that struck Germany after the end of the Second World War, focusing on the work of Theodor Adorno, who explains this lack of memory not as absence but rather as *masked permanence*. Medina argues that melancholia itself is a critical tool, an instrument of power that inhabits the space left by an affective void (16–17). He explains the political transformation that took place in Spain as a process of co-optation: '[f]rente a la "ruptura democrática," propuesta en principio por las fuerzas de la oposición, la cual habría supuesto una total fractura y discontinuidad con las instituciones del régimen, se impondrá la "ruptura pactada" un proceso de reconversión desde dentro llevado a cabo a través de una política de consenso' (17). For Medina, the loss of the Caudillo represents the moment at which the continuity of the political structure of Francoism (along with its institutions) was guaranteed.

The effort to craft a new Spanish identity—one that had shed its former ties to an outdated dictatorship and ideology—materialised in the writing of a new constitution, but this effort, too, ultimately failed to achieve a clean break from Spain's past and its related trauma. Medina argues that the new democratic constitution of 1978 was nothing more than apocryphal writing, a project hijacked by an elite that, despite its message of democratic participation and the rhetoric of consensus, only served to confirm its own view and priorities regarding Spain's new political (and legal) structure (56–57). In particular, he finds an inextricable connection between the notion of 'consensus' and 'disenchantment': a narrative of utopic harmony projected by those in power in which all is negotiable and where everything can be discussed in order to reach a compromise. The problem is that, in undertaking such a process, the past is dissolved and, ultimately, erased (Medina: 57–58). The 1977 Moncloa Pacts and the 1978 constitution become representative gestures, part of the civic attempt to cleanse the country of past linguistic and political practices, as if the new government were created out of (or based on) thin air (Medina: 57–58).[10] Similarly, the transformation of the media landscape through the elimination of censorship was taken

---

pasado es modelado a imagen del presente' (14). Recovered representations of Franco depict him minimised and domesticated: playing cards, talking with his wife, etc. In tracing the thread of this restoration, Medina highlights Manuel Vázquez Montalbán's *Autobiografía del general Franco* (1992) and Fernando Vizcaíno Casas's *Y al tercer año resucitó* (1978), as well as the films *Madregilda* (Dir. Francisco Regueiro, 1993), *Espérame en el cielo* (Dir. Antonio Mercero, 1988), and *Dragon Rapide* (Dir. Jaime Camino, 1986).

10　See Song (2005: 223–25) for an examination of the 1978 constitution and the later effort to guarantee its untouchability by invoking the concept of constitutional patriotism.

as further evidence of freedom; again, however, this apparent transparency was only an illusion.[11]

Following a similar train of reasoning, Cristina Moreiras-Menor interrogates the end of Francoism by highlighting the desire, present in many works published during the *Transición*, to recover the past. She analyses this desire as a reflection of the need to make history a part of one's own story: 'a través de una puesta en duda, de una manifiesta y dolorosa incertidumbre, de que la experiencia del presente, la realidad contemporánea, está constituida sobre las ruinas precisamente de unos fantasmas que siguen vivos y sin enterrar' (17).[12] Examining the legacy of the dictatorship within the narrative of freedom and modernity that marked the arrival of democracy in Spain, Moreiras-Menor argues that the spectacle, trauma, and violence that characterises the works of this time is connected to the way Spanish history has been narrated and silenced since Franco's death. She uses the term 'herida', an open wound, to point to the experience of the contemporary Spanish subject: a body in crisis that rises from a world of contradictions, 'de la coexistencia de modos antagónicos de articular la realidad' (19). This lack of closure is also brought up by Joan Ramon Resina, who argues that the remembering that took place during the years of the *Transición* was already tainted: '[f]orgiveness implies forgetting and starting anew; whereas to rehabilitate is to bring forth prostrate memories of good character and intrinsic worth. In either case, a change of consciousness is involved, not so much of the subject but of those who forget or else reconstruct the master narrative ...' (2000: 8). Given that the discourse on political transformation is 'overwhelmingly a matter of narrative', Resina argues that a better way of approaching this period 'would be to study it in reference to what it leaves out, what substracts [*sic*] from what we know from experience or what can be learned from less popular and more inaccessible sources (2000: 9).[13]

11 Paul Julian Smith offers a different reading of the Valle de los Caídos: '[w]hile Alberto Medina deplores the neglect of the Valle as a sign of historical amnesia, I would celebrate that neglect as proof of Spanish culture's successful engagement with or working through the past. I thus try to examine nostalgia sympathetically in this book (to read it for its complex fusion of time, space, and feeling)' (2006: 9).

12 For Moreiras-Menor, the erasure of memory (or history) results in violence, which can be read as a lasting trace of those deletions that become manifest in later generations. Her study demonstrates how this violence, as a new cultural expression, thrives in a postmodern and democratic Spain where the hegemony of the market and mass media rules (17).

13 In this case, Resina is referring to works of fiction published after the end of the dictatorship. The question of the legacy of Francoism was tackled in *Traces of Contamination* (2005), which I co-edited with Eloy E. Merino. In this collection of

To talk about trauma, melancholia, or lack of closure is to talk about memory. In post-Franco Spain, memories have been described as spectres that continue to haunt the present. Jo Labanyi works with 'history as hauntology' to examine the films and fictions produced between 1970 and 2000 and to pose the following question: 'what does a society—in particular, Spanish society of the transition and since—do with history; that is, what does it do with the ghosts of the past?' (2000: 65). When a society that imagines itself to be young and modern is confronted with the burdens of its past, the outcomes of negotiation with its memories (or ghosts) can be varied: they can be refused, expressed through melancholia (as analysed by Medina), or be acknowledged—and it is only the latter path that allows one to live with its traces (Labanyi 2000: 65–66). Labanyi is, perhaps, the first scholar to clearly identify these ghosts. She names them as the victims of the past who have disappeared from social space and can only appear in virtual spaces (2000: 66).[14] In her analyses of works by Víctor Érice, Julio Llamazares, Juan Marsé, and others, she finds these ghosts in ruins: spaces that are useful not only to dig up the past, but to conjure up its spectres (2000: 71).

Labanyi's early search for ghosts has taken a literal turn amid recent debates concerning the exhumation of mass Civil War graves demanded by relatives searching for the physical remnants of their kin. The creation of civil associations, such as the Asociación para la Recuperación de la Memoria Histórica, and the public debate around the 'Ley de Memoria Histórica' (Law of Historical Memory) proposed by the PSOE in 2004 and approved by Congress in 2007, reveals that the key issue at stake in this dispute is the memory of the violence of the Civil War and the dictatorship. As I discuss in the next chapter, this remembering—once kept a private matter thanks to Francoist repression—has now started to enter the public sphere (Labanyi 2008b: 119–20). As Noël Valis points out, this memory is inevitably linked to conflict: the highly politicised rhetoric of the Spanish Civil War focuses on 'what was at stake at this war ... the very identity of a nation and its

---

essays, we aimed to examine the traces of the concrete experiences of Francoism that shaped a great part of Spain's contemporary history and culture (11–26).

14 Labanyi connects the idea of ghosts with 'spaces where the possibility of collectivity and communication is denied or at best curtailed' (2000: 67). Films like *El Sur* (Dir. Víctor Érice, 1983) and *El espíritu de la colmena* (Dir. Víctor Érice, 1973) or novels like Julio Llamazares's *Luna de lobos* (1985) and *Escenas de cine mudo* (1993) and the works of Antonio Muñoz Molina are read for their geographical displacements as well as for their feeling of loss. Another important work that embodies this emotion is Basilio Martín Patino's *Canciones para después de una guerra* (1976) (Labanyi 2000: 70–71).

people. The war was a battle over the future history of the country and who would represent that history' (11). In the aftermath of the war and the official Francoist version of this history, the past is a disputed territory filled with subjective recollections (Valis: 11)—and, ghostly or not, the memories connected to this past are highly contested and continue to haunt Spain's present.[15]

Beneath the current and ongoing criticism of the conservative PP's fiscal policy during the financial crisis that began in 2008 and the tension-filled relationship between the central and regional governments in the peninsula, there remains a thread of general dissatisfaction traceable to the country's failure to deal with its memories of the past. From this perspective, 'memory' in Spain has not only become a critical term, but a paradoxical one whose constant presence actually exposes its complete absence. This contradiction is compelling for it allows us a closer look into how memories—transformed, mediated, and manipulated—circulate in contemporary Spain. While some recollections are deployed to misconstrue the past (for instance, in the revisionist works of writers like Pío Moa or César Vidal), the majority are perceived as morally grounded and requiring no justification. These memories are valued for their ability to recover stories and even material traces of those who were disappeared during the war and the dictatorship, revealing a situation that, according to historian Paul Preston, demands moral reparation (2004: 20).

While these stories are welcomed into the collective consciousness, their continued presence also signals a structural condition that both creates the need for and sustains the production of recovered memories. Curiously, it is the *Transición* itself that, despite rejecting the past ideologically, has enabled the continuation of this production of memory. Resina argues that political change in Spain was not about revolution but about obeying the rules of the capitalist market. For him, it was the market's 'implacable logic that pushed Spain, from the sixties on, out of the autarchy and into reformist policies'—towards a position that deemed history, seen as a commodity, to be old-fashioned and irrelevant (2000b: 93). The transition worked as the 'special effect (in the cinematographic sense too) of a collective installation in a present that wished itself absolute: the present of the market' (Resina 2000b: 93). The constant sense of a present era driven incessantly by change also established a particular relationship with history. The past was to be

---

15 Ángel Loureiro, for instance, has criticised this interest in the past for creating a public discourse based on victimhood, ignoring the real events that took place during the Francoist dictatorship and its aftermath. I will return to his work in the next chapter.

amputated as the needs of the present demanded, but, as Resina points out, 'the battleground for remembrance is not so much the field of historiography as the everyday experiences through which the collective memory is shaped, reformed, or erased' (2000b: 104). Logically, once Spain had been integrated into the world market, memories of the Spanish Civil War and the dictatorship should have become superfluous and even counterproductive (Resina 2000b: 104), yet publication about both is still going strong, and despite many judicial and political failures involving family members searching for traces of disappeared family members, the news and stories about their suffering (and, ultimately, death) have not vanished. Instead, these memories have created an industry of their own[16]—or, to put it differently, these battles have become part of an everyday experience. As part of the country's current political and cultural debate, the *Transición* drives and sustains the production of the memory of a troubled past.

The study of memory in contemporary Spain has generated an extensive discussion on how the process of recollection works and the different forms in which it endures. For example, there has been an insistence on distinguishing between historical and collective memory. The former, according to Resina, is a specialised recollection based on research and documentation, which should be 'treated as witnesses of events and must be scrupulously reconstructed before their meaning and validity can be formally established' (2000b: 83-84). In contrast, collective memory, following Maurice Halbwachs's definition, should be understood as a collection of different memories across generations and social groups (38-39). José F. Colmeiro's definition of memory is more inclusive and comprises all experiences, traditions, practices, rituals, and myths shared by a collective group (17-18). The range of this memory, however, exposes a dilemma detected earlier by Resina, who argues that multiplicity, assumed to rely on historical truth, only evinces an 'erosion of the past' (2000b: 84). Colmeiro echoes this belief in his writing on the 'memory crisis' in Spain. For him, historical memory implies historical consciousness, a part of a collective event in which memory is activated individually (18). What is absent in Spain, then, is the link between memory at the individual level and memory as part of a collective historical consciousness.

Talking about a memory crisis in Spain is, indeed, another way of pointing to the lack of connection between subjective and institutional memories.

---

16 Memory, in this sense, fell prey to the logic of the capitalist market in which memories themselves have become commodities. Many critics, including the aforementioned Loureiro, have pointed to this overproduction and consumption of memories.

This absence is often explained by what happened during the years of the *Transición*; as described above, the political amnesty granted to those involved in the previous regime led to a wilful act of forgetting which in turn resulted in fragmented memories, private memories, and the replacement of memory with nostalgia (Colmeiro: 18–19). Many critics have identified this deliberate erasure of history as the impetus behind the excessive number of first-person accounts about the past in contemporary Spain.

More recently, Txetxu Aguado has raised the issue of the exhaustion brought on by the abundant and repetitive nature of these works, observing that the memories contained in these historical works seem emptied of real experiences. Aguado contends that the ever-present, self-congratulatory memories of the successful *Transición* preclude the existence of other recollections, and thus prevent the promulgation of an alternative history (12–13). As Colmeiro explains, the *Transición* has come to serve as an essential historical reference point in the production of collective memory, as a foundational myth on which the present has been built (25). While I agree with Colmeiro's and Aguado's assessment of the preferential treatment of the *Transición* as a site of memory and a point of origin for Spain's present national identity, I also believe that we need to find a new way to engage with contemporary Spanish cultural production about the recent past. Rather than emphasising the referential value of these recollections as accurate, accountable memories, we should consider their affective value. It is affect, rather than truthful representation, that insists on, and provides, an enduring connection between past and present. By conceiving the private as an extension of the public—by examining how subjects experience the public privately—we can appreciate how subjective experiences become relevant collectively and glimpse the affective structure that sustains this connection. The cultural and political circumstances that reinforce affective structures teach us how to produce and preserve meaning in our contemporary world.

The perception of a crisis of memory in Spain has led critics like Ulrich Winter to examine the notion of 'performative memory'. Winter argues that the necessity to recover memories has transformed knowledge of the past into a component of present reality (249). In other words, a present-day form of the past ('presentificación', or what Winter calls the 'ontologización de la memoria') is created in order to ensure that the past becomes an essential part of the present (249–51). The performance of this past-in-the-present is invoked by Winter to explain the current social and judicial activism around the memory and legacy of the Spanish Civil War and the Franco dictatorship. Likewise, cultural representations through literary texts have started 'performing' as historiographical studies (Winter: 253).

While continuing to regard the historical content of literary texts as a 'contribution' to the recovery of the past, Winter correctly recognises how the treatment of memory in contemporary Spain has changed. Perhaps this shift also challenges the way in which historical recollections are currently understood.

If a 'crisis of memory' can point to the *absence* of memory, it can also suggest its distortion. After all, there are always competing interests when it comes to producing and circulating memories of the past and 'experiences attended by the powerful social institutions are likely to be better preserved than experiences less favoured by rich institutional rememberers' (Resina 2000b: 85). Discussion about historical amnesia in Spain, then, is not so much about the actual loss of the past but, as already discussed, its politics of memory: '[t]he dispute is really over which fragments of the past are being refloated and which are allowed to sink' (Resina 2000b: 86). The *Transición* played an important political role in the production and preservation of past experiences. As an active moment of 'forgetting', this period has become synonymous with progress, democracy, and the normalisation of the previously abnormal, signalling a need for reconciliation and the manufacturing of a broad consensus (Resina 2000b: 88).[17] However, as Resina notes, it also demonstrates how 'just as memory reaches back over relatively long stretches of time, its dissipation does not occur overnight' (2000b: 91). To put it differently, though a discourse of change prevailed during the transition, there lingered beneath it a host of memories not yet fully processed. This contradiction explains, on the one hand, the persistence of memories about the past and, on the other, the time lag between the critical discourse of the *Transición* of the 1980s and the current recollections of this era. These memories did not dissipate, but instead turned into what I have characterised as 'memory projects'. The years of Spain's political transformation were opened for examination, part of an unfinished task. In fact, the *Transición* now shares the same status as the Spanish Civil War and the Franco dictatorship: all three eras have become inexorably linked to troubled memory, deployed at will to explain and to criticise any aspect of Spain's current political or cultural situation.

17 Resina sees the election of the Partido Popular in 1996 as the final moment of respite for democracy: 'Casting his party as a political Schlemil, he [Vice President of the Government Francisco Álvarez-Cascos] hoped that no one would notice that it was precisely the Partido Popular's coming to power that finally put temptations of unconstitutional adventures to rest' (2000b: 90).

It is too obvious to state that the ongoing memory of the *Transición* is flanked by many different narratives. Faced with the official account of this political process (sanctioned by the government and other interested political parties to offer an historically cohesive and coherent recollection), critical accounts of this experience, often originating from academic circles, have insisted on offering an alternative account.[18] As this process has continued, the term *Transición* itself has come to encompass a wider significance. Germán Labrador, for instance, has argued that the term *Transición* has come to imply not just a process of political (and institutional) change, but a collective will that unites the habits, languages, and values of a time. As such, it belongs to a larger story that contains not only the end of the Francoist world but a projection into the present and into the future, 'en esa ampliación del marco de referencia se ha ido disolviendo una historia personalista, muy vinculada a los artífices de la ingeniería política, en favor de una genealogía ciudadana, colectiva de todo ese proceso' (Labrador: 64). Debunking the idea that it was a time of dialogue and consensus-building, Labrador insists on adopting a comprehensive approach to the *Transición* that acknowledges the continuation of Francoist social, political, and cultural structures. Politics during the transition, according to Labrador, worked more like a *simulacrum*, a stage where the spectacle of democracy was performed (70).[19] Ultimately, Labrador's reading of this time echoes the same sense of loss and trauma already examined, traceable in the ghosts of memory present in the works of artists like Juan Goytisolo, Carlos Saura, Jaime Chávarri, and Leopoldo María Panero. In particular, these works reveal how the past is summoned by a sense of loss that eventually replaces memory, projecting instead an alternative construction of history that thrusts 'la lógica histórica de lo político hacia el terreno del imaginario, hacia el cuerpo simbólico social' (Labrador: 70–71).[20] The lack of accountability in politics is questioned, thus, in works such as Almodóvar's *¿Qué he hecho yo para merecer esto?* (1984) or

18 Germán Labrador Méndez identifies Victoria Prego's work in *Así se hizo la transición* (1995) as embodying the officially sanctioned view (63).

19 He builds on Eduardo Subirats's *Después de la lluvia: sobre la ambigua modernidad española* (1993) to offer a critical view of the *Transición*.

20 Labrador argues that these works shift the discussion from the discipline of history to that of literary and cultural studies. The works of Goytisolo, Saura, Chávarri, and Panero represent a confrontation between the official history and an alternative one: 'Frente a las operaciones colectivas de la memoria, amparadas por una fuerte producción de textualidad legitimadora, en el estudio de la producción de algunos intelectuales y algunos artistas será posible encontrar miradas diferentes al proceso histórico que, lejos de ceder al olvido, se edifiquen en la reflexión sobre el proceso transicional' (71).

Manuel Vázquez Montalbán's Pepe Carvalho detective series. These fictional recreations of history insist on the need to revisit the past as an integral part of our cultural and personal identity.

This need to revisit the past foregrounds the relevance of our discussion of generational experience and identity for it highlights the connections a group can share, consciously and subconsciously; whether in terms of worldview or memory of past events, a cohort, despite its individual differences, is affected temporally and historically in comparable ways. This resemblance, in turn, leads to common cultural or political practices. In terms of aesthetics, the authors examined in this book reflect a strong preference for storytelling and the use of subjective voice and experience. They also express a clear faith in the value of historical documentation despite their awareness of the infinite possibilities for its manipulation. Historiographic veracity, in turn, gives way to private ties to the past, where the work of memory is not focused on recovering stories but on converting historical experiences into personal ones. One could argue that this obsession with narration, with getting the story 'right', is symptomatic of a contentious relationship with the past. Yet it could also be viewed as the consequence of confronting a past as yet unburied. As Cristina Moreiras-Menor argues in *Cultura herida* (2002), a past that remains unresolved prevents trauma from being overcome, as it prevents the victims of trauma from imagining or engaging with the idea of a more hopeful future. It is difficult not to identify a sense of impasse in these recent works about the *Transición*— yet this impasse itself translates into a greater interest in the present, a perspective from which one can attempt to make peace with the past. At the same time, the difficulty of achieving such a resolution is palpable in these works and in the uncertainty they express about the future. As we shall see, all of the works examined embody this conundrum in a very particular way: the memories recreated in them do not express any doubt about the past, but approach it methodically and exhaustively, driven by an impulse to establish a clear connection between past conflicts and present troubles. The uncertainty that arises from this quest is not about the past (even if an accurate recollection of its experiences proves to be impossible) or even the present, but always about the future. This is, for example, the case for Benjamín Prado's *Operación Gladio* (2011), which I discuss in the last chapter of the book. The investigative journalism undertaken by the female protagonist paints a very detailed account of the murder of the lawyers in the 1977 Atocha massacre. The connection between this violent past and the present is clear; the ambiguity in the novel directs the reader towards a suspended or uncertain future, one hanging by a thread, where all depends on the final outcome of digging into the past.

The favouring of subjective recollections over historical facts is a strong feature in the recent works of memory about the *Transición*. Perhaps because these memories are constantly challenged, these recollections insist on research, documentation, journalistic investigation, and—above all—on a personal and direct experience that connects past and present. Rather than focusing on the material traces of the past—lost photographs, forgotten objects—these recollections manufacture an affective relationship with the past, one in which the present is shaped emotionally by previous experiences. While the persistence of memory can be understood as the result of repression—the trauma of the Spanish Civil War and the violence of the dictatorship—it also offers the opportunity to understand a particular period of history through the lens of what Raymond Williams called a 'structure of feeling'. For Labanyi, this means the possibility of creating new relationships with the past from the present (2000: 70). In Juan Marsé's use of 'aventis' in *Si te dicen que caí* (1973) and in Basilio Martín Patino's use of archival material in *Canciones para después de una guerra* (1976), we find alternative stories of the past, full of trivia and pieces of information that send tendrils into the present, exposing the remaining traces of history (Labanyi 2000: 70). In contrast, the 'structure of feeling' provided by the recollection of the transition years examined here focuses not on the traces or remnants of the past but on the emotions attached to its memories. Memories, in other words, are not important for what they recall or represent, but for the emotional connection they allow.

I begin my investigation of the shift in this referential relationship in the next chapter by examining the debate over the 2007 'Law of Historical Memory' and how memory in Spain has been forced into private spaces. The perception of memory as a personal concern has shaped the social structures that sustain recollections of the past. The privileging of subjective accounts results in a narrative charged with emotions and couched in an intimate view of the past. I begin my discussion of 'affect' as a general framework for examining how these memories are produced and how they endure socially and culturally.

Each of the subsequent chapters provides specific theoretical approaches to analysing the affect found in the works examined in this book. I begin with a close look at the dominant historical account of the transformation of Spain as one of change and political success. Missing from this narrative of the *Transición* is the political instability and popular apprehension about the future of the country in the years surrounding the death of Franco. The key political event that helped to forge this view was the failed coup d'état of Colonel Antonio Tejero on 23 February 1981. I revisit this episode by examining Javier Cercas's critically acclaimed non-fiction essay *Anatomía de un instante* (2009); two miniseries for television, 23-F: *El día más difícil del Rey* (Dir. Silvia Quer, 2009), 23-F: *Historia de una traición* (Dir. Antonio Recio, 2009); and the feature-length film adaptation of the event, 23-F: *La película* (Dir. Chema de la Peña, 2011). In these works, the events of 23 February 1981 are shaped through narratives that rely on archival materials and personal experiences to document the hours in which the Spanish government was held hostage by Colonel Tejero, while King Juan Carlos and the Spanish military manoeuvred to bring the coup to an end. I suggest how the 23-F has been transformed into a sign, a Peircean index that sustains multiple significations.

I continue with an analysis of the television series *Cuéntame cómo pasó* (2001–) and *La chica de ayer* (2009), which are good examples of how the past is transformed into a memory project to be narrated, remembered, and recreated. They also illustrate the important role that the popular media play today in shaping a person's view of the past and the memories of historical events. In the same chapter, I highlight the way popular culture mediates an affective relationship with the past, borrowing from the concept of media memory. Finally, I examine four novels about the *Transición* published in 2011. Their authors, all born between 1960 and 1963, experienced these years as young adults. I examine the experiences and memories of the *Transición* as narrated in Benjamín Prado's *Operación Gladio* (2011), Ignacio Martínez de Pisón's *El día de mañana* (2011), Antonio Orejudo's *Un momento de descanso* (2011), and Rafael Reig's *Todo está perdonado* (2011). In a close reading of these novels, I consider new ways of analysing this continued obsession with the past.

These chapters offer a renewed perspective on the recent memories of the *Transición*. Rather than focusing on the critical view these works may express about the politics of the time, I have chosen to closely examine their positioning towards the past. Thus, I do not engage with these narratives in terms of their depiction of important political events of that time, such as the tension between the central government of Spain and its culturally and linguistically diverse regions. Equally, I do not address directly the gender politics of the *Transición* or the important women's rights that were hard won during those years. All of these events remain in the background of the recollections I discuss in the book; although they are important historical and political moments, they are not the focus of these narratives. Instead, what these narratives bring forward is the subjective relationship of the authors with the events they depict and recollect. Ultimately, I argue for the importance of political and cultural context in recent recollections of the *Transición*; I show how these works are deeply connected to the ongoing political, historical, and cultural debate about the legacy of the Civil War and the political and economic crisis in contemporary Spain.[21] The generational interest in this period has developed into an exercise of affect in which the past is transformed into a political present and personal feelings and individual experiences replace ideology. While reading the experiential can be a messy endeavour, it opens new lines of inquiry. The intersection of memory and emotion reveals how the latter makes the former relevant in our present.

In *Radical Justice*, Luis Martín-Cabrera draws attention to the sheer number of academic works that have been published about cultural memory and amnesia, while simultaneously reflecting on how this public interest has been insufficient to actually overcome that amnesia or come to terms with the traumatic past. He explains this failure by pointing out that 'the struggle for the recuperation of historical memory is trapped between the inability or unwillingness of the "new" democratic state to assume responsibility for its violent origins and because of the rapid commodification of memory via the spectacular action of the media' (9). To avoid the effects of market commodification and the politics of oblivion, Martín-Cabrera chooses not to consider memory from an abstract, neutral vantage point, 'but rather in a battlefield of multiple meanings that affect the present. As a collective social construction, memory is anchored in economic realities and thus subject to different power pressures, including but not limited to the vested interests of the state and the spectacular logic of the market' (9). The sheer complexity of memory's effect on the present is reflected in the brief review on the topic I have offered thus far. The debate about its meaning, social relevance, and political manipulation continue to shape the way memory is understood in Spain. As this discussion is increasingly connected to current events, as well as a future conditioned by the uncertainties of an unresolved past, it is important to continue to examine the complicated relationship between past and present in contemporary Spanish society. It is this perspective that drives my focus on the memories produced around the political transition in Spain.

21 A direct relationship between the period of the *Transición* and Spain's economic crisis is explored by Bryan Cameron in 'Spain in Crisis: 15-M and the Culture of Indignation', in the recent special issue of the *Journal of Spanish Cultural Studies* (2015).

CHAPTER TWO

Ordinary Memories: Feeling the Past

Insisto en que, a mi juicio, hoy en España no puede hablarse de otra
cosa: hoy vivimos en un momento especial, donde la referencia a la
Transición, explícita o implícita es constante ... Es decir, lo que hoy nos
preocupa está ligado a lo que ocurrió entonces, a treinta años vista de
aquel proceso de los años centrales de la década de los setenta. Pero
esta percepción empieza hoy un evidente proceso de cambio.
Julio Aróstegui Sánchez, 'La Transición a la democracia,
"matriz" de nuestro tiempo presente', 37

In examining current recollections about the *Transición*, it is crucial to understand, first, how memories are constructed and transmitted, and second, how they are embodied, forging deep connections between personal and collective experiences. One of the main criticisms of the political transition, as I show in the previous chapter, concerns the lack of discussion about the legacy of the Spanish Civil War and the violence that continued after its end. The so-called 'peaceful' years over which Franco's dictatorship presided were not the result of consensus or reconciliation. As historians have documented, Franco ruled over a divided society in which the regime's opponents suffered death, incarceration, torture, or exile.[1] Even those who did not actively resist the regime but belonged to the losing side of the war lived in constant fear of retaliation. In Spain, the end of the dictatorship did not bring a Truth and Reconciliation Commission but a consensus politics that chose amnesia (and silence) in matters of its past. As Paloma Aguilar has demonstrated, this deliberate act of forgetting was rooted in fear, successfully instilled in the population by the Franco dictatorship, about the possibility of another war. In other words, the silence that followed Franco's death in 1975 had more to do with the war that had happened

---

1 More recently, see Paul Preston's *The Spanish Holocaust* (2012). For a collection of essays on the topic, see Julián Casanova et al., *Morir, matar, sobrevivir* (2004).

almost forty years earlier than with the dictatorship (Aguilar 2002: 26–27). Critical readings of Spanish culture and fictional recreations of this period have taken note of this silence, but this 'pacto de silencio' has only been challenged publicly since 2000 (Alonso and Muro: 5). The civic work done by the grandchildren of the victims of the war and the dictatorship, demanding moral and economic compensation, has become visible to the public. The creation of groups like the Asociación para la Recuperación de la Memoria Histórica has allowed private petitions for public exhumations, and these activities have in turn directly influenced the debate about the 2007 'Law of Historical Memory'.

One consequence of this public discussion has been the exposure of the political, social, and cultural complexity of the issue of memory in Spain in relation to the Spanish Civil War. The law proposed by the PSOE in 2004, which came to be known as the 'Ley de Memoria Histórica', crystallised the many paradoxes surrounding the question of how to address the memory of Spain's recent past. The law itself, whose title does not contain the term 'memory', was designed to extend the rights of victims of the Spanish Civil War and the dictatorship and to remove Francoist symbols from public places. After much heated debate and opposition, led by the conservative right, a considerably watered-down version of the law was approved by Congress on 31 October 2007 and implemented on 26 December of the same year.[2] In fact, the current law has such a limited scope and budget that, in practice, it cannot efficiently deal with the issue of memory or do justice to the victims of the war and the dictatorship on either side of the ideological divide (Labanyi 2008b: 119).

The key issue at stake in the dispute over the so-called 'Law of Historical Memory' was the memory of the war as preserved during the dictatorship. This memory, as explained by Jo Labanyi, had been maintained only privately, thanks to the Francoist repression. It was only when this memory started to enter the public sphere that the trouble began, as this shift forced Spaniards to recognise how their experiences had been suppressed during the dictatorship and ignored during the transition (Labanyi 2008: 119–20). Accepting the narrative about a peaceful democratic transformation meant accepting a political system that ultimately decided to ignore the trauma of past oppression. The 2007 debate about law and memory quickly turned

2   The actual title of the law is 'Ley por la que se reconocen y amplían derechos y se establecen medidas en favor de quienes padecieron persecución o violencia durante la guerra civil y la dictadura' [Law by which the rights of those who were persecuted or were victims of violence during the Civil War and the dictatorship are recognised and expanded]. Available in pdf format at http://www.boe.es/boe/dias/2007/12/27/pdfs/A53410-53416.pdf.

into a political war when the conservative PP, then in the minority, tried to undermine the socialist PSOE by attacking the law. As a result, the discussion about the legacy of the past turned into a sparring match, with each party more interested in scoring political points than enacting good policy (Labanyi 2008b: 119).

The first casualty of this exchange was the term 'memory', which was actually excluded from the law's title by the Comisión Interministerial, the body responsible for drafting the text. This commission decided that it was not the job of the government to interfere with the memory of its citizens (Labanyi 2008b: 125); nevertheless, the unofficial title 'Ley de Memoria Histórica' stuck in the media. (As we shall see, however, this attachment is peculiar, for the law does not really address what the popular title seems to suggest: collective memory.) Also vociferously attacked by politicians on the right were clauses of the law concerning the removal of Francoist symbols, such as street names, plaques, statues, and monuments (Labanyi 2008b: 125).[3] The desire to defend and preserve these emblems as part of the national history exposed an ideological position that was, at best, ambivalent about its authoritarian past.

The popularity of the term 'memory' in the press and in the public debate led to criticisms over a growing industry generating public interest about Spain's troubled past for profit.[4] The disapproval, in this case, was not about political or editorial manoeuvring, but the media's over-reliance on phrases such as the 'recuperación de la memoria histórica' [recovery of historical memory] or 'reconciliación nacional' [national reconciliation], the repeated use of which rendered these phrases ineffectual clichés without any power to urge a more reflective approach towards the past. One example of the banality resulting from this over-use was its impact on the work of exhuming common graves, where the phrase 'graveside testimony' quickly came to indicate a popular media subgenre (Labanyi 2008b: 119).

Literary critics like Ángel Loureiro have criticised this 'interest' in the past as deliberately creating a public discourse based on victimhood, while ignoring the real events that took place during and after the Franco dictatorship. Loureiro expresses deep suspicion over the appeal to

---

3 The removal is still an ongoing process. The recently elected mayor of Madrid, Manuela Carmena, ordered the removal of Francoist names from the streets of Madrid in July 2015 ('Spanish Dictator Franco names to go from Madrid Streets'. Available at http://www.bbc.co.uk/news/world-europe-33425995).

4 It is rather ironic that Javier Cercas has written about this so-called industry, given the huge success of his 2001 novel *Soldados de Salamina* ('Javier Cercas: "La memoria histórica se ha vuelto una industria"'. Available at http://cultura.elpais.com/cultura/2014/11/12/babelia/1415819975_800516.html).

sentimentality and the role that emotion can or should play in our present understanding of history. He questions the notion of 'historical memory', arguing that this phrase only alludes to the *construction* of memory, rather than actually engaging in the *act* of remembering, and thus undermines the overall concept of memory (226). Memory does play a role in contesting history, however; as Labanyi correctly argues, 'historical memory' does not indicate specific memory, but rather a collective form of memory that brings the past to the public sphere (2008b: 120).

Forcing the issue of remembrance into a public space opens the possibility of creating social frameworks in which individual memories can be placed; it was Maurice Halbwachs who first wrote about the way collective memory works and the way such memory is preserved through social structures (38). While no actual remembering takes place in collective memory, Labanyi argues that the term is appropriate because 'the shared (and contested) understandings of the past that comprise it do connect individuals with the past, and are transmitted across generations in the same way that private memories are' (2008b: 121–22). More precisely, as demonstrated by the criticism of the Law of Historical Memory by supporters like Emilio Silva (co-founder of the Asociación para la Recuperación de la Memoria Histórica), in insisting that memory is a private matter, we allow the law to avoid questions such as the teaching of history in the educational system (Labanyi 2008b: 120). As Labanyi and Silva point out, the law fails to acknowledge that 'historical memory' is a form of collective, and not personal, memory (Labanyi 2008a: 154; Labanyi 2008b: 120). Memory of the violence of the Spanish Civil War has become conflicted precisely because it has been forced to remain a private matter; ultimately, the debate about the Law of Historical Memory did not manage to shift this view politically.

In the final assessment, the debate about 'historical memory', and the 2007 law that grew out of it, was telling in two ways. First, it confirmed the unresolved nature of the legacy of the Spanish Civil War and the dictatorship in Spanish society. Second, it revealed a political impasse within which questioning of the past had become synonymous with criticising democracy in Spain: recognising the failure to address injustices committed in the past was seen as akin to admitting that the nation's political transformation was deficient. The discussion about memory in Spain endures as the disparity between opposing sides of the conflict becomes increasingly clear; the losses suffered by the winners and the losers of the conflict during the war and the dictatorship cannot be considered equal. The fact that these losses are officially deemed equal fuels the perception of continued injustice and the view that the past has not been fully settled. This realisation, in turn, points to the need to come to terms with the shortcomings of the *Transición*.

Curiously, the recent crises faced by the state in economics, corruption, and regional politics have become part of the same narrative of Spain's transitional failure. The inability to address the country's troubled past has also come to be seen as another reflection of the government's incapacity to face its own political struggles.

The suspicion and negativity surrounding the *Transición* has led to a renewed interest in the early post-Franco years. As we have seen above, the memory of this political period has undeniably been influenced by the experience of remembering the war. I contend that the familiarity (and practice) of keeping memories of the past private has shaped Spaniards' relationship with the past. The lack of a public or official venue to deal with painful memories and experiences has forced people to keep the act of remembering private. Ironically, many decades later, the intimate character of these recollections has made them more widely accepted. In other words, because these memories are defined by their private and personal connections, they are perceived as authentic and credible. The appeal of this personalised style of remembering explains the explosion of contemporary Spanish narratives dealing with intimate memories of the past. The memories these works narrate are intimate stories of pain and loss that present themselves as true voices of the past. As social media extols the cultural importance of individual experience, the subjective is reinforced and legitimised over and over in these narratives, which thrive on multiplicity, not in terms of variety, but in the recurrence of similar experiences. These memories can be understood as rehashed versions of the same story, told as separate and distinct episodes by different characters.

While the recollections of the years of the transition are not as traumatic as those of the war or the dictatorship, they are equally subjective. Since they focus on the personal perspective of a political moment, these memories tend to be deeply intimate. Historical events are perceived as everyday experiences by the individuals who lived through them; remembering what has taken place becomes a quest to define and create a memory of one's identity. The multiple retelling of the 23-F, which I discuss in the next chapter, for example, offers a fascinating glimpse into the practice of connecting with the past. When an event is repeatedly reconstructed in an attempt to fully understand what took place, this process creates a narrative about a subjective experience. Ultimately, this insistent storytelling does not result in a better understanding of past political developments, but it does allow for a better comprehension of one's own identity and how it has been affected by the past.

Historical traumas persist because of the incapacity of a society to officially address the losses of the past. In the case of contemporary Spain, the failure of discussions about the past to lead to a present resolution reveals a structural problem; the process of addressing past trauma has become a blame game in which both political parties along the ideological divide engage in a rhetoric that only emphasises lost opportunities instead of focusing on the possibility of creating new ones. In Spain's current sociocultural configuration, the more frequent the discussion about the past, the stronger the perceived effects on the present. Recent recollections of the *Transición* reinforce feelings of both loss and nostalgia—nostalgia for a time when change seemed possible, despite the uncertainty, fear, and violence of those years. Fuelled by the regret of missed opportunities and the frustration that not much has changed politically, the current attitude towards Spain's democratisation is one of disenchantment. Yet there is also an acknowledgement that, perhaps, the legacy and ideology of Francoism was so entrenched during the years after his death that little else could have been done. Ironically, while temporal distance from these political decisions provides a clear view of their shortcomings, it has also made those shortcomings harder to articulate. As a consequence, present political and cultural circumstances are often blamed on the past without concrete justification. Historical and political facts are hard to remember accurately, but the feelings they evoke are still very present.[5]

Perhaps it is the abundance of emotion *despite* the lack of tangible political consequences that makes comprehending the recent memories of the *Transición* challenging. How should we understand recurring narratives of this period that rehash familiar events and add little or nothing to what is already known? Tinted with nostalgia and longing, these narratives are suspicious for offering an uncritical view of the past. Indeed, it is easier to disregard them as irrelevant or as part of the recent cultural fad of 'historical memory'—a fad that has been disparaged, as I mentioned before, because of its focus on victimhood and its lack of critical perspective. Yet the insistent popularity of these works demands that we pay critical attention to them. We should examine the emotion they project, the familiarity with

---

5 For instance, politicians from the Franco regime, like Manuel Fraga, continued to be part of that political world until their deaths, sometimes well into the democratic era. The purging of politicians and the dismantling of the Franco regime was never quite completed, and their disappearance was due to time and social change more than political intervention after the end of the dictatorship. The missed opportunity to 'break' with the past has since been identified as proof of Spain's troubled political system, manifested in its many levels of corruption, tense relationships between regional autonomies and the central government, etc.

which they approach previous political events, the way the memory of these events permeates the experience of the everyday. Though a large part of the Spanish population has close ties to these years, structurally speaking, the political and cultural significance of this connection is hard to assess from the present. In other words, while it is clear that important changes have occurred, those changes have been multiple and complex and their experience resists simplification into a linear narrative that connects past and present. Yet some of the recent narratives about Spain's democratisation, in privileging a subjective account, are able to construct an almost linear progression that explains the past and links it to the immediate present. While this body of work has generally been examined for its historical veracity and ability to complement our understanding or recover forgotten events of the past, previous critical analysis has paid insufficient attention to the emotion that saturates these works.

It is within this critical context that I find Kathleen Stewart's notion of 'ordinary affects'—defined as 'public feelings that begin and end in broad circulation'—useful (2). I link the emotion that permeates recollections of the *Transición* with Spain's current inability—real or manufactured—to provide closure for the traumatic memories of the Spanish Civil War and the Franco dictatorship. Recollections of these years often produce a visceral reaction in those who lived through them; affect theory offers the possibility of detecting these widely circulating feelings, considering them in context, and envisioning a public role that they can play in helping us understand the past.

Stewart describes ordinary affects as the 'varied, surging capacities to affect and to be affected that give everyday life the quality of a continual motion of relations, scenes, contingencies, and emergences. They are things that happen ... that catch people up in something that feels like *something*' (1-2). This is precisely the manner in which recent recollections communicate the political change that took place during the *Transición* period. The importance of the story does not lie in the particular historical or political event being remembered or narrated, but in the small ways in which that event ends up shaping the everyday. The pace of change is sometimes so slow that the transformation is only palpable when seen from decades later. Hindsight is important in these narrations: the small emotions, the protagonists' tiny gestures, the fleeting thoughts of the narrators provide meaning to the act of remembering. More than the story told in these memories, what is important is the *act of recollection itself*—the affect that this activity produces. It is from this perspective that I analyse the *Transición* narratives, paying attention to intimations rather than full actions, noting the way these small signs suddenly disrupt an otherwise normalised structure of existence.

The circulation of critical narratives of the *Transición* opens up the past as a contested space and offers a chance to re-examine previous political events. Probing the years of political change has also offered the opportunity to retell stories—perhaps better ones than those already told, more comprehensive, or stories that can set the record straight. Earlier, I characterised the recent recollections about the Spanish transition as 'memory projects', arguing that their attempt to retell familiar stories reflects the viewpoint that this period is unfinished. Their goal is not so much to offer a perfect or final version of the past (the authors are clearly aware of the multiple ways in which history can be recalled), but to expose the process by which remembering takes place: how past experiences become meaningful and how they remain relevant and connected to the present. The stories should be understood, therefore, as a symptomatic condition, one that points to a contested relationship between past and present. They are the consequences of the collective effect of memory on the Spanish populace; remembering the past has become part of Spain's contemporary social fabric.

The Spanish people's relationship with the *Transición* has become a 'thing'—a cultural, historical, and political referent in the present. While artists continue to produce textual and visual recreations that address the deficiencies of this period, the perception that remains is one of absence—as if there were no awareness of these works, or as though the existing ones were not deemed sufficient. Intriguingly, this response mirrors that to memories of the Civil War and the dictatorship. Even when the perceived political and historical vacuum has been filled and addressed by historians, political scientists, and cultural critics alike, it continues to be sensed as a reality that affects contemporary society. It is this impression that shapes the way Spaniards react to their current politics and their shared realities.

Seen in this context, Stewart's 'ordinary affects' pertain not only to public perception, but also to people's private lives, which 'can be experienced as a pleasure and a shock, as an empty pause or a dragging undertow, as a sensibility that snaps into place or profound disorientation'; more importantly, they are not 'in fixed conditions of possibility but in the actual lines of potential that a *something* coming together calls to mind and sets in motion' and can be understood 'as both the pressure points of events or banalities suffered and the trajectories that forces might take if they were to go unchecked' (2). In my analysis of the memories presented in this book, I seek to examine precisely those moments in which public feelings become private moments, experienced in subtle ways. As separate incidents, these memories may seem to hold no meaning and belong to ordinary moments of everyday life, but together they expose a very particular world view. On the one hand, the persistent belief that Spain's troubled history remains unresolved creates a particular relationship with the past; on the other, the continuation of this relationship is a direct consequence of actions (or even non-actions) taking place in the present, which keeps the connection between the present and the past active. In contemporary Spain, this sustained linking has led many to feel that they inhabit *both periods at the same time*. The social fabric in which people exist, think, and feel belongs equally to the present and the past.

Kathleen Stewart's concept of ordinary affects is connected to Raymond Williams's notion of 'structures of feelings'. Stewart employs Williams's concept to talk about 'social experiences in solution', which do not need to be defined or explained before they exert palpable pressures:

> [ordinary affects] work not through 'meanings' per se, but rather in the way that they pick up density and texture as they move through bodies, dreams, dramas, and social worldings of all kinds. Their significance lies in the intensities they build and in what thoughts and feelings they make possible. The question they beg is not what they might mean in an order of representations, or whether they are good or bad in an overarching scheme of things, but where they might go and what potential modes of knowing, relating, and attending to things are already somehow present in them in a state of potentiality and resonance. (3)

The notion of a break between representation and meaning provides a useful structure for thinking about recent recollections of the *Transición*. Because these recollections usually recreate and revisit familiar historical events, trying to assess their historical or political accuracy becomes repetitive and even exhausting. Trying to find meaning in these works— either by identifying the intersection between fiction and reality or by creating particular categories for these crossovers—is a rather limiting activity. Accepting the fluidity (or even the ambiguity) of the meaning of these narrations, on the other hand, allows us to shift our focus to other characteristics, such as how the 'feeling' of an unresolved past directly affects how the future is viewed from the present. Instead of simply identifying which stories or events from the past are told in the present, I am interested in tracing a narrative flow that opens up an unlimited and continued link between the two periods. Rather than exposing the all-too-familiar stories of war, repression, dictatorship, and disillusionment, I focus on comprehending the affective ways in which these narratives maintain their interest and relevance in contemporary Spain.

By reading texts for affect—in this case, specifically 'ordinary affect'— we undertake an important shift in our understanding of how ideologies work. What become visible are not political examples or historical events, but the ways 'different instances of a relationship with the past' can be '[a]t once abstract and concrete ... more directly completing than ideologies, as well as more fractious, multiplicitous, and unpredictable than symbolic meaning' (Stewart: 3). The diverse connections between present moments and past experiences render the relationship between them tangible—if not politically, then certainly in terms of the raw emotions they produce. Feelings, epiphanies, expectations, and/or frustrations function as real and material traces of the past. They cannot always be logically explained or identified, and sometimes they have no relevance at all; sometimes, however, they are full of significance. It is the unexpected nature of these instances that makes their presence harder to identify and to articulate.

All of the works examined in this book are similar in the way they depict the past as continuing to affect the present (and even the future). Connections between current problems and the events of the *Transición* can be made patently obvious or subtle; the works may be thematically oriented to recount the past from the perspective of the present or they may be situated within the past itself or even in other times. More than the actual stories these works tell, what is important is the way these accounts are made familiar to readers. The stories weave between past and present, set up so that characters physically experience and relive historical events. Couching the experiences of the past within the context of the physicality of everyday life—going to the market, drinking coffee, or going for a walk— makes these experiences easier to understand for readers. Memory here becomes physical and emotional, and it is this physicality that creates an affective relationship with the past.

Moving away from what Stewart calls 'representational thinking and evaluative critique', my interest in these works derives from the complexity that the phrase 'interest in the past' entails (Stewart: 4). I focus on the pull exerted by the years of the *Transición*, using this phenomenon as an opportunity to look into the singularities of the interest in this past. The fact that none of these recent recollections provides any closure or offers a clear understanding of this experience demands a closer look. As part of the so-called 'crisis of memory' in Spain, these works are in need of a new critical approach, one that can map out a new set of connections, a 'new contact zone' between present and past:

Ideologies happen. Power snaps into place. Structures grow entrenched. Identities take place. Ways of knowing become habitual at the drop of a hat. But it's ordinary affects that give things the quality of a *something* to inhabit and animate. Politics starts in the animated inhabitations of things, not way downstream in the various dreamboats and horror shows that get moving. The first step in thinking about the force of things is the open question of what counts as an event, a movement, an impact, a reason to react. There's a politics to being/feeling, connected (or not), to impacts that are shared (or not), to energies spent worrying or scheming (or not), to affective contagion, and to all the forms of attunement and attaching. (Stewart: 15–16)

Understanding the *Transición* as an event and as a shared experience opens up the possibility of rethinking the significance of the period for the generation of Spaniards marked by this historical process.

Thinking back to Raymond Williams's notion of 'structures of feelings', it is important to note the connotation of temporality encoded within it. Williams uses the term 'feeling' instead of 'world view' or 'ideology' in order to refer to the 'meanings and values as they are actively lived and felt' (132). Although he considers 'experience' perhaps a better word to express this idea, he chooses 'feeling' to connote 'thought as felt and feeling as thought: practical consciousness of a present kind, in a living and interrelating continuity' (Williams: 132). Using the moment of the present to communicate a social experience that is 'still in process' allows an understanding of the connections that exist in a generation or a period; for Williams, this process has a 'special relevance to art and literature, where the true social content is in a significant number of cases of this present and affective kind' (132–33).

The production of memory work around the *Transición* in recent years offers us the opportunity to investigate how the generation that came of age during that time works to comprehend its experiences by recreating this living process out of its own social material. As Williams explains, this experience can be characterised 'not by derivations from other social forms and pre-forms, but as social formations of a specific kind which may in turn be seen as the articulation (often the only fully available articulation) of structures of feeling which as living processes are much more widely experienced' (133).

The experience of shared living processes is part of what we could call a 'normalised' structure of existence. But this structure is under constant political, financial, and cultural pressure. It is constantly disrupted or shifted, with the result that individuals must make continued adjustments to maintain their sense of normalcy. Lauren Berlant introduces the notion of 'cruel optimism' to understand this process of adjustment as it relates to fantasies of the 'good life'. She explains how subjects negotiate expectations through affective structures that help to sustain their ideals. For Berlant, optimism is ambitious and continuous and 'involves a sustaining inclination to return to the scene of fantasy that enables you to expect that *this* time, nearness to *this* thing will help you or a world to become different in just the right way' (2011: 2). At the same time, optimism is cruel 'when the object/scene that ignites a sense of possibility actually makes it impossible to attain the expansive transformation for which a person or a people risks thriving ...' (Berlant 2011: 2). While this particular discussion applies to ideals of the 'good life' in the context of the US, it is equally relevant to other fantasy scenarios. In the case of contemporary Spain, for instance, the possibility of addressing the wrongs of the past may itself be understood as the 'desired object' of cruel optimism. As Berlant writes, it is important to ask what happens when these fantasy scenarios—including good political systems, functioning institutions, fair markets, and fulfilling work—reveal themselves to be unstable, fragile, or costly (2011: 2): '[f]antasy is the means by which people hoard idealising theories and tableaux about how they and the world "add up to something". What happens when those fantasies start to fray—depression, dissociation, pragmatism, cynicism, optimism, activism, or an incoherent mash?' (2011: 2). An important exercise is to read the now—this moment, when the fantasy is no longer sustainable—by focusing on the affective components of citizenship and the public sphere (Berlant 2011: 2–3).

Berlant's description of fantasy maintenance, and the question of what happens when a fantasy is no longer sustainable, are useful tools in our discussion about contemporary Spain and its relationship with the past. How might the current interest in memory and ongoing recollection of the past be interpreted as an effort to sustain an ideal democracy for Spain? Or, is the obsessive need to remember the past evidence that the democratic project initiated by Spain after the Franco dictatorship has yet to be achieved? In other words, can the recent obsessive remembering of the Spanish political transition be understood as a critical juncture in terms of affect? I suggest that the current situation can be seen as a moment in which a generation marked by a narrative of political change is confronting its world view and the emotional consequences of living with the rhetoric of a successful *Transición*.

Affect theory provides a useful framework for rethinking the relationship between past and present in contemporary Spain, and particularly the recent treatment of the years of the country's political transformation.[6] The works

6 The theoretical framework of this book reflects the scholarship I engage with as an academic working outside of Spain. While I give attention to research published in Spain on the *Transición* from the perspective of cultural studies, the connection between Iberian culture and affect theory has not yet been widely explored in

of Stewart and Berlant suggest helpful new ways to detect the intensities present in narratives that touch on familiar topics or easily recognisable political beliefs. I focus on Berlant's notion of 'cruel optimism' in the last chapter of the book, but her discussion of good life fantasies and Stewart's concept of 'ordinary affect' function as valuable starting points to begin shifting the critical approach to the study of memory in the context of the Spanish transition. This shift, I contend, will help us to understand the fluidity of the ongoing discourse about the past—the sense in which these memories constitute ongoing projects to find a generational experience and to grasp for meaning in the present by actively recalling or creating private memories. This examination of feelings and expectations turns my critical focus away from representation (challenging the link between memory, fiction, and history) and towards the individualised interaction between past and present. Berlant argues that:

> If the present is not at first an object but a mediated affect, it is also a thing that is sensed and under constant revision, a temporal genre whose convention emerges from the personal and public filtering of the situations and events that are happening in an extended now whose very parameters (when did the "present" begin?) are also always there for debate. (2011: 4)

In the case of the works I analyse in this book, the past is perceived in the same manner. There is a 'presentness' in all of the recollections of the past that seems to undergo constant revision, its parameters continuously challenged. Berlant refers to this emphasis on the present as 'the narcissism of the now' because 'it involves anxiety about how to assess various knowledges and intuitions about what's happening and how to eke out a sense of what follows from those assessments' (2011: 3). It could be argued that, in Spain, the narcissism is of the past, where every incident or event is examined and determined for its consequences, material or otherwise. It is through this constant challenge and assessment that past and present become intimately linked and even temporally blended as a continued 'now' whose origins are found more than three decades ago.

One question that needs to be answered is the 'why' behind this need to link past and present. The affective identification with the past that is found in the recent recollections of the *Transición* encourages the audiences of these works to enter the same relationship, participating in a shared and

scholarship published in Spanish. Luisa Elena Delgado's *La nación singular* (2014) is one of the first books to incorporate affect as an interpretive tool in examining contemporary Spanish society.

collective experience of the past. The reason for this desire is not clear, but it may be indicative of a symptomatic interest, rather than a logical enterprise. These memories can be seen as a reaction to present-day perceptions of daily obstacles with no clear solutions in sight. News about political and financial corruption, austerity measures, the lack of job opportunities, and the continued fraying of standards of living are fuelling the need for an explanation. Searching for a reason for the deterioration of the democratic values of a state than once seemed committed to care for its citizens means looking for an account of what went wrong. In a way, the years of Spain's political transition represent a point of origin for many of these social and financial structures. A careful look at this period also reveals how its democratic project was burdened by its history. Incapable of breaking with the past, the state instead chose to forget the trauma of that time, and in its place to foster a narrative of successful political and cultural change. Such actions, however, also open up the possibility of looking nostalgically to the past and mourning the end of a time full of promises. Both views are equally present in the memories of the Spanish transition; indeed, sometimes they are shared simultaneously and ambiguously by the subjects who engage in remembering the past. To identify a shared experience is also to recognise one's condition and understand the collective journey that has created the social and political structures in which one exists. Finally, these first-person accounts of the past serve as models for remembering. The past, a period intimately linked to one's personal biography, is always more accessible, more easily understood, and, most importantly, easier to connect with emotionally than the present.

Andreas Huyssen opens his *Present Pasts: Urban Palimpsests and the Politics of Memory* with the observation that '[h]istorical memory today is not what is used to be', explaining that it used to 'mark the relation of a community or a nation to its past' and that 'the boundary between past and present used to be stronger and more stable' than today (1). The technological possibilities that allow us to 'access' the past (film, photography, recorded music, the Internet, historical scholarship, museum culture) have guaranteed that the past is now more than ever part of the present, both temporally and experientially. According to Huyssen, the previously strict boundaries meant that the discourse of history, for instance, was necessary to guarantee the stability of the past; it also meant that the boundaries for 'history' were clear, always belonging to the narrative of historical time, whose purpose was to strengthen and legitimise the nation-state to insure its future— culturally, politically, and socially. Memory, by contrast, was relegated to works of literature or the arts. More recently, Huyssen argues, memory and history have collapsed into a single entity:

> Whatever the specific content of the many contemporary debates about history and memory may be, underlying them is a fundamental disturbance not just of the relationship between history as objective and scientific, and memory as subjective and personal, but of history itself and its promises. At stake in the current history/memory debate is not only a disturbance of our notions of the past, but a fundamental crisis in our imagination of alternative futures. (2)

It is important to note that, although this debate is framed in terms of the past and its memory, what is at stake is actually the future.

An important caveat to Huyssen's reading of memory work is his own recognition of the impossibility of knowing how contemporary memory discourses and cultural products will fare in shaping public debate (for better or for worse) in comparison to traditional historical texts (10). Any result would be a consequence of the paradox of memory, since memory participates in processes that erase temporality and '[m]emory as re-presentation, as making present, is always in danger of collapsing the constitutive tension between past and present, especially when the imagined past is sucked into the timeless present of the all-pervasive virtual space of consumer culture' (Huyssen: 10).

In addition to providing a clear framework within which to discuss the confrontation between past and present, Huyssen's concept of 'present pasts' is useful for identifying a type of memory work done in Spain that is ubiquitous in everyday life. He believes that our modern societies are characterised by their strong yearning for the past and show a favourable response to a 'memory market'. This preference, according to Huyssen, has caused a 'palpable transformation of temporality in our lives, brought on by the complex intersections of technological change, mass media, and new patterns of consumption, work, and global mobility' (21). The change in temporal sensibility is not about loss, but rather the recognition of 'the fundamental shift in structures of feeling, experience, and perception as they characterize our simultaneously expanding and shrinking present' (Huyssen: 24). We must accept that, although space and time are fundamental categories of human experience and perception, they are also subject to historical change. In an optimistic reading, Huyssen suggests that:

> In the best-case scenario, the cultures of memory are intimately linked, in many parts of the world, to processes of democratization and struggles for human rights, to expanding and strengthening the

public spheres of civil society. Slowing down rather than speeding up, expanding the nature of the public debate, trying to heal the wounds inflicted in the past, nurturing and expanding livable space rather than destroy it for the sake of some future promise, securing 'quality time'—those seem to be unmet cultural needs in a globalizing world, and local memories are intimately linked to their articulation. (27)

The idea that memory work 'slows down' time is significant in the context of the recent fictional works on the *Transición*. As an historical period and as an object of memory, the *Transición* is currently undergoing a process of scrutiny that stretches and expands its temporal parameters. The effort to fully comprehend, to document, or to imagine the totality of its shortcomings and accomplishments has changed the perception of its time and duration. Obsessing about the past is not the same as mourning the possible failures of a future that has yet to arrive; according to Huyssen, this memory work is important for our societies, which continue to be increasingly in need of productive remembering than productive forgetting.

More than a decade ago, Joan Ramon Resina pointed to the abundance of memorialistic literature on the Spanish Civil War and the Franco dictatorship that flooded the publishing industry during the *Transición*. Years later, it is interesting to observe how this production anticipated the later debate over historical memory and the relationship between narrativity and historiographic legitimacy (2000b: 104). Resina referred to C. Nadia Serematakis' work in his discussion of the apparent paradox in the coexistence of amnesia and memory in post-Franco Spain. He quotes from her work 'The Memory of the Senses': '[a]s the zones of amnesia and the unsaid expand in tandem with the increasingly formulaic and selective reproduction of public memory, the issue of narrativity becomes a zone of increasing political and cultural tension' (2000b: 105). Expanding on this observation, Resina argues that '[d]espite the rhetoric about the disappearance of historical memory, we are far more conscious about the past than at any other time ... who does the remembering? For whom? ... In short, this surplus of memories and remembering agents raises the question about the legitimacy of the memory deployed' (2000b: 109). In other words, in the persistent production and circulation of memories of the Civil War, the dictatorship, and now the transition in Spain, the issue at stake is no longer the identity or the validity of such memories but the structural context that has created the situation that requires this memory work and continues to perpetuate it. A focus on the affective structure that sustains the recent memory work about the *Transición* can help us better comprehend the enduring interest in Spain's troubled past.

A key criticism of the Spanish democratisation process has been the politicians' failure to address regional differences in the peninsula. In fact, discussion of this topic during the transition quickly led to the restatement of a unified vision of the nation that mirrored the one embraced during the Francoist regime. Indeed, part of the 'forgetting' that took place during this period can be understood as an effort to maintain a homogenous national identity. As Resina notes, Spain, then emerging from a 'self-imposed ostracism and international disrepute, [did] not need historical memories—above all, it [did] not need an accurate representation of its past—but resonant ones, and those are accrued through heritage building' (2000: 13–14).[7] In this fierce criticism, Resina emphasises the difficulty of remembering the *Transición* and notes that the successful master narrative of this period 'not only contain[ed] its own subplots as a mushroom houses its spores, but also establishe[d] the rules of plausibility for each retelling' (2000: 13). It is important to keep the notion of this 'successful master narrative' in mind when taking stock of the political transformation that took place in Spain. Despite the criticism surrounding the political transition, Spain has since sustained a democratic government for over 30 years, during which both conservatives and socialists have been elected to office. What is more, Spain has achieved international status as a desirable military ally and an economic partner. Even as the recent financial crisis has identified the country as an economically weaker nation alongside Italy, Ireland, and Greece, Spain has firmly maintained its identity (in the short-termed memory of world politics) as a member of the tradition of Western democracy. The enduring relevance of this effort at identity crafting is illustrated by the way the narratives of these accomplishments are routinely connected to the *Transición*. In the works I analyse in this book, regionalism is not a frequent topic of discussion; likewise, minority identities or rights are not usually the central theme of these memories, although their discussion surfaces as part of the social fabric of the moment.

The final key approach I will take to the recent memories of the Spanish transition picks up on the notion that the *Transición* has become a 'thing'. What does this mean? Primarily, it signifies that this period of history is now itself a referent capable of containing multiple significations. Explicit identification between the referent and the political period is no longer necessary to communicate its importance. The relevance of the period can thus be multiple and complex, referring to political or historical events in

7 I have discussed in my own work the idea of Spain in connection with the writing of the Spanish constitution of 1978 which reflects a unified view of the nation (Song 2014).

the past and the present or to personal and collective emotional states. The Spanish transition has become experiential not only for the generation who came of age during those years, but also for others who have lived under the rhetoric of this period's political success. It is the affect produced, subjectively and collectively, by this experience that makes this historical period relevant to the present. Focusing on the Spanish transition as an empirical event (or at least acknowledging that it is perceived as such by those who remember it) opens the possibility of reading it as a Peircean 'index': a sign that not only *refers* to the object but is modified and affected by it (Peirce: 143). While I specifically use the concept of the 'index' in my analysis of the 23-F in the next chapter, it is also useful to think about an indexical relationship more generally when discussing how the past is regarded in contemporary Spain. In *Making Memory Matter*, Lisa Saltzman explores the relationship between memory and visual culture and how artists engage in the cultural production of memory when history is no longer understood as 'straightforwardly referential' (6). While examining visual strategies that create a place in the present where a material trace of the past can be contained, Saltzman turns to Peirce's index to articulate 'a mode of making meaning in relation to the world that is predicated on physical contiguity, on material relation, on the trace of touch' (12). Saltzman argues that the index should be understood 'as a form rather than a function of representation, the index as a point of reference rather than a referential structure of representation, the index as a vestige rather than a viable means of representation' (12-13). When art objects move from being purely indexical or purely iconic (based on physical relation or resemblance), they reveal that forms are just conventions and structures. Saltzman raises an important question about this relationship, asking, '[w]hat do we call the empty index, the impotent index, the index at one remove, the index that is no longer a sign, but instead, pure signifier? Perhaps, as a start, we can address the specific forms that such work takes' (13).[8]

The notion of an 'empty index' is relevant to the discussion of the process by which the troubled past continues to be revisited in contemporary Spain. As temporal distance from specific political or historical moments increases, their representation and signification are constantly changing. In fact, it could be argued that Spain's unrelenting interest in the past has evolved into memory works where events such as the Spanish Civil War, the dictatorship, and now the *Transición* have become pure signifiers—empty

---

8 Ulrich Winter has written about examples of memory work in Spain that move beyond the symbolic and should be read as 'indexes', replacing reality with the sign itself (256-57).

indexes that can be used to recreate multiple significations, implications, or relationships with the present. As discussed earlier, the trauma of the war begat other traumas, giving rise to a specific view of the past that complicates its understanding by turning it into an endlessly rewritten, recreated, and remembered time, and in which ultimately the question of historical veracity is no longer relevant.

This is the case with the recent works of memory on the Spanish transition. As the motivation for the relationships between past and present loses its referentiality, the discussion of these works of memory can take into account their conventions and structures. The notion of physical contiguity that is implied in the index is also relevant in the analysis of these memories in terms of affect as they can be examined for their bodily and emotional output. Remembering, in these works, becomes a physical act that carries an affective toll, in terms of both generational and personal experience. The works also emphasise the sheer physicality of the act of remembering, employing archival documents as well as photographic and filmic images that remind us of the material traces of the past that are still present today. Indeed, recent works on the Spanish transition highlight how the relationship with the past has changed from referential to indexical.

This transformation, which has been in the making for some time, can be illustrated by contrasting two early works by Manuel Vázquez Montalbán: *Asesinato en el Comité Central* (1981) and *Crónica sentimental de la Transición* (1985). Vázquez Montalbán was one of the earliest critics of the transition, a process in which he detected the gradual abandonment of the left-wing ideologies that structured the political opposition under the dictatorship. His multiple chronicles, as well as his popular detective fiction, the 'Carvalho' series, can be seen as a prolonged criticism of the speed at which the immediate past was forgotten during the political transformation in Spain.[9] Vázquez Montalbán's writing reflects a new approach to capturing this change in a wide range of social, cultural, and political instances that often extend beyond national borders. His chronicling of everyday events traces a shift that, while difficult to pin down, perfectly captures a sense that 'something' is taking place. This could be a general sense of malaise (as Pepe Carvalho expresses in the collection *Historias de política ficción* [1987]), a geographical disorientation, or a sense of the absurdity that infuses national and regional

9 The 24 titles that comprise the Pepe Carvalho detective series function as a chronicle of the political transition and its continued relevance to Spanish politics and culture. The titles span a period extending from the mid-1970s to 2000, with a posthumously published two-part title in 2004 that takes the detective away from Spain.

politics (as is the case in *El hombre de mi vida* [2000)], a continuation of an earlier story told in *Los mares del Sur* [1979]). In addition to these fictional works, the collection of Vázquez Montalbán's columns, published later as *Crónica sentimental de la Transición* (1985), provides a good example of the type of writing that addresses the everyday. The interviews contained in *Mis almuerzos con gente inquietante* (1984) also showcase how change is sometimes visible in little junctures during the political transformation in Spain. The politically and culturally recognisable characters of the time that share a meal with the author embody this difference by making comments, offering observations, or sharing a feeling or a reaction. These texts capture the 'structure of feeling' discussed by Raymond Williams: they describe a social experience in progress, exemplifying the ideology of the moment. Vázquez Montalbán's many chronicles paint an early picture of the experience of Spain's political transition. His texts attest to the belated memories of a generation that became adults during these years and are only now taking stock of the social and political turmoil of that time.[10]

Separated by a period of only four years, Vázquez Montalbán's two disparate works reveal that the shift in popular perception of Spain's political transformation began more than three decades ago and confirm the author's status as a shrewd reader of his time and the finest chronicler of the *Transición*. Using the genre of the detective novel to narrate the murder of the General Secretary of the Spanish Communist Party after the end of the dictatorship, Vázquez Montalbán employs fiction to unveil the internal problems of the party. His political criticisms were in part a settling of old scores, denouncing the failure of the political left after Franco's death (Hart 1987: 97). The thinly veiled references to the political struggles during the dictatorship and the real individuals who populate the plot make it possible to read this novel as an historical narrative that not only informs about the past but also complements existing historiographical works about this period. The story of the failure of the Communist Party in the novel echoes the criticism of the shortcomings of the real political transformation in Spain.

Crónica sentimental, on the other hand, reflects a different referential relationship. The chronicles that comprise this volume cover a wide range of political and cultural events, including reports about politicians, socialites,

---

10 Their intensive documentation of this political process is symptomatic of this later awareness. Ironically, the need to explain and to comprehend every detail of the *Transición* actually reveals an incapacity to fully understand what took place during those years. An example of this condition could be the journalistic work done by Victoria Prego on the transition, especially her *Diccionario de la transición* (1999).

bishops, royalty, their dinners and meetings, and social and cultural topics circulating during the period which later came to be identified as the *Transición*. No clear story is told about this period in these vignettes yet, at the same time, these casual but incisive texts reveal everything. On the one hand, the collection constitutes an example of Stewart's 'ordinary affect'; on the other, perhaps more importantly, the multiplicity of its texts evinces the ways in which the *Transición* was already starting to turn into a signifier by the mid-1980s—a transformation that continues to this day.

Sara Ahmed has written that emotions are intentions *about something*, and this 'aboutness' means that 'they involve a stance on the world, or a way of apprehending the world' (7). To consider memory not for its referentiality to an historical event but rather for its emotional content and affective structure requires that we also examine the role memories play in establishing relationships between past and present. As Ahmed argues, '[t]he memory can be the object of my feeling in both senses: the feeling is shaped by contact with the memory, and also involves an orientation towards what is remembered' (7). Orientation rather than cognition, feeling rather than meaning: memories as affect can be mediated, visceral, immediate, and they are always about disturbing and creating movement. These are the interruptions examined in this book: looking to the affective side of recent memories of the *Transición*; looking at them as ongoing projects that tell more about the present than the past; considering the subjectivity of their narrators and their vision for the future.

CHAPTER THREE

The Moment of Memory

¡Se sienten, coño!
Lieutenant Colonel Tejero on 23 February 1981
in the Spanish Congress

I f there is one moment that has come to epitomise the political transition in Spain, it is the failed coup d'état of 1981. On the afternoon of 23 February, during the investiture vote of Leopoldo Calvo Sotelo as President of the Spanish government, Lieutenant Colonel Antonio Tejero burst into the chambers of the Spanish Congress with a small group of civil guards armed with submachine guns. Holding the politicians present hostage, along with the staff and journalists covering the event, Tejero remained in the building throughout the evening waiting for the military support he had been promised. After approximately 18 hours, when it became clear that his coup lacked the necessary political and military backing, he was finally persuaded to surrender. While the interpretation of this event has been varied, its outcome has generally been understood as evidence that Spain had finally overcome its authoritarian past and was firmly set on its path to democracy. The victory of the socialist PSOE in the general election later the same year was seen as the official arrival of democracy in Spain.

The 'tejerazo', as the coup was termed colloquially, gave a face to the deep-seated troubles that beset the political transformation taking place in Spain in the years following the death of Francisco Franco. At the time, neither end of the newly visible political spectrum seemed happy with the way that 'democracy' was being implemented in the country. The day of the coup, 23 February, later became known as the '23-F', coined by the only civilian jailed after the coup, Juan García Carrés.[1] This failed uprising, which

---

1 A man known for his extreme right-wing ideology, García Carrés barricaded himself in a bar with a group of sympathisers during the first moments of the coup.

kept the entire country awake for a night, was adopted into the popular culture as evidence that Spain was truly no longer the same country as the one governed by Franco. Confirmation of this transformation came in the form of the televised speech of King Juan Carlos, who commanded the military to step down and vehemently denied that he had in any way desired or authorised the coup. This intervention was interpreted as a decisive moment in Spanish politics and a redeeming moment for a monarch whose power, forged under the dictatorship, was one of the lasting legacies of the Franco regime. The king's speech signalled a break from this history and came to represent a new dawn in Spanish politics. The image of the king expressing his position circulated widely, both nationally and internationally, and was later used as proof of the country's new-found democracy. In the wake of this dramatic event, the ensuing socialist victory in the general elections was ultimately interpreted as simply the final confirmation of Spain's new political reality.

Amid the recent debate over the shortcomings of the country's transition to democracy, it is not surprising to find in many works a focus on the events and significance of the 23-F.[2] Javier Cercas's critically acclaimed *Anatomía de un instante* (2009) pursues this path in a work that blends novel, personal essay, and historical study. To gain insight into the events of this fateful day, the narrator obsessively watches the recorded live TV feed of the Spanish Congress, along with footage from the press gallery shot before the guards commanded journalists to stop filming. He pores over the visual remnants of the day, striving to understand what happened that remarkable afternoon, piecing together what he and other Spaniards remember of the event. This examination quickly leads the narrator to conclude that what many Spaniards claim to remember about the day does not truly coincide with what actually took place.

Part of the motivation for Cercas's work was his desire to revisit his own memory and to challenge the existing popular account of the events of the 23-F, both as a stand-alone event and through the lens of its ultimate significance within the context of the *Transición*. He obsesses over the most emblematic visual image of that day: a single frozen image from the TV footage of the failed coup (footage that lasted only 34 minutes and 24 seconds). Starting from this image, Cercas narrates a story of more than

When the uprising did not go as planned, he returned to his house and mediated between the members of the military holding hostages in the Congress and those in command of the takeover (Prego 1999: 619).

2 The significance of this event has been examined critically in the collection *Cartografías del 23-F*, edited by Francisca López and Enric Castelló and published in 2014.

400 pages, recounting the intricacies of what took place that afternoon and during the early hours of the following day as though it were the plot of a detective story. The frozen frame captures the confrontation between Lieutenant Colonel Tejero and three prominent politicians of the time: Adolfo Suárez, the outgoing President of Spain; Santiago Carrillo, the leader of the Communist Party and a mythical figure in the opposition against Franco; and General Gutiérrez Mellado, a key figure in the structural transformation of the military in Spain, which facilitated the country's shift to a civilian government. These figures representing three very different historical trajectories together embody the tensions of the political moment of the *Transición*.[3]

In *Anatomía de un instante*, Cercas obsesses over every detail of this TV frame, dissecting the past into particles that not only allow the reader to relive the moment of this confrontation but also to focus on its emotions. The precision with which Cercas tries to communicate the significance of this frozen TV frame is characteristic of current memory production in Spain: repetitive, detailed, excessively documented, subjectively narrated, seductively deducted. Cercas's almost surgical look into the past uses political speculation as a tool to compile a coherent narrative of the coup and, by extension, of the Spanish political transition. Curiously, what comes into focus in this story is not so much the partisan machinations of the time, but the singular moments that connect the very public event to the private life of the narrator. Ultimately, the significance of this incident rests in the intimate story the narrator tells about his own relationship with his father. The past only becomes comprehensible at the intersection between the historical and the personal, where the interpretation of this experience can be multiple, repetitive, and, above all, emotional.

Although, as we have seen, the triumphant reading of the *Transición* was questioned early on, the renewed criticism of this period seen recently reveals an interesting development in the country's relationship with its past. While the early disapproval focused on questions about the true nature of the 'democratic' process, the persistence of the power apparatus of the old regime, and the abandonment of Marxist ideology on the political left, the current examination of this period is directly linked to present-day politics. Despite being separated by decades from the *Transición*, Spanish society still perceives itself as suffering from the consequences of the

3 After the abdication of King Juan Carlos in the summer of 2014, Cercas presented himself as a monarchist, espousing the belief that there would have been no transition without the king ('Sin el Rey no habría democracia'. Available at http:// politica.elpais.com/politica/2014/06/02/actualidad/1401719800_079533.html).

political decisions of that time. This perception has to do, in part, with the lingering debate about the legacy of the Franco dictatorship and the Spanish Civil War, and the trauma these events inflicted. Both experiences continue to shape generations of Spaniards and their understanding of their past and present. The current political and financial crisis facing the country is clearly connected to this renewed critical look at the past, as it forces Spaniards—especially younger generations—to take a closer look at current political manoeuvres.[4] In both instances, the criticism of the *Transición* is expressed as a denunciation of the crisis of memory, which ignores a past full of unresolved issues. Despite the remarkable number of works produced about Spain's recent past in reaction to this criticism, the persevering perception is nevertheless that there is a lack of critical response regarding the past.[5]

In addition to Cercas's book, this chapter also discusses three filmic works made close to the thirtieth anniversary of the coup: two television miniseries, *23-F: El día más difícil del Rey* (Dir. Silvia Quer, 2009) and *23-F: Historia de una traición* (Dir. Antonio Recio, 2009), and the motion picture *23-F: La película* (Dir. Chema de la Peña, 2011). Finally, I will briefly talk about a recent mockumentary directed by Jordi Évole, *Operación Palace* (2014), which stirred up quite a storm after its airing on Antena 3 on the thirty-third anniversary of the failed coup. In these works, as in Cercas's book, the events of 23 February 1981, are shaped through narratives that rely on archival materials to document the hours in which the Spanish government was held hostage by Colonel Tejero. The focus on the past in these three filmic works ranges from a faithful reproduction of events, including a recreation of the Spanish king's private life, to a fictional adaption of the coup in the format of a criminal investigation. The three representations approach the story from three notably distinct perspectives. Silvia Quer's TV miniseries scrutinises the constitutional aspects of the coup and offers us a glimpse into the workings of the Spanish monarchy. In this version, it is the Spanish monarchy that draws a clear victory from the coup; King Juan Carlos emerges as the hero in the eyes of both the democrats and the Spanish military. The motion picture *23-F*, on the other hand, focuses

4 Teresa Vilarós's *El mono del desencanto* (1998) cleverly articulates the idea of the disillusionment that followed the dictatorship.

5 It is in this disconnection that Colmeiro detects a crisis of memory (22). He also argues that the transition has become an object of memory: 'La transición ha venido a ocupar el lugar histórico preferencial en la memoria colectiva, como nuevo mito fundacional sobre el que se ha construido el presente, borrando efectivamente los rastros del pasado y con ello una pieza fundamental de nuestra identidad histórica' (25).

on the political machinations of the event, following the way in which the political parties strove to suppress the coup. Here the starring role belongs to the Spanish media as they tried to perform their work during the hostage situation, the Spanish TV station under the watchful eye of the Guardia Civil. Finally, Recio's version offers a fictionalised account of the 23-F, told as a military drama where we follow the story of the friendship between two officers who end up on opposite sides of the coup. Following the storyline of a police investigation, this two-part made-for-TV film reveals a divided Spanish army and alludes to a previous attempt by the military to overthrow the Spanish government. The story uncovered by the investigation is one of uneven reactions to the process of democratisation in Spain.

Each of the stories examined here reprises the events of the 23-F, restating a familiar version with some variations. In contrast, Évole's mockumentary weaves a very different story of the failed coup. Based on archival materials and interviews with politicians and journalists, it offers a surprising twist to the story that unleashed a media turmoil after its airing. The nature of this outcry itself is revealing of the enduring significance of this event. The obsession with the 23-F raises questions about one of the most enduring and successful stories of post-Franco Spain. The failed attempt to overthrow a young and very inexperienced civilian government by a military with a very long history of political intervention necessarily takes on symbolic significance in the context of the *Transición*. After a long, repressive, and authoritarian dictatorship, the democratic 'triumph' of the failed coup came to be used as a defence against criticisms of the imperfect nature of the country's political transformation. More than three decades later, the successful narrative of the *Transición* faces even stronger criticisms.[6]

Javier Cercas (b. 1962) rose to literary prominence with the publication of his instant bestseller *Soldados de Salamina* (2001), which sold more than half a million copies and was translated into more than 30 languages. The commercial success of this work was surprising given its conspicuous topic, the Spanish Civil War, an ever-present plotline in the literature of contemporary Spain. Author of six novels including, most recently, *Las leyes de la frontera* (2012) and *El impostor* (2014), Cercas has received numerous literary awards and is currently considered one of Spain's most notable writers. His writing, which often blends fiction with reality to produce

6 While critical works exist, the official version and the collective narrative of the coup emphasise a positive end to the conflict and serve as a testament to the successful democratisation of Spain.

stories that he terms 'relato real', tends to be nearly impossible to classify in general literary terms.[7]

Such is the case with his acclaimed *Anatomía de un instante* (2009), in which he narrates the failed coup of 1981. Cercas received critical praise for mixing fiction and history to narrate an already familiar story in an innovative way, relying on personal experience to bridge gaps in historical evidence. When archival documentation and research are exhausted, the personal is always there to produce a story about the past that is fitting for the present. This same philosophy is reflected in Cercas's story of the 23-F, which reveals how the intersection between reality and fiction yields access to a level of understanding that history alone has been unable to communicate. Essential to this narrative are the personal impulses that guide the story of the failed coup and reveal a new dimension of the memory work being done in Spain.

Awarded the Premio Nacional de Narrativa in 2010, *Anatomía de un instante* focuses on a traumatic (and yet triumphant) moment of the transition, codified, as we have noted, in one frozen TV image from the footage of the failed coup of 1981. From this image, Cercas reconstructs more than three decades of Spanish history, spanning from the Franco dictatorship to the present. If the 23-F initially acquired a cathartic significance in the political transformation of Spain as 'the event that allowed a democratic resolution', it was later identified as a clear symbol of the many problems inherent in this process. The failed coup has been reimagined as a sign of the failures of the *Transición*, a touchstone for acknowledging the civic discontent with Spain's democratisation process. In other words, the 23-F has come to be understood as a point of return, an origin site for current conflicts, guided by personal memories that connect the present with the past. The possibility of 'unpacking' an instant into almost countless moments reflects the Spanish conception of the past as a 'project', an open task that not only requires a great deal of historiographical research, but also exacts a high personal toll from the narrator, who undergoes a deep, transformative process.

In *Anatomía de un instante*, the narrator, whom we identify as Cercas himself, is only able to 'tell' the story of the 23-F after reading extensively on the topic and 'mediating' the research he has completed by translating this experience into a well-documented personal reflection about the past. While the skeletal structure of the account is constructed from historical evidence, the version of events told is based mainly on conjectures. What the narrator actually points to is the absence of hard documentation about the

7 His latest controversial novel about Enric Marco, the man from Barcelona who for three decades pretended to be a survivor of Nazi concentration camps, pushes Cercas's usual interplay between truth and fiction even further.

23-F; most of the works he consults come to be seen as historical speculation against which his own estimation gains more credibility. Ultimately, Cercas crafts a generational response to the crisis that exposes the mechanisms of an intimate recollection of the past by linking collective and personal events and merging public and private experiences.

Through its 'messy' and complex memory work, *Anatomía de un instante* uncovers the tension between the impulse to control the narrative of the *Transición* and the multiple details and glimpses of the period that surface unexpectedly. The impulse for control is evident in the way the realities of violence and instability are conveniently forgotten in the official version of the 'model transition'. Cercas's own account, obsessive in its details and evocative of the official version of the past, is exceedingly organised and symmetrical.

Kathleen Stewart's concept of 'ordinary affect' gains relevance here: despite its coherent structure and historically tight argument, what matters in Cercas's memory work is not the recollection of the events of the 23-F itself, but the *way* in which these events are remembered. In fact, his narration seems to suggest that the failed coup can only be remembered from the present in such detail because of the visceral reaction it still causes today. The drive to tell a story—or at least attempt to craft a satisfying narrative—about the past is fraught with failures; part of the memory work is to recognise and accept the uncertainty that prevails even in the telling of the perfect tale.

To understand the past as a 'memory project', it is necessary to see its contradictory impulses: despite favouring imagination to capture historical experience, there remains a clear need for documentation, a compulsion to obsessively return to the archive to validate the past (or at least the version of the past presented in these works).[8] Subjective memories are presented as essential links to the past, but the longing for historical evidence to legitimise them is intense. As a result, these works can often be read as confrontations between reality and fiction, and as meditations on the way the latter can contribute to the understanding or the narrating of history. The end result, however, blends fiction and fact so tightly that it becomes impossible to distinguish one from the other.

Recent renewed interest in experiences of the war and the dictatorship in Spanish fiction and film has been interpreted as the manifestation of historical trauma. In the case of the recollection of the *Transición*, however, there is no longer a recognisable traumatic subject. Instead, what we find is

---

8 In this case, the archive is used more as a reference, a 'quote' rather than an historical source, as though its mere mention can validate a claim. I say this because these works use many of the same archival images.

a determined and clear-eyed examination: ghostly appearances, unconscious manifestations, and uncontrolled utterances give way to methodical and rational approaches, precise organisation, and purposeful versions of the past. This attitude conveys the impression that the past is no longer dormant and given to unruly disruptions but rather a resource for explaining the present.

Cercas's methodical inquiry into the past, identifying and (re)collecting memories, is part of a work that aims at providing 'defining' narratives rather than 'definitive' ones. Put differently, the narrator is always aware of the multiplicity of perspectives that are involved in telling a story. The goal is not to provide a 'unique' and historically accurate version of what took place, but to reveal one that is personally meaningful and relevant to the present. Telling the story in this manner enables the narrator to define his own identity and his place in history. The stories themselves, however, do not provide earth-shattering insights or effect any significant change in the narrator. On the contrary, they lead to *more* ambiguity: a messy process of trying to understand what took place and to communicate it appropriately. Ultimately, the stories recovered or 'successfully' told still fail to capture the past's defining moments—yet it is precisely this incapacity to perfectly articulate or grasp this experience that turns these attempts into compelling narratives. Within this context, the term 'project' appropriately captures the rational approach of this work while also conveying its unfinished (or unfinishable) nature. Given the impossibility of relaying the past in any satisfactory way, remembering becomes an ongoing effort in search of new rhetorical strategies. The sheer number of publications about the Spanish political transition is proof of this continued labour.

By locating his narrative in the space between reality and fiction, Cercas seeks to fully capture and explain the events of the past. His obsession with recovering the past through archival work, historiographical research, and profuse documentation is less about providing a truthful version of past events and more about establishing a personal connection with this past. The author himself has explained that his texts, and especially his novels, cannot be labelled 'historical' as they are really not about the past, but about the relationship between past and present (de Eusebio 2013: 112). He calls the past 'una dimensión del presente' (de Eusebio 2013: 105): the connection to the personal is what makes the past accessible. This philosophical approach explains why Cercas always uses a first-person narrator; the autobiographical voice used in *Soldados de Salamina*, *La velocidad de la luz* (2005), or *Anatomía de un instante* serves to ground the significance of the past in the present, the moment where the 'I' exists.

Cercas makes his personal connection to the past relevant in the present by posing questions he considers 'moral' (Cercas 2011: 'La tercera verdad').

Morality is a poor lens through which to evaluate controversial events and that is exactly why Cercas uses it. The aim of his writing is not to illuminate past events, but to boil them down to small instances through which he can bring into focus specific feelings (or beliefs). Historical events are recast as timeless questions, a rhetorical manoeuvre that transforms the past into a field to be ploughed for answers. In other words, the morality implied in Cercas's interrogation of the past should be recognised for the subjectivity it represents. As the past only becomes available through one's own connection to it, it becomes necessary to examine the relevance of the personal and the many possibilities for communicating historical experiences created by a subjective inquiry.

Cercas's story highlights everyday experiences by revealing the complex way in which past events transform or touch different lives. Stories cast in the 'personal' are also helpful in aiding us to recognise how generational responses to historical events tread between facts and emotions. In this process, the members of this generation get to establish their own historical and political identities. Cercas's work exposes an impulse to tell a story about one's own past that is simultaneously private and public. Dealing with what is known, but also with what is not, Cercas's narrators are always capable of explaining, informing, and speculating. They are ultimately able to offer organised and meaningful information, but also 'lo ignorado, el repertorio de lo desconocido: lo que los relatores no saben con certeza, lo que sospechan, los hechos posibles que jamás podrán documentar y su sentido probable' (Serna: 98). This uncertainty is outweighed by the categorical 'I', which convinces the reader to follow the narrator's instincts and deductions.

The trust developed through this first-person perspective is an important aspect of Cercas's aesthetic. Trust is achieved because of the narrator's willingness to reveal his weaknesses and his use of self-deprecating language. Cercas's narrators are always very upfront about the many things they ignore; they put themselves and the reader on equal ground at the beginning of the book, embarking on a journey together to learn about an event of the past. The back story narrated in these texts is always one of personal growth, where history is reflected both physically and emotionally in the narrator's 'I'.[9]

---

9 I am not interested in Cercas's knowledge about the past or the moral questions that his narrators pose. I am equally not interested in analysing his humorous language or the virtues reflected in his characters, as some critics have done. What I focus on here is the way historical events affect his narrators emotionally and physically.

As in his other works, Cercas bases the writing of *Anatomía de un instante* on an 'historia minúscula'. This 'tiny' tale, however, quickly uncovers a mystery in need of a resolution. His telling of this story—captivating in its scope and its misleading simplicity—allows the narrator to pile many more stories atop the original small piece.[10] The failed coup of the 23-F, for instance, is boiled down to one TV frame and one gesture, repeated three times by three different characters who each represent an important part of Spain's recent history. The seated figures of Adolfo Suárez, General Gutiérrez Mellado, and Santiago Carrillo encompass the political scenario of the *Transición*, which the narrator—whom we assume to be Cercas—is able to describe for us based on his extensive reading on the subject.

As Serna observes, Cercas's narrators are always about to reveal something to the reader that only they are able to discover (103).[11] The narrative structure employed in *Anatomía de un instante* allows the reader to accompany the narrator on his journey and to share his closely guarded historical insight. This process, predictably, always raises new questions. For instance, it never becomes clear how exactly King Juan Carlos was involved in the planning of the coup (whether he tacitly approved of it or whether the military misinterpreted his words) or what real role the Spanish intelligence, the CESID (Centro Superior de Información de la Defensa), played. Even as Cercas's journey into the backstory of the 23-F offers a compelling version of events where symmetry and logic prevail, the end result is well reasoned and deftly composed historical guesswork, which must be considered with caution. In fact, although his work raises new questions about the official explanation of the coup, it does little to settle the many doubts the author himself has at the beginning of the story.[12]

The only clarity achieved in Cercas's narration pertains to his own insight. His intimate understanding of Suárez as an historical and political figure (and, ultimately, as a human being), is made possible through Cercas's reflection

10 Serna explains how Cercas's narrators are 'trapped' by their objects of interest, and how the complexity and the enthusiasm with which they embark upon uncovering their back story infects the reader. This interest is presented as a 'natural' reaction to the topic in question, although we realise that this is not the case. This fascination derives from 'la manera en que [Cercas] administra la información, al modo en que presenta esas indagaciones aparentemente minúsculas' (103).

11 This is clearly expressed by Serna's explanation of how Cercas writes: '[p]ara llegar con bien a una cima que es meta y enigma. No le vale que otros hayan coronado ese objetivo con anterioridad ... Es él mismo quien ha de recorrer el itinerario, quien ha de leer toda la bibliografía disponible para averiguar lo que él solo puede descubrir' (103).

12 The version that Cercas follows most closely is Jesús Palacios's book, *23-F, el Rey y su secreto* (2010).

on the words of his own father. Here, the link between history and the personal is absolute, and suggests that the past cannot be understood except through subjective experience, no matter how much historical research or reading of archival documents one is able to undertake. This rather limiting view throws into doubt the possibility of ever understanding a history one does not belong to or hold a special connection with. Yet, in the Spanish context, this exceptionality is unsurprising. The need to subjectively explain what happened in a way that validates an historical claim stems directly from the country's long and complicated relationship with its troubled past. Ultimately, historical distance and rational analyses give way to an emotional understanding of what took place. The past only becomes meaningful once the narrator is able to connect with it emotionally. There are two sides to this memory work: one highlights an affective reaction to an historical event, while the other points at how this affective response ends up conditioning the way the past is perceived and re-interpreted in the present.

Anatomía de un instante begins with a prologue and concludes with an epilogue that work inversely; that is, the prologue is the epilogue of a failed novel about the 23-F, while the epilogue becomes, in fact, the prologue of a successful one, after a thorough five-chapter account of the failed coup of 1981.[13] In the prologue, the narrator explains the reasons behind the failure of his novel and, in a confessional tone, shares his realisation about the events of the 23-F: that this political episode is already so full of improbable elements that trying to narrate a fictional account about it is useless. Instead, he decides to capture the compelling and very 'real' story behind the events of this day. The result, as his 'epilogue' suggests, is the most captivating novel about the Spanish transition.

Through his writing process, Cercas reflects on the way the memories of this day have been archived and circulated. He considers how these materials were mediated by technology and wonders how other Spaniards remember the event. Most importantly, his recollections of the day, and his conjectures about what the 23-F was really about, shed light on the most important story of the book: the narrator's relationship with his father. The personal element of his narration allows us to read the political intrigue as a tale about Cercas's father. The historical analysis of the 23-F offered in *Anatomía de un instante* provides a chance to consider, not what is actually

---

13 The 'transformation' of an historical essay or a chronicle into a novel is reflected in the debate about the nature of Cercas's work. Should *Anatomía de un instante* be read as fiction or history? Just a quick glance at the praise offered in the inside leaf of the book are enough to make this point: 'a perfect chronicle', 'an essay', 'the best history book', 'new journalism', 'literary work', 'splendid story', etc.

being told, but the *reason* behind the telling of the story. It also exposes what happens in the process of trying to narrate an historical event.[14] This will be an important distinction as I move away from questioning the historical veracity of Cercas's work and focus instead on the way the past is remembered and narrated as a reflection of the present.

Cercas starts his examination of the 23-F by considering the fictional qualities of the protagonists involved in the failed coup. Discussing Lieutenant Colonel Tejero, he writes: '[a]unque sabemos que es un personaje real, es un personaje irreal; aunque sabemos que es una imagen real, es una imagen irreal: la escena de una españolada recién salida del cerebro envenenado de clichés de un mediano imitador de Luis García Berlanga' (2009: 14).[15] Three elements of this observation deserve further consideration: first, the transformation of a real person into a fictional character mediated by television, which Cercas calls 'el principal fabricante de realidad a la vez que el principal fabricante de irrealidad del planeta' (2009: 13). Second, the use of the first-person plural, which Cercas employs to universalise the experience he describes as part of a collective consciousness. This position is quickly accepted by critics like Serna: '[t]odos hemos contemplado la irrupción de las tropas del teniente Antonio Tejero en el Congreso de los Diputados. En algún momento, cuando vimos a esos individuos por primera vez, sentimos vergüenza, repudio, frustración: de nuevo el pretorianismo español parecía imponerse con ignominia y fatalidad' (104). Finally, Cercas points to the phenomenon in which historical memories are facilitated by visual images provided by popular culture. I will discuss the relationship between popular culture and memory in more detail in the next chapter, but it is important to point out here that, in the case of Spain, this relationship is strong. As already mentioned, although mostly absent from official discourse, memories of the Spanish Civil War and the Franco dictatorship have circulated predominantly through fictional recreations in literature as well as in film and television programmes.

The mediated nature of the 23-F shapes Cercas's characterisation of the event and his own memory of that day. He explains that everyone in Spain remembers 'seeing' the coup on live TV, but this never actually happened. The television feed was not made public until after the liberation of the Spanish Congress on the morning of 24 February. The coup was broadcast live on

14 In this narration, what becomes visible or detectable is not always articulable, but recognising or 'feeling' its presence is essential. An example is the significance of Suárez's gesture, captured on film on the day of the attempted coup.

15 The play on opposites is a constant feature in Cercas's writing. By confronting two distant possibilities, he is always able to offer a more plausible version. The 'middle of the road' approach makes his accounts more credible.

the radio, but its images were only seen by a few journalists and technicians from Televisión Española.[16] Cercas emphasises these details to demonstrate how history is often recalled incorrectly: 'Eso fue lo que ocurrió, pero todos nos resistimos a que nos extirpen los recuerdos, que son el asidero de la identidad, y algunos anteponen lo que recuerdan a lo que ocurrió, así que siguen recordando que vieron el golpe de estado en directo' (2009: 15).

Cercas insists on the relationship between memory and identity, and the need to privilege the first as a way of establishing the latter. The questioning of this memory is a challenge to one's identity and, in this case, it is a challenge closely related to the outcome of the *Transición*. As part of the generation that 'remembers' the failed coup, Cercas probes his own identity and memory in order to establish a narrative of his own coming of age. The act of correcting his memory of the events surrounding the coup is used as an opportunity to reassess his own self, in this case in relation to the story of his father. This recognition also means the surrender of his own sense of independence, as Cercas finds that he is not so different from his father; both men are free-thinking subjects in a rapidly changing country affected by the same political realities.

The belief Spaniards hold about having witnessed the coup in front of their TV sets is, according to Cercas, evidence of how the 23-F has evolved into fiction:

> Al fin y al cabo hay razones para entender el golpe del 23 de febrero como el fruto de una neurosis colectiva. O de una paranoia colectiva. O, más precisamente, de una novela colectiva. En la sociedad del espectáculo fue, en todo caso, un espectáculo más. Pero eso no significa que fuera una ficción: el golpe del 23 de febrero existió, y veintisiete años después de aquel día, cuando sus principales protagonistas ya habían tal vez empezado a perder para muchos su estatuto de personajes históricos y a ingresar en el reino de lo ficticio, yo acababa de terminar el borrador de una novela en que intentaba convertir el 23 de febrero en ficción. Y estaba lleno de dudas. (2009: 15)[17]

The collective neurosis or paranoia that results from this fiction contributes to the event's unsettling qualities. As a member of the young generation

---

16 The cameras present at the Congress usually recorded the sessions; images were then distributed internally and later edited and used during the afternoon and evening news programmes (Cercas 2009: 15).

17 For instance, in the film *El calentito* (Dir. Chus Gutiérrez, 2005), in which a group of young Spaniards decide to go ahead with their rock concert despite the unfolding coup, the parents of the young characters are at home glued to their TV sets.

that lived through the coup, Cercas shares the feeling that matters related to this incident have never been fully resolved. The solidarity of this belief is expressed in the use of the collective 'we', intimately connected to the 'I' of the narrator. The narrator's doubts about the failed coup function as an invitation to further examine the political moment of the 23-F. Cercas's inquiry into the details of Spanish democratisation works as a memory project because of his belief that achieving a narrative about the past is doable and ethically necessary. It is the same desire and belief present in the other recent works about the transition.

Cercas writes about the feeling that 'la realidad le está reclamando una novela de que no es él quien busca una novela, sino una novela quien lo está buscando a él' (2009: 16). Cercas's sentiment—an invitation to consider the close relationship between reality and fiction—materialises after he writes an essay detailing three personalised versions of the coup, slated for publication near the anniversary of the event. In the story he tells, he is considered a hero for having run to the university after he heard about the coup from his mother; however, he does not consider himself a 'real' hero because the true motivation behind his action was to find a classmate with whom he was hopelessly smitten. Finally, he realises that, despite the rhetoric, no one was truly a hero on that day since, rather than going out into the streets to confront the military, everyone simply stayed at home, awaiting the outcome of the coup (2009: 16–17). Cercas remarks on how his own story of personal failure contrasts with the ones told in the Spanish media, where the botched coup is declared to be the 'triunfo total de la democracia' (2009: 17).[18] At first, Cercas reacts to the successful narrative, condemning it as a lie, but he is quickly pulled into the official version of the story through his reaction to a single image. This image is shown repeatedly during each anniversary of the 23-F, yet Cercas suddenly finds himself captivated by what he has seen over many years: the image of the solitary figures of Adolfo Suárez, Gutiérrez Mellado, and Santiago Carrillo sitting while all the other politicians are hiding under their seats as the Guardia Civil shoot their guns. On rediscovering this image, Cercas finds to his surprise that this familiar scene has suddenly become enigmatic:

> De repente me pareció una imagen hipnótica y radiante, minuciosamente compleja, cebada de sentido; tal vez porque lo verdaderamente enigmático no es lo que nadie ha visto, sino lo que todos hemos visto

18 Cercas's essay ultimately agrees with this narrative of a successful *Transición*. Despite acknowledging the shortcomings of this historical version, the author's final recognition of the merits of the process of democratisation in Spain has to do with the acceptance of his own family history.

muchas veces y pese a ello se niega a entregar su significado, de repente me pareció una imagen enigmática. (2009: 18)

The phenomenon of a suddenly incomprehensible gesture singled out from a familiar image resonates with Kathleen Stewart's notion of 'ordinary affects'. As 'public feelings that begin and end in broad circulation', such affects are also part of what 'intimate lives are made of' (2). Public and private feelings and events are not always connected by causality; their flows are unpredictable and their relationship is complex and subtle, reflecting the multiplicity that characterises everyday life. When these feelings intersect, they can be experienced as a 'pleasure and a shock, as an empty pause or a dragging undertow, as a sensibility that snaps into place or profound disorientation' that allows the identification of 'a *something* coming together'; as a result, these colliding feelings 'can be seen as both the pressure points of events or banalities suffered and the trajectories that forces might take if they were to go unchecked' (Stewart: 2).

The sudden impact of Suárez's image on Cercas (or the way the politician's loneliness grabs hold of the narrator) captures the moment when 'something' comes together. Affect is what transforms an over-circulated and all-too-familiar image into a relevant document of the past. It offers the possibility of 'reading' an historical event through a moment of empathy; in other words, the significance of the event stems from exploring the feelings it arouses. Stewart explains that ordinary affects do not work through meanings, but rather through the intensities those meanings build and the emotions they raise. Ultimately:

The question they beg is not what they might mean in an order of representations, or whether they are good or bad in an overarching scheme of things, but where they might go and what potential modes of knowing, relating, and attending to things are already somehow present in them in a state of potentiality and resonance. (3)

The feeling that first piques Cercas's interest ends up resisting his attempt to narrate it rationally. His initial effort to write a novel about the 23-F is a failure, and his story only becomes plausible once he is able to connect his reaction to Suárez's image to his own emotions towards his father. Cercas's first impression of Suárez is judgmental—'un escalador del franquismo', 'un político oportunista, reaccionario, beatón, superficial y marrullero'—because he sees in the politician a reflection of his own father, a 'suarista pertinaz' (2009: 18–19). His opinion of Suárez changes, however, once he sees the man through the eyes of his own father. What the gesture of the politician ultimately reveals is an intimate story about a father and a son.

To 'remember' the *Transición* in this context, then, is to turn to and acknowledge its affective side. No longer perceived only as a political process, this period is now understood as a complex set of circumstances that gained importance through the emotion(s) it inspired. Its unresolvedness 'feels' relevant to the present, encouraging the inquiry into this past to extend beyond the mere understanding of historical facts. Remembering is an act of subjective interpretation and a process of self-examination. The past becomes relevant when it is recognised as part of one's intimate current, and possibly future, history.[19] Suárez's gesture and the familiar TV image of the coup are 'ordinary affects' of the *Transición* that continue to circulate in contemporary Spain. As such, these iconic elements can contribute to the creation of 'an animate circuit that conducts force and maps connections, routes, and disjunctures' (Stewart: 3). The connections and fragmentations that these affects produce bring new relevance to the past. At once abstract and concrete, Stewart argues that these affects are more 'completing than ideologies, as well as more fractious, multiplicitous, and unpredictable than symbolic meanings' (3). Since the early 1980s, the *Transición* has been read as a general failure of the political left and the progressive ideology once embodied by the Spanish Communist Party. An examination of the affective side of this political process opens the opportunity to understand this past anew, even if in fragmentary and arbitrary ways, and to reassess the meanings that have since been attached to the 23-F.

Cercas's obsession with Adolfo Suárez and his gesture develops into a complex reading of the politician himself and the events of the 23-F. The 34 minutes and 24 seconds of the video-recording of the coup become an infinite source of meaning:

> Cuando se emitieron por televisión ... el filósofo Julián Marías opinó que merecían el premio a la mejor película del año; casi tres décadas después yo sentí que era un elogio escaso: son imágenes densísimas, de una potencia visual extraordinaria, rebosantes de historia y electrificadas por la verdad que contemplé muchas veces sin deshacer su sortilegio. (2009: 19)

Cercas obsesses over the visual documentation of the event, searching for clues as though the 23-F were a giant puzzle. He writes about seeking meaning in a random sequence of images which, seen through the lens of the ensuing three decades, acquires immeasurable meaning. But Cercas's search is misleading. We later find out that most of the questions he has

---

19 In fact, instances of this memory should sometimes be read as gestures that attempt to connect with the future.

been trying to answer through his close examination of the images of the 23-F had already been answered by Javier Pradera. The journalist describes the coup as a novel, a police fiction: 'Porque el golpe de estado es una novela. Una novela policíaca. El argumento es el siguiente: Cortina monta el golpe y Cortina lo desmonta. Por lealtad al Rey' (Cercas 2009: 20). Cercas finds this hypothesis irresistible because of its symmetry: 'de repente el caos del 23 de febrero cuadraba; de repente todo era coherente, simétrico, geométrico, igual que en las novelas' (2009: 21). It is the proximity of the 23-F to fiction that helps Cercas to narrate its 'reality'—a reality composed of theories, conspiracies, false memories, and uncertainties. In this 'laberinto espejeante de memorias', he realises that the magnitude of what happened on the 23-F cannot be contained in a work of fiction. Instead of a totalising and all-encompassing story, what remains of the event are its details:

> comprendí que los hechos del 23 de febrero poseían por sí mismos toda la fuerza dramática y el potencial simbólico que exigimos de la literatura y comprendí que, aunque yo fuera un escritor de ficciones, por una vez la realidad me importaba más que la ficción o me importaba demasiado como para querer reinventarla sustituyéndola por una realidad alternativa, porque nada de lo que yo pudiera imaginar sobre el 23 de febrero me atañía y me exaltaba tanto y podría resultar más completo y persuasivo que la pura realidad del 23 de febrero. (2009: 24)

Cercas's flirtation with the intersection between fiction and reality invites critics to engage in a discussion about their relationship to the past and the nature of this author's work. *Anatomía de un instante* has been read as a work of fiction, an essay, a fine piece of journalistic investigation, and a (popular) history book. However, for me, what is most important about Cercas's writing on the 23-F is the way he chooses to connect with the object of his literary and intellectual attention.

The five chapters of *Anatomía de un instante* are organised in a circular way, each section beginning with a description of what the narrator has seen (or is presently seeing) in those 34 minutes of video footage of the Spanish Congress. The narration takes place in the present tense and is visually marked by the use of italics. Each description focuses on a different detail of the goings-on in the time between the irruption of Lieutenant Colonel Tejero and the stopping of the recording by the Guardia Civil. The description ends each time with the narrator zooming in, as if he himself were the lens of the camera, on the subject that will be developed in that segment of the book. The chapters are similarly divided by numbered sections, in which we learn about the chosen politician (or the military officer) as a man and a public figure: his actions, the political and social background of the moment, and how it all comes together (described in the last section of every chapter, dated '23 de febrero'). The different perspectives explored in this narration move circularly and repetitively to add complexity to what took place, to emphasise details, to tease out connections, and to provide the overarching symmetry initially described in the prologue.[20] This is how characters like Gutiérrez Mellado, Carrillo, and finally Suárez come into focus. The same narrative strategy is also employed to convey information about the machinations of the Spanish intelligence service, the CESID, and the role played by figures like José Luis Cortina Prieto and Torcuato Fernández Miranda during this time. The contemporary political ensemble that Cercas draws together through these chapters is impressive, but this is not what makes the story of the 23-F compelling. The abundance of names, dates, and political details of the Spanish transition are certainly evidence of the effort Cercas has put into preparing himself to tell his story. But what makes each section of his narrative compelling is the human side of the characters, onto which the narrator projects his own (real and imagined) emotions: '[t]al vez fue eso lo que sintió con los años Adolfo Suárez; eso o una parte de eso o algo muy semejante a eso ...' (2009: 374). The narrator is moved by the tiny gestures of these subjects, 'ordinary affects' full of potential meaning and historical resonance:

> permaneciendo en su escaño mientras las balas zumbaban a su alrededor en el hemiciclo durante la tarde del 23 de febrero, Suárez no solo se redimía él, sino de que de algún modo redimía a todo su país de haber colaborado masivamente con el franquismo. Quién sabe: quizá por eso—quizá también por eso—Suárez no se tiró. (2009: 385)

The obsessive documentation pursued in *Anatomía de un instante* points to Cercas's need to visualise and experience first-hand what took place during the *Transición*. The interviews he conducts, the transcripts he obtains with difficulty, the newspapers and academic books he combs through for new information, all speak to the importance of a physical connection in understanding the past. A logical approach to an object of study, it reveals the belief that the past is *knowable*; learning and remembering seems to be an accomplishable project. His work also evinces a moment of generational

---

20 It is ironic that, despite choosing 'reality' over fiction, Cercas organises his information symmetrically, a practice he attributes to fiction writing: 'como cualquiera buena ficción, había sido construida a base de datos, fechas, nombres, análisis y conjeturas exactos seleccionados y dispuestos con astucias de novelista hasta conseguir que todo conectase con todo y la realidad adquiriera un sentido homogéneo (2009: 23).

awareness of how the events of the Spanish transition influenced the population's relationship with politics. Most importantly, Cercas's attempt to narrate the 23-F proves that no amount of rational labour can fully capture past experiences. The attempt to understand the past turns into a search for different ways of knowing. For Cercas, this quest to knowledge leads him to the story of his father. The initial connection he offers in *Anatomía de un instante* between his father and Suárez comes full circle at the end of the book, where he explains how, on the day before the last public photograph of Adolfo Suárez appeared in the Spanish press, he buried his own father. The now-famous picture of the ex-Prime Minister walking away with this back turned to us accompanied by King Juan Carlos, who has an arm around his shoulder, captures the end of a hotly contested historical period and serves as an intimate reference to Cercas's own loss.[21] It is not surprising that the last words of *Anatomía de un instante* are about the narrator's father, who, despite the mistakes he may have made, should be remembered as a decent man: 'No incurriré en la presunción de afirmar que no cometió ninguna de las trapacerías de aquella época trapacera, pero puedo asegurar que, hasta donde sé, no hubo nadie que no lo tuviese por un hombre decente' (2009: 435).

Cercas's generous depiction of his father extends, in turn, to the political period of the transition. In particular, it extends to Suárez, with whom the author establishes first a personal and later a generational connection. He confesses that the real reason behind his dislike for Suárez was the politician's resemblance to his own father: 'es posible que pensase algo parecido de mi padre, y que por eso me avergonzase un poco de ser su hijo' (2009: 435). Cercas (or his narrator) also reflects that perhaps his troubled relationship with his father can be attributed to his own arrogance. The narrator has always thought of himself as better than his progenitor—or, at least, has always felt sure that he would *become* better over time. He now realises that this has not been the case. Looking back, Cercas comes to realise that he and his father were only able to communicate with each

21 This photograph, taken by Suárez's son, acquired new meaning, first when Suárez died, and thereafter when King Juan Carlos I abdicated his throne. The photo was printed again in the Spanish press after both incidents as an iconic image of the *Transición* and of both the ex-President and the ex-King of Spain. I requested permission to use this photograph here to illustrate Cercas's story and also to use it as part of my book's cover However, Suárez's son vehemently declined my request when he learned about the content of my book, expressing his strong dislike for *Anatomía de un instante* and its author. Ironically, Suárez's son seemed to perceive Cercas's text as an objectionable history book. I tried to explain, without success, that I do not read Cercas's book as an historical study. The photograph can be seen online at http://periodistas-es.com/el-rey-con-suarez-mision-cumplida-31666.

other through their discussions of politics. In the light of this revelation, the narrator's desire to re-examine the *Transición* becomes an attempt to understand his father: 'para intentar entender a mi padre' (2009: 437). The intent with which Cercas examines and interprets Suárez's gesture stems from his father's trust of this politician, '[p]orque era como nosotros' and 'no iba a hacer nada malo' (2009: 436–37). In the end, the academic and journalistic research done for the book is trumped by Cercas's own personal interpretation and understanding of history. The past, he concludes, is a collective and generational experience:

> En fin, el franquismo fue una mala historia, pero el final de aquella historia no ha sido malo. Pudo haberlo sido: la prueba es que a mediados de los setenta muchos de los más lúcidos analistas extranjeros auguraban una salida catastrófica de la dictadura; quizá la mejor prueba es el 23 de febrero. Pudo haberlo sido, pero no lo fue, y no veo ninguna razón para quienes por edad no intervinimos en aquella historia no debamos celebrarlo; tampoco para pensar que, de haber tenido edad para intervenir, nosotros hubiésemos cometido los mismos errores que los que cometieron nuestros padres. (2009: 434)

The endorsement of this political change, which parallels the official discourse about the Spanish transition, is certainly questionable, but the focus on the personal, the move from the 'I' to the 'we', emphasises a lasting connection with the past. Cercas's choice of turning to an intimate relationship to imbue the past with meaning is characteristic of the way history is recalled in contemporary Spain. Cognition is replaced with emotion as the existing frameworks are challenged to discuss memory works. No longer solely focused on historiographical accuracy or a critical reading of nostalgia, the act of remembering is now required to provide a physical and intimate connection to the past. A close look into other recent representations of the 23-F also reveals this epistemological shift. As Alonso and Muro's collection has raised new questions about Spain's political transition, the current memories about this period have become fertile ground from which to assess the continued obsession with the *Transición*.

The footage of Lieutenant Colonel Tejero's irruption into the Spanish Congress with the Guardia Civil is the visual component of the 23-F that unites all narratives of the failed coup. The way the images of this event have been deployed to recreate and narrate the *Transición* tells us something about the way visual elements function to provide and create meaning and the relationship between the constructed images of fiction and real-world images. Laura U. Marks turns to the semiotic theory of Charles Sanders Peirce to elucidate the connection between images and reality. This theory, which departs from a linguistic focus to talk more generally about how signs work, leads Marks to consider how documentaries make generalisations about the world based on intimate contact (196).

Peirce defines a sign as 'something which stands to somebody for something in some respect or capacity' (135). In tandem with this understanding of signs, Peirce develops the notion of the 'index' to describe a sign that is affected by its object or necessarily has some quality in common with it (143). This idea of an 'index' has been used to analyse visual materials and identify the physical connection between images (such as photographs) and signs (Pierce: 159). The real connection that the index provides between one's mind and an object is further emphasised by its ability to influence mood (Peirce: 165). The index, from this perspective, is a complex sign that provides a 'dynamical (including spatial) connection both with the individual object ... and with the senses of memory of the person for whom it serves as a sign' (Peirce: 170). Moreover, the index is not limited in reference to individual objects but also applies to imaginary constructions, to 'images in the mind which previous words have created' (Peirce: 172).

Marks explains that Gilles Deleuze's theory of images, which depicts them as actualisations of the virtual, is based on Peirce's sign system. In other words, images are considered to be signs and, therefore, real. While documentaries per se are not encompassed in Deleuze's thinking, for Marks, the implication of the real in documentary images helps us to understand how signification works and the way fictional and real-world images interact with each other to create meaning. Considering that footage of the 23-F comprises real-world images and is used in documentaries, fictional films, 'mockumentaries', and even in an extensive narrative essay, its process of signification helps us to recognise the way we have come to understand, deploy, and narrate these images.

Building on Peirce's system of signs, Marks identifies three different modes in which the 'real' appears: Firstness, Secondness, and Thirdness. Firstness is a 'mere quality', a first impression that indicates 'something so emergent that it is not yet quite a sign' or a 'sign of possibility' (196). Marks describes Firstness as the sign itself, a relation to the object that is 'iconic', a sign that 'denotes the object', and, in Deleuze's terms, the '*affection-image*, an image of barely contained feeling or affect' (196–97).[22] For Marks, this is the

---

22 She further explains that '[i]n the affection-image, a becoming-other occurs; for as soon as we have sensation or feeling, we change. Thus, in the affection-image there is an enfolding of perceiving self into perceived world' (Marks: 197).

realm where documentaries kindle their relationship; first, with reality, as 'we observe the birth of affection-images from the world-itself', and second, with the 'sense of possibility', as 'affection-image precedes perception, for affection conjures an anonymous quality of feeling' (197). The footage of the 23-F, only released after the fact, on the afternoon of 24 February 1981, captures this idea of affection-image—not only quickly becoming the sign of the failed coup, but also emerging as a departure point from which to explore the affective reaction to these images.

Secondness, according to Marks, is the sign that 'denotes the object through an existential connection to it', that is, an indexical relationship that reflects the basic attributes of object and events (197). She explains that this is where documentary works best, 'the realm of relations—not of causality, but of brute matter in contact with brute matter—that the documentary must claim to accurately record' (198). Finally, Thirdness is the realm of interpretation and symbolisation, 'where signs take part in mental operations that make general statements about qualities and events' (198). Here, the relationship between sign and object is symbolic: the sign denotes the object (through interpretation, representation, or an argument) as well as what Deleuze calls a 'mental image' or 'relation image'. Marks describes how a mental image 'mediates affection-images or *qualisigns* (feelings, sensations) and action-images or *sinsigns* (facts, events) and builds an argument from them' (198).[23] What the description of these realms reveals is a pattern of significations and a process by which we understand (or engage with) reality through its representation.

Mental images help to form associations, which in turn generate totalising narratives. Marks, however, focuses on quite the opposite process: on the meta moment in which 'the mental image of a film begins to reflect upon itself' (199). The result is a need to look beyond the symbol, to acknowledge that there are elements that cannot be symbolised and that, '[b]y forestalling symbolic action ... the mental image begins to probe the affective components that are enfolded in the action-image, breaking the action-image down to its component affections' (Marks: 199–200).[24] Marks examines this return to the primary qualities of the sign as she analyses the way in which the creators of false documentaries exploit the affective potential of fabricated footage: '[w]hen the people's experience cannot be

23 It is important to understand that the relationship between these three realms is fluid; as Deleuze points out, affection-image and action-image may already have elements of thought in them (Marks: 198–99).

24 Movement-image is a Deleuzian term that broadly defines an unbroken, linear narrative 'based upon the continuity editing rules established by the Hollywood studio system' (Martin-Jones: 2).

represented in discourse, *the story must be creatively falsified in order to reach the truth*' (201–02, emphasis original). This discussion highlights how we think about the process by which documentary footage becomes meaningful, and provides a constructive space to consider the ways in which the footage of the 23-F has been used and how that usage has evolved in the last three decades. These images—from which Cercas extracts over 400 pages of meaning about the *Transición*, impossibly real and fictitious at the same time—reveal a desire to offer a totalising narrative about the past, one that thrives in multiplicity rather than offering an overarching account of what took place. But this apparent complexity is misleading; the meaning of what happened, its 'truth', ends up being much simpler. From the first moment the footage of the 23-F was aired on Spanish television and seen around the world, the images of the coup exemplified how signification can move fluidly across the Peircean sign system. Ultimately, this flexibility signals that, at every level of this system of signification, 'an enfoldment takes place, so every image enfolds a heterogeneous elements'; Deleuze refers to this phenomenon as 'peaks of present', that is, 'those points where two or more pasts are enfolded in an image' (Marks: 202). In the multiple enfolding of the images of the 23-F, meanings are created and read to emphasise their importance both in the past and the present.

José Carlos Rueda Laffond and Carlota Coronado Ruiz characterise the images of the 23-F as exemplars of the visual paradigm of the Spanish political crisis of the *Transición*. These images belong to personal memories, inasmuch as individuals have appropriated details of the event as part of their own experience (Rueda Laffond and Coronado Ruiz: 135). The authors describe how emotional qualities of the event—unexpected, shocking—quickly became attached to the now-familiar images of the coup. It is important to remember that these images started circulating on Spanish TV much later than the actual press coverage of the event, which was mainly covered by radio stations like SER and Radio Intercontinental. As Rueda Laffond and Coronado Ruiz point out, the public history of this footage began only once the public and the press together recognised it as an opportunity to witness an historical moment of great transcendence (135–38).[25] It is ironic that, even as the images of the 23-F are so well known, most of the political details of the events of that day are still unknown.[26] The widespread circulation

25 Rueda Laffond and Coronado Ruiz compare the experience of watching the footage of the 23-F with seeing a live broadcast of history (137). This concept has been studied by Daniel Dayan and Elihu Katz in *Media Events: The Live Broadcasting of History* (1994).

26 Most documents related to the event that came out during the trial after the failed coup are still under seal.

of these images has inspired a number of efforts to recreate and narrate Spain's political transition visually.[27] My intention here is not to examine every documentary made about the 23-F but to acknowledge titles like *23-F: se rompe el silencio* (Antena 3, 1994) and its sequel *Los silencios del 23-F* (Antena 3, 1997), *El 23-F desde dentro* (TV3, 2001), and *El 23-F a Catalunya* (TV3, 2004), which reflect the way documentaries explore the indexical relationship between the images of an event and the event itself. Recognising their efforts to accurately record and explain what took place historically and personally anticipates an eventual turn from documentation to fiction.[28] Curiously, the later recreations of the 23-F, despite their fictional nature, consistently tap into the qualities of the affection-image. Directors always include the real footage of the 23-F or produce meticulous replicas. All the representations of the 23-F which I examine offer fictional accounts that nevertheless aim to create realistic narratives of the failed coup. In the process, they expose how the images used and composed for these recreations contain and visualise different significations for this political event.

The film *23-F* is shot from the perspective of a political plot; within this plot, Tejero is presented as a pawn, a soldier manipulated by the greater powers behind the uprising. The heroes of the day in this case are the Spanish media: the journalists, producers, and editors who bravely continued to work during the hostage situation. Part of the film takes place in the Televisión Española (TVE) station, where the Guardia Civil has arrived to monitor the journalists' activities. The film's emphasis, however, remains on Tejero, humanising him and presenting the coup from his personal point of view. The narrative of *23-F* does not excuse the coup, but it does provide a context for understanding the frustration that motivated this military action. In particular, the film is sympathetic to the figure of Tejero (Paco Tous), who is portrayed as a man acting on the principles instilled in him by his military training. His involvement in the 23-F is a direct result of his loyalty and his sense of duty rather than any political ambition or ideology.

The image of Tejero as a puppet being manipulated from behind the scenes is visually strengthened in the film by his constant communication with Juan García Carrés (Juanma Lara), the only civilian involved in the coup. He appears on the screen on the other end of the telephone line in the shadows of a dark office. During most of the film, we can only identify him by his voice. García Carrés's job is to convince Tejero that everything is

---

27 Rueda Laffond and Coronado Ruiz offer a very useful list of documentaries on the 23-F (148–65).

28 Marks would explain this situation by pointing to 'the fragments of the real contained in the affection-image' (201).

going according to plan and that military, political, and public support for the coup is growing. He is the sole mediator between Tejero and the outside world, including the other officers and his own family.

That Tejero is being lied to is made clear when García Carrés puts the receiver of the telephone to the radio so he can hear the military marches that are being played. When the coup began, the radio stations stopped their broadcasts and played only military music, which offered a strong reminder of the years of the Franco dictatorship. García Carrés uses the military marches to convince Tejero that the government overthrow is succeeding and that the good old times are about to return. The way Tejero blindly believes his handler re-enforces his naïveté. The officer's credulity is again emphasised during his confrontation with Adolfo Suárez (Ginés García Millán). Tejero blames the politician for the ongoing military action, accusing Suárez of ignoring the losses suffered by the Guardia Civil at the hands of terrorist groups. The officer is deeply hurt by the Prime Minister's failure to attend the funerals of these servicemen, taking his absence as proof that the military is being abandoned by a cowardly government that ignores the servicemen's sacrifices and their love for the country.

In this encounter, Adolfo Suárez is also given the opportunity to express his personal feelings about the situation. He confesses to the powerlessness he experiences when confronted with the grieving families, giving this as the reason he stopped attending the services. The sympathetic portrayal of these two figures echoes the reading of both men offered by Cercas in *Anatomía de un instante*. In fact, the film clearly nods to this author's version of events; for instance, in the beginning of the film we are offered close-ups and long and medium shots of the key figures detailed in Cercas's essay, allowing the viewer to identify them as important characters in the story. In the initial sequences of the film, amid the casual conversation that takes place inside the chamber preceding the vote, the camera offers a shot of Adolfo Suárez entering the room from the side. He occupies the frame by himself, while all previous frames are shared by two or three characters. The film parts from Cercas's book, however, in emphasising the actions of Tejero rather than those of Suárez.

As director Chema de la Peña and his crew explain in the interviews available on the DVD release, the purpose of the movie was to recreate as faithfully as possible what took place on the day of the 23-F. On the cover of the DVD, the movie is described as the first motion picture to try to tell, in all of its complexity, the story of the coup d'état of 1981: '[d]esde la toma del Congreso, usada como arranque, hasta la liberación de los diputados, se reviven las diecisiete horas y media que hicieron temblar los cimientos de una joven democracia'. The message is clear: the film reaffirms the triumphal narrative of the political transition in Spain and reinforces the belief that democracy succeeds because the personal reactions of the key figures of the event are not, in the end, completely misguided. What is remarkable here is the director's desire to faithfully recreate the footage of the irruption of Lieutenant Colonel Tejero into the chambers of the Spanish Congress even though he is mainly restating the official version of events. As the extra materials on the DVD document, this is an extremely meticulous process: each camera had to be placed in the exact location and at the correct angle in order to reproduce some of the now very familiar images of that day. Both this set up and the way the coup is narrated by the journalists inside the chamber signal the importance of the press in documenting this historical event and rescuing (and protecting) its visual evidence.

The belief here is that these images, despite their staged quality, will have the same impact as the originals and inspire the same reaction. In order to achieve the same effect, the film begins with an extensive montage of archival footage of the period. On the one hand, the political incidents visualised in this footage serve as an explanation for the political uprising the audience is about to witness. On the other, the initial montage serves as a visual reference for the later recreations of historical scenes. *23-F* builds its own historical credibility by appealing to and using historical footage as the starting point for its story. Combining the original footage with a slow dramatisation of Tejero's preparation as he gets ready to leave his house to assault the Spanish Congress, the film becomes charged with suspense. Ironically, the viewer is already cognisant of what is about to happen and visually familiar with its details. Even when the plot is already known, it is hard for viewers not to be pulled into the emotional build-up of the film, with the contrast in colour and brightness in its initial scenes as they move between inside and outside shots. The cold blue and grey tones that dominate the shots following the Guardia Civil as they prepare their entrance into the Congress building are sharply contrasted with the yellow and red warm tones of the inside shots, which capture politicians and journalists lingering around the chamber. This visual contrast prepares the viewer for the imminent violence. What ultimately drives the emotional narrative of this film, however, is the in-between archival imagery that prepares the viewer for what is about to come. The irruption into the Congress is, in a way, triggered by the montage of black-and-white images, reminding the viewer of the key moments in the country's political life after the end of the dictatorship.

In the film's script, written by Joaquín Andújar, the trust in the strength of these affection-images is such that the initial sequence lacks any meaningful dialogue. The film starts with an extreme close-up of two hands buttoning a shirt, cut to a similar shot of an unknown person tying a shoelace, adjusting a tie, putting on a jacket, winding a wristwatch, putting on a belt with a pistol holster and checking a weapon. As the camera moves up to focus on the face of the man dressing himself—with a little pause en route as he touches his military pins, adjusts his jacket, and retrieves the iconic Guardia Civil hat, the *tricornio*—we finally realise we are seeing an officer of the Spanish gendarmerie. We see him briefly in the kitchen saying goodbye to his wife; she asks him if everything is alright and he responds that he will call her later. Getting ready to exit the flat, he stops by a mirror in the hall to adjust his hat, look at himself slowly, and make the sign of the cross, head slightly bowed.

As he leaves his home, the film cuts to a montage of black-and-white archival footage that visually organises the most important events of the early seventies into a seamless narrative. The montage begins with the assassination of Franco's heir, Carrero Blanco, the death of the dictator himself, the street protests, the terrorist groups and their attacks, the Atocha murders and the first elections, then ends with the speech of Adolfo Suárez resigning as President of the Spanish government. From this brief visual historical recap, the film moves to the inside of the Spanish Congress, where journalists are congregating, chatting informally, and getting ready for the afternoon session. The initial focus on these journalists signals their importance in this story, yet they quickly fade into the background as the camera and the script favour the story of Tejero and the other historical figures involved in the day's events.[29] The scenes inside the building and the chamber are intercut with shots of military officers, telephone conversations, and a brief look inside the dressing room of King Juan Carlos, as the viewer begins to recognise the sequence of events leading to the arrival of Tejero and his men. As the scenes unfold, the already familiar images of the 23-F set up the beginning of a totalising narrative of the coup. In this supposedly accurate retelling of the events of the day, the specific viewpoint we encounter not only shapes the actions of the day, but clearly takes for granted the privilege of the virtual image to deliver a 'real' version of a past event.

Laura Marks points to the blurring of the distinction between documentary and fiction, echoing Patricia Pisters's argument that cinema is increasingly a 'becoming-time-image' (Marks: 201). The Deleuzean time-image, which Pisters explains as 'crystals through which the actual and the virtual rotate, sometimes even in indistinguishable ways', establishes a connection between

---

29 Towards the end of the film, when the coup is nearing its final hours, it finally becomes clear how important was the role played by the journalists on that day.

virtual and actual images that work together to create a sense of the real (58). As Marks clarifies, for Deleuze, the virtual image—'what may or may not be recorded in memory'—is opposed to the actual image ('what was recorded') but not 'to the real' (207). This complexity is encapsulated by the crystal-image in which actual and virtual images reflect each other, producing 'a widening circuit of actual and virtual images like a hall of mirrors' (Marks: 207). This multiplication of images (as signs and, therefore, as forms of signification) in the use of both archival and fictional images creates fertile ground for the association of mental images with the affection-image of the 23-F.

What one should take from this complexity is not a suspicious view of the manipulation of archival footage, but an appreciation for how cinema (and television) combine these images to allow the visualisation of different elements as they unfold (and enfold) the details of an historical event. These images continue to create meaning and memory, connected not only to the distant past but also to other moments in time, perpetuating their relevance. Each new (re)interpretation of the 23-F, including (past) documentaries, contemporary narratives such as Cercas's work, and the television miniseries about the coup, speaks to the importance of the event. What is more, the fact that the movie version of the 23-F cannot be separated from either of these renditions, or from the archival footage itself, is a testament to the persistence of the history of the Spanish transition and how it continues to remain intertwined with current events.

23-F: *La película* and the recent television miniseries clearly illustrate the moment at which the documentary approach to this event is abandoned in favour of other forms of narration (Rueda Laffond and Coronado Ruiz: 167). In the case of Silvia Quer's 23-F: *El día más difícil del Rey* (TVE, 2009), the story of the uprising is developed through the figure of King Juan Carlos, tracing what went on inside the palace that day. Antonio Recio's 23-F: *Historia de una traición* (Antena 3, 2009) tells the story from the perspective of the present, recounting the 23-F as a present-day police investigation that recovers the story (and memory) of an old friendship between two military officers.

El día más difícil and *Historia de una traición*, both two-part miniseries, share the narrative qualities of a melodrama: the former a family drama; the latter a tale about the falling out of two close friends, one of whom loves the other's wife. The TVE production *El día más difícil* was overwhelmingly more successful than Antena 3's *Historia de una traición*, and is considered the most watched miniseries in the history of Spanish television. The first episode had 6,491,000 viewers and its conclusion 6,920,000, an audience share of 31.5% and 35.5%, respectively (Smith 2012: 57). During the last episode and the golden minute for television rating, the 'minuto de oro' at 11:20 pm, it achieved around 8.5 million viewers (Rueda Laffond and Coronado Ruiz:

178). In comparison, 23-F: *Historia de una traición* achieved only 2.8 million viewers (a share of 14.3%) for its first episode, which dropped to 1.5 million (a share of 7.6%) when it shared the same time slot as the initial episode of 23-F: *El día más difícil del Rey* (Rueda Laffond and Coronado Ruiz: 189–90).

The success of the TVE production has been attributed to its stellar cast of very well-known actors, including Lluís Homar, who played King Juan Carlos. In addition, the art design and the general production was considered to be of a much higher quality than the programme produced by Antena 3. In addition to TVE's experience in producing high-quality historical dramas, the media work involved in promoting the series, including interviews with the actors before they started shooting, helped to create expectations around this show (Rueda Laffond and Coronado Ruiz: 178–79). It also marked a key moment in television history, as the Spanish crown had, up to that moment, been hidden from public representation (Rueda Laffond and Coronado Ruiz: 180). It was only after this miniseries that other programming began to involve the Spanish royalty—as in the case of *Felipe y Letizia* (2010, Telecinco), a series dramatising the love of the recently crowned Felipe VI and his wife.

These titles are only part of a long list of miniseries in recent Spanish television history which, for Smith, are the unintended consequence of government legislation of the media (2012: 54).[30] What these successful programmes show is that 'Spanish viewers are increasingly offered the opportunity to experience widely varying re-workings of the national past at the same moment of consumption' (Smith 2012: 54). As Smith points out, this phenomenon is currently attractive for both producers and the public in Spain, because such historical programmes are profitable and serve 'as a focus for historical memory: for group creation and social cohesion, as [much as] for continuing grievance and contention' (2012: 54).

Rueda Laffond and Coronado Ruiz argue that both of these miniseries exemplify how television (and popular culture) is the site of a dominant ideology that recreates narratives enforcing its viewpoint. Their critical reading of the TVE production tackles its view of the monarchy in a teleological and ahistorical reading of the past that enforces its place in Spanish politics and that repeats, 'la metanarrativa televisiva sobre el proceso de cambio político en la España de los años sesenta y ochenta' (180). This reading of the past is reinforced by the 'presentism' favoured in historical adaptations for television. Critics oppose this practice because they see in it a clear intention to simplify history and codify an official

30 Smith explains that 'the revival of mini-series is derived from the Ley del Cine (Law of Cinema), whose provisions were reinforced in 2007, obliging television companies to invest in feature film production' (2012: 54).

Figure 3.1   The king sits down to read his speech while his son is watching him. *El día más dificil del Rey* (TVE, 2009)

version. In the case of the adaptation of the 23-F, the king is presented as a family-oriented and courageous man who was misled by some of his closest followers (Rueda Laffond and Coronado Ruiz: 182).

Smith notes how the connection of the past to the present is identified in TVE's *El día más difícil* by its engagement with current television genres that foreground everyday life. He highlights the connection between the portrayal of the royal family in this miniseries and the typical attitude of transnational reality franchises, noting how '[p]ublic policy is consistently shown in terms of private loyalty and rivalry' (2012: 58). During the 23-F, the Spanish king's most public and important performance was his speech, but in Quer's television adaptation, this speech is visualised as a private event, one dedicated first and foremost to his own family. The creation of a private space during the king's speech is visually paired with reverse shots of both his son (Lluís Bou) and his wife (Mónica López), who are listening to him attentively and approvingly (Smith 2012: 60). Smith observes that, in its climatic moments, the emotional engagement of *El día más difícil* reminds the viewer of a *telenovela*; moreover, the show undertakes a clear 'feminisation' of the monarch, whose listening audience in the palace is overwhelmingly female (2012: 59). In the end, this miniseries casts the story of the 23-F as a family drama in which the father succeeds in protecting his family and taking advantage of the adversity represented by the coup to teach his son a political lesson (Figs 3.1, 3.2, and 3.3). Susana Díaz emphasises this point, going so far as to contend that the miniseries is but an excuse to legitimise the monarchy of King Juan Carlos and to show the political education of

Figures 3.2 and 3.3   The reverse shots of the king's speech are of his family members, mainly of his son (the future king) and his wife and daughters. *El día más difícil del Rey* (TVE, 2009)

the prince who, as heir to the throne, will have to follow in the footsteps of his father (169).[31]

31 The Spanish monarchy is currently under much scrutiny in light of recent scandals, including the now-infamous elephant hunting trip of 2012, on which the former king broke his hip, and the corruption charges against his eldest daughter Infanta Cristina and her husband Iñaki Urdagarín. The historical trial of a princess in the Spanish court stands as a testament to how the discourse about the Spanish monarchy has changed. The reading of the relationship between father and son in Quer's adaptation of the 23-F, in particular, has acquired a new significance in light of the abdication of King Juan Carlos and the coronation of his son as Felipe VI in June 2014.

The shift to the personal and private as a mode of narration of the 23-F is apparent in both the TVE production and the series produced by Antonio Recio for Antena 3, *23-F: Historia de una traición*. In Recio's series, the police investigation that discovers the plot surrounding the 1981 coup is recast as a (clearly fictionalised) story of unrequited love. Tracing the falling out between two friends whose relationship ends when one of them falls in love with the other's wife, the intense emotions of loyalty, betrayal, jealousy, friendship, love, and sacrifice are mixed into the uncovering of the planning and aftermath of the coup. The audience discovers this story through the lens of a police investigation taking place in the present day. Throughout the series, sequences shot in the past are woven together with sequences shot in the present to produce a story that connects two eras and two generations.

23-F: Historia de una traición traces the experience of Ignacio Zárate (played as a young man by Sergio Peris-Mencheta and in later years by Héctor Colomé), who tries to protect his friend Antonio Leal (played by Pau Cólera and Manuel Zarzo) from becoming personally involved in the coup. Zárate first attempts to get Leal to leave Madrid on the day of the coup, but his plan fails and his friend is jailed with the other military men involved in the uprising. Zárate then gives Leal secret documents related to the 23-F in an attempt to help him avoid a heavy sentence from the court. Over the course of the events, the deep involvement of the CESID in the coup is uncovered; the show stresses the way the Spanish intelligence service's role has remained hidden. The closely guarded secret of this involvement is revealed when the children of Zárate and Leal, Arantza (Bárbara Goenaga) and Gonzalo (Rodrigo García), come under attack during their efforts to recover the documents that Arantza's father gave to Leal's wife, Pilar (Xenia Tostado and Inés Morales).

Although Rueda Laffond and Coronado Ruiz dismiss this series as a fictional account of modest production value (195–97), I contend that this fictionalised recreation of the coup engages with the standard historical narrative just as the (more clearly historical) version produced by TVE does. In fact, *23-F: Historia de una traición* should be understood as another instance of television's 'presentism', which establishes a direct connection between the coup and the present day. This connection, made explicit in the temporal slant of the series's narration, is fully articulated in the final scenes, when Zárate comes clean about his involvement in the coup. He reflects on his long silence and justifies it by asserting that when everything ended, 'pasó algo más', something important: 'nacieron nuestros mitos'.

The myths that he recounts echo the characterisations of the political and military figures of the 23-F discussed above. Most significantly, Zárate acknowledges that these stories directly affect the future generations, including that of his own daughter and the son of his now-deceased best friend. Zárate's own future is made possible through his acceptance of what took place more than three decades ago. Only when he agrees to a version of history that justifies the actions of his best friend is he finally able to pursue his now-reciprocated love for Pilar.

In the motion picture 23-F, the irruption of Tejero into the chamber of the Spanish Congress is fully restaged, as are the radio broadcasts of that day. In the case of the television series, the only actual re-enactment is that of the king's speech in the TVE production.[32] Given the focus on the king in Quer's adaptation of the 23-F, it is not surprising that the most carefully restaged scene of the series is the monarch's most recognised and admired action. The intimate setting in which the now-famous address is delivered and taped suggests a change in the audience for whom these words were intended. In 23-F: *El día más difícil del Rey*, contrary to what the title indicates, the challenge the king must overcome is not a national crisis but a personal one. He is able to emerge triumphantly thanks to the support of his loved ones and because he succeeds in fulfilling his familial duties. His words are meant to calm and protect his family, who are the first to listen to the speech. The visual recreation of this scene suggests that each Spanish household is an extension of the royal one. When the monarch gives his speech, he is providing the leadership that is required of him as a father, stepping up at a perilous moment for his family and, by extension, the country as a whole.

While a similar level of dramatisation is missing from the Antena 3 production, the reliance on archival footage to provide the narrative of the 23-F and the period of the *Transición* is common to all three recreations. As I have already noted, in de la Peña's motion picture, the original, grainy, black-and-white archival footage is incorporated in the early part of the film. The violence and the historical significance of the Spanish transition depicted in those familiar affection-images establishes the political (and fictional) context of the film. In the case of the TVE production, the first use of archival material is a sound file, introduced when the king and his staff first realise what is happening on hearing the radio broadcast from the Congress. The only visual image of the coup is the real footage of the closed-circuit cameras of the day, which is seen first (and only) from the television station. The lack of visual footage actually helps to create the impression that the palace was completely isolated and that the king's

---

32 By 'actual', I mean the events of the day known thanks to the available visual footage such as the video from the closed-circuit television in the Spanish Congress or the televised address of King Juan Carlos on the day of the coup.

difficult decisions had to be made by him alone.[33] The radio broadcast is also the first piece of archival material included in Recio's 23-F: Leal hears about the coup on the car radio and quickly turns his car around to return to the capital. Paradoxically, the most fictionalised version of the events, the miniseries produced by Antena 3, is the one that uses the largest amount of archival footage of events around the 23-F, including film of King Juan Carlos I being booed during his appearance in the Basque Country on 5 February 1981, General Milans del Bosch taking the tanks out on the streets of Valencia on the day of the coup, and the king's speech. In a seamless mix between actual and virtual images (this time recast in colour), Recio's miniseries creates a fictionally dramatic and historically authentic narrative about the Spanish transition.

All three recreations of the 23-F successfully blend real and virtual material to create a memory of the event. The fluidity with which these images are used and deployed points to their signification. At the same time, the use of these images also reveals how signs become symbolised through a reliance on their basic affective qualities. The visual narratives found in all three works recall the way time-image operates. As Marks explains, it 'disintegrates the distinction between actual and virtual because it renders indiscernible the very distinction between present (actual) and past (virtual)' (195). Even the (deluxe DVD) packaging of TVE's *23-F: El día más difícil del Rey* features a combination of fictional and actual visual material, providing a physical demonstration of how the distinction between the actual and the virtual can be reduced: both documentary and fictional accounts of the past are presented as equally valid in a relationship that is collaborative rather than antagonistic (Fig. 3.4). Engaging with these forms of narration should not mean that one merely lists and acknowledges the opposing qualities between them, but should rather entail an exploration of what each form accomplishes and how they work together and separately.[34] At the same time, the erasure of the distinction between these narrative frameworks exposes a new aspect in the indexical relationship between the sign and its object, where signification is no longer exclusively based on the latter.

When thinking about the relationship between visual objects and memory, it is useful to return to the Peircean index. The connection this index establishes between object and sign can be expanded to encompass

33 In the early scenes of the first episode, as the coup is taking place in the Spanish Congress, a technician informs the king that the palace lacks a direct telephone line. The palace can therefore easily be cut off from any outside contact.

34 I follow Marks's lead here, agreeing with Pisters's opinion that, rather than questioning the morality of mixing virtual and actual images, we should learn to ask other critical questions (210).

Figure 3.4   The description on the DVD packaging equates *El día más difícil del Rey* with documentary and archival footage (see the back of the cover, bottom right)

the way in which memory works evolve into other forms of representation. Lisa Saltzman examines how works of art are able to bear witness to past traumas 'belatedly and obliquely', even when they no longer 'represent' or are 'straightforwardly referential' (5–6). The continued production of both fictional and non-fictional works of memory in Spain which repeatedly and insistently revisit the country's difficult past can also, perhaps, be thought of as belonging to a relationship that has lost its referentiality over time. Once this loss is acknowledged, the discussion shifts from a consideration of how history and fiction fail each other to an investigation of ways in which the recreation of the past produces new meaning about previous experiences.

Cercas's work on the 23-F, for instance, provides a good example of how an apparent referential relationship between a book and an historical event can acquire significance, not through a detailed account of what took place, but rather through the personalised way in which the author understands this past. The many recreations related to this political episode are *indexical*, rather than fully referential. In the case of visual art, we often talk about how the referential connection is broken by a process of abstraction; in the case of Spain's relationship with the past, the opposite is true.[35] Rather

35 Saltzman explains the process of abstraction in contemporary works of art as a coping mechanism to help deal with painful histories (7–8).

than a progressive disappearance of concrete references to the object of representation (consider minimalist or abstract sculptures that commemorate a traumatic event such as the Holocaust), what we find in works on the 23-F is an overload of concrete details and historical references, so rich that they end up diffusing their connection to the original referent. Seen in this light, it is hardly to be wondered that critical discussions of these works that focus on their historiographical accuracy ultimately arrive at a negative valuation of their content.

This negative view is present in José F. Colmeiro's discussion of memory in contemporary Spain. In *Memoria histórica e identidad cultural*, Colmeiro argues that the country is experiencing a 'crisis of memory', in which true historical memory is being replaced by a surfeit of memory both weak and fragmented. He describes this process as an 'inflación cuantitativa y devaluación cualitativa de la memoria' (19). Memory becomes a fetish, an objectified and commodified substitute for real memory, tainted by nostalgia (Colmeiro: 22-23). The overproduction of this reductive memory is symptomatic of an unsettled past; while Colmeiro recognises instances of historical memory taking place, he concludes that in order to overcome the past, Spain must 'rehistorificar la memoria colectiva' (25). For Colmeiro, the *Transición* is a favoured site for collective memory, 'como mito fundacional sobre el que se ha construido el presente, borrando efectivamente los rastros del pasado y con ello una pieza fundamental de nuestra identidad histórica (25).

Even if the loss of memory leads to an eventual loss of identity, I would argue that this reductive critical perspective hinders a necessary full examination of ongoing memory production in contemporary Spain. Colmeiro is correct in identifying the period of the transition as a key moment in which the traumas and memories of the past were ignored rather than acknowledged and settled. But these memories have not been forgotten: they have reproduced and multiplied. And no matter how commodified or fetishised these memories are, they challenge us to pay attention to them. Even if we regard these nostalgic recollections of the past as detrimental to proper historical memory, they represent an insistent relationship with the past. The recollections of the 23-F discussed in this chapter should not be casually dismissed as narrations that reinforce the triumphal account of Spain's political transformation; instead, these works should be analysed as examples of how memories are constructed from the present, personalising, fictionalising, and physically internalising the past to fit current discursive needs. Seen in this light, our scholarly emphasis should not be on the memories themselves, but on the intense relationships with the past that are established through the process of either recalling or creating

Figure 3.5 Cover of the DVD
of *23-F: la película* (2001)

remembrances. As the past and its memories become but a token, an index, their true significance settles into an iconic dimension.[36]

Saltzman writes that contemporary artists pursue the indexical capacity of the image; she characterises this index 'as a form rather than a function of representation ... as a point of reference rather than a referential structure of representation ... as a vestige rather than a viable means of representation' (12–13). Each new reading of the Spanish Civil War, the Franco dictatorship, and, now, the *Transición* generates its own new-found meaning for the original referent. What we see in the discussion of the 23-F is precisely the 'emptying' of its referent, to be refilled with a multiplicity of significations about the past and the present. Even if the political significance of this event does not challenge the existing official version of the Spanish transition, what remains is the iconic dimension of the failed coup, codified in that black-and-white silhouette of Tejero holding his gun and lifting his arm (Fig. 3.5).[37]

36 Writing about the complexity of Peirce's sign theory, James Elkins remarks that in this system, 'there is a *ruleless* dialectic between a desire for the absolute, categorical order ... and the equal, and incommensurate, interest in happy phenomenal chaos' (19).

37 I include the poster for the film *23-F* as an example of the iconic dimension of Tejero's image.

Understanding the 23-F as an 'empty index' allows us to read its multiple narratives as a coherent *structure of feeling*, a critical conjuncture from which to question the successful story of the *Transición*. Now distant from the earlier 'desencanto', the current criticism of this period can be read as a generational story that is intimate and personal, a mediating narrative that connects the conflicts of the past with those of the present.

Perhaps the greatest example of the indexical quality of the 23-F and its melding of the actual and virtual is Jordi Évole's recent mockumentary about the coup, *Operación Palace* (Antena 3, 2014), released during the writing of this chapter on the thirty-third anniversary of the failed uprising. In this supposed documentary, a journalist recreates the events of the 23-F by interviewing politicians, journalists, guards, and civilians present during that day. Gradually, the compiled evidence of the documentary begins to suggest that the entire incident was planned by politicians, the military, the press, the Spanish intelligence, and the king in response to the political discontent of that time, which threatened the democratic process taking place in Spain. Everyone interviewed in this fake documentary alludes to the fact that the Spanish transition was not as peaceful as Spaniards like to remember; they point to the many crises that necessitated both political and police action, such as the confrontations between regional interests and the central government, the wave of violence unleashed by terrorist groups, and the financial recession of the time. In a quest to achieve a democratic state, Évole's mockumentary suggests, extreme means were needed to jolt the country and to discipline the political class, the military, and civilians alike. A failed coup becomes a *deus ex machina* through which to address the instability of the period. Using archival footage and interviewees' statements, Évole creates a plausible explanation of the coup according to which the only ones unaware of the conspiracy behind the unsuccessful overthrow were Colonel Tejero and the Spanish people.

Adding to the intrigue of this account, the producers of *Operación Palace* delayed revealing its fictional nature until the very last minutes. The mockumentary's airing was immediately followed by an hour-long roundtable moderated by Évole, who started the discussion by apologising to viewers. His position was that, by showing viewers how easily the past could be manipulated, the film could open up a serious conversation about what the coup meant, and the way Spaniards remember it. The participants of the roundtable had different opinions about the event, yet each reflected a similar perspective: one that questioned the narrative that has been used to explain the successful arrival of democracy in Spain. What was most remarkable about this stunt was the immediate reaction in the media and in multiple discussion forums (including Facebook and Twitter), where opinions ranged from absolute indignation to the celebration of what many thought was a filmic coup in its own right, reflective of the fictional nature of the Spanish transition to democracy.

Rather than focusing on the merits (or lack thereof) of this mockumentary or the reactions to it, I wish simply to suggest that this incident be read as indicative of a particular moment in Spanish society where past legacies are being confronted in the midst of present-day crises. The urge to continue to engage with these narratives, whether fictional or actual, points to the reality that the process of the *Transición* is not yet complete. Spain's indexical relationship with its past finds its signification in the present, where the physical materiality of historical events can be traced and mediated by personal day-to-day experiences. This process, aided by the blending of archival and fictional materials, lets us see that the work of recovering memories from the past is also one of gaining knowledge and awareness about the present while (attempting to) confront the future.

CHAPTER FOUR

Mediating Memory
(or Telling How It Happened)

The television series *Cuéntame cómo pasó* (2001–) has achieved unprecedented success in Spain since it began its run in the fall of 2001. Now in its fifteenth season with 271 episodes broadcast, the series has won countless awards and has broken ratings records for TVE, Spain's national state-owned public service television broadcaster.[1] The evolving nature of the programme is reflected on its website, which has grown to include interactive features that allow viewers to play an active role in watching the series. The site's visitors can learn about the different characters as well as the historical, cultural, and social context of each episode. They can view complementary documentaries about the time period, additional features such as behind-the-scenes clips and script-reading sessions, and media coverage of the series and its principal actors.

The popularity of the series, which appeals to viewers because of its focus on a 'regular family' with experiences similar to their own, has gone beyond the local market and reached audiences around the globe, leading to its adaptation in other countries.[2]

A series that reaches millions of spectators weekly (more than 10 million in Spain at its peak, by some accounts), *Cuéntame cómo pasó* has so far covered the period from the year 1968 until the 1980s (it is still unclear when the series will end), and therefore tackles many of the changes that occurred in Spanish politics and society from the later years of the Franco

---

1 TVE belongs to the RTVE Corporation, which is responsible for national public radio and television under a general manager appointed by the Spanish Parliament. This official reports to both a board of directors and an all-party committee, as dictated by the Public Radio and Television Law of 2006. Adolfo Suárez worked as programme director for TVE in the 1960s.

2 This appeal to audiences beyond the local context of Spanish television is confirmed by the many international awards the show has received, including in South Korea. So far, this series has been adapted in Portugal as *Conta-me como foi*, in Italy as *Raccontami*, and in Mexico, where it is still in production.

dictatorship to the *Transición*. These experiences are narrated through the lives of the Alcántara family, comprising parents Antonio (Imanol Arias) and Mercedes (Ana Duato), Mercedes's mother, Herminia (María Galiana), and the children, Inés (Irene Visedo, Pilar Punzano), Toni (Pablo Rivero), and Carlos (Ricardo Gómez), as well as the family's many neighbours and friends from San Genaro, the Madrid *barrio* where they reside. The story is framed by a voice-over narration (provided by Carlos Hipólito) from the perspective of the youngest son, Carlos, who comments on each episode of the series from an unidentified present. This voice-over often helps to situate the plot by explaining the social or political context of the time and its relationship to the present. The imminent changes that will affect the family reflect the greater social changes taking place in the country. As Ana Corbalán points out, the infantile perspective of this narrator gives the series a playful and deceptively naïve tone, but the narration also allows the series to focus on some of the most important social and political events of the time (341).[3] These changes are always experienced physically by the members of the family and connected to the present via the voice-over narration.

In this chapter, I examine the success of this series and its treatment of the past as symptomatic of the popularity of memory-related works in contemporary Spain. I am particularly interested in how recent recreations of past experiences are made relevant to the present. In addition to *Cuéntame cómo pasó*, I analyse the miniseries *La chica de ayer* (2009), the Spanish adaptation of the British TV series *Life on Mars* (2006–07),[4] which tells the story of a modern-day police officer, Samuel Santos (Ernesto Alterio), who finds himself transported to the late 1970s. Originally set in 1973, the Spanish version had to be reworked to include women in the Spanish police force. The year chosen for the show was 1977: the year of the first democratic elections since the Second Republic. The fact that this year was also one of unparalleled violence is alluded to in the show, although it is often forgotten in the many narratives that assert the success of Spain's political transition.

3 The nostalgia expressed in this voice-over is clearly connected to the longing tone of the series as a whole. This voice, speaking in the present, is trying to connect with an irretrievable past. But it also implies a somewhat negative, if not nihilistic, view of the present and the future. In a way, we could say that this series looks backwards for a temporal escape which, in turn, makes us question the conditions of life in the present. I am grateful to William Nichols for this observation.

4 The Spanish series was cancelled after its first season, while the British version ran for two. *Life on Mars* was later rebooted in the series *Ashes to Ashes* (2008–10), using the same characters from 1973, but taking place in the 1980s.

In these two series, the past is transformed into a memory project to be narrated, remembered, and recreated. The urgency demonstrated by these shows—their need to account for this lost time—betrays the same contradictory impulses examined in the previous chapter. Evidence of this contradiction includes the overuse of archival material to document a fantasised past, the scrutiny with which that past is examined, and a belief that if its experiences and memories cannot be fully recovered, they can at least be satisfactorily accessed. These series also demonstrate the important role that popular media play in shaping the audience's view of the past and their memories of historical events.

My intention here is to highlight the way popular culture mediates the viewer's relationship with the past, and how it affects the creation of both cultural and private memories. In particular, we shall see how subjective experiences are narrated in these series in order to create an affective archive of the past. The stories told in *Cuéntame* and *La chica* are, above all, personal stories that deal with easily recognisable family crises. As domestic predicaments are imbricated with the narration of the political events of the dictatorship and the *Transición*, it becomes impossible to understand the sociopolitical goings on without (or separate from) this intimate component. This focus on everyday stories—a dominant feature of all coming-of-age tales—has clear relevance for the understanding of this political moment.

The chronological unfolding of the narratives in these TV series is also significant. Both are able to offer a temporal experience that, unlike that of feature films, allows spectators to immerse themselves in extended and complicated storylines.[5] Long formats like *Cuéntame* and, to a lesser extent, *La chica* permit the creation of extensive narratives that help viewers remember the past. Through the 'mediation' of these memories, the past is connected to the present of the audience. The perception of each time is affected by the other; watching the past from the emotional and intellectual framework of the present makes it easier to identify points of contact between two moments in history, and allows relationships of causality to be established between present problems and past decisions.

From the moment the small screen entered the family space, to talk about television was also to talk about everyday life. The series *Cuéntame* starts in

5 The way in which TV series take their time to develop characters and storylines is comparable to the pace of serialised novels. The popularisation of the serial format in both literary fiction in the nineteenth century and television in the twentieth and twenty-first centuries could offer an interesting comparison.

1968, and of course the significance of this year is obvious, but what truly initiates the story of this family is the arrival of a TV set in the Alcántara household. Part of the show is actually about the Alcántara family watching on their TV set what is happening in Spain during the late 1960s and 1970s. The audience joins them, watching, on their own TV, the programmes aired during that time: daily news, commercials, and live shows.[6] As the show progresses, viewers witness how the family's radio slowly fades into the background as the Alcántaras spend more time watching television and receiving their news through this medium. Even when radio broadcasting is given its own storyline in the series—Carlos works at his school's radio station and later Toni works as a journalist at a local station—it is television that is central to Alcántara family life.

Radio is used in this series as a way to remember the past and to reflect on the changes occurring in Spanish society from the perspective of the elder generation of the neighbourhood. The television in the Alcántaras' living room represents the country's move towards the future. The viewer accompanies the family as they watch the unfolding of contemporary national and international news, popular shows, and programmes about new technologies and social practices. The experience of scheduled and communal television portrayed in the show is no longer part of the viewers' lives. Nevertheless, in the current TV era—available in multiple formats, on multiple devices—television is more present in our daily lives than ever before.

Everyday life is about order and identity—an identity that we construct and maintain through social relationships, responsibilities, and institutions: family, household, community, school, nation. Roger Silverstone argues that television has become an ontological and phenomenological reality of our everyday experience: because of its 'dailiness and factuality', we can talk about the '*experience* of television' (2). The almost complete integration of television into our daily routine can be attested by:

> its emotional significance, both as disturber and comforter; its cognitive significance, both as an informer and a misinformer; its spatial and temporal significance, ingrained as it is into the routines of daily life; its visibility ...; its impact, both remembered and forgotten; its political significance as a core institution of the modern state. (Silverstone: 3)

Silverstone sees TV as a 'transitional object' that offers ontological security (18-19). The physical presence of the TV set in the small living room and the way it shapes the lives of the Alcántaras speaks to its key role in narrating the

---

6 All these programmes are available in the archival collection of TVE.

family's experience during the years covered by the series. After all, most of the significant moments 'remembered' in this programme are either transmitted by television or confirmed by it.[7] At one point, as I will discuss in detail in this chapter, the images transmitted by television help the father 'settle' into his newly fashioned personality after the end of the Franco dictatorship.[8] In the same manner, in the miniseries *La chica*, the television set allows the main character, Samuel, to get in touch with his past life as he embarks upon a personal journey into his childhood memories and experiences.[9]

The centrality of television in our daily lives helps to shape our relationship with the past. Gary R. Edgerton states that '*television is the principal means by which most people learn about history today*' (1; emphasis original). Taking into account the primacy of television in disseminating and understanding the past, one has to consider how non-fictional and fictional portrayals in this medium 'have transformed the way tens of millions of viewers think about historical figures and events' (Edgerton: 1).

What is more, television is a big business which has identified and capitalised on the past as a profitable resource; non-fictional programmes such as documentaries are cost-effective to produce and historical dimensions are a great draw for audiences (Edgerton: 2). In the case of Spain between 1975 and 1990, the revision of the country's immediate past has frequently served as the subject matter for television programmes. Emeterio Díez suggests that the Spanish viewership's interest in the past actually reflects the media monopoly of TVE, influenced during the socialist government after Franco by left-leaning creators; furthermore, he points to a dramatic shift in this situation with the emergence of privately owned television channels, where 'los ejecutivos consideran que la Guerra Civil, la posguerra, las luchas de clases o la pugna de partidos son veneno para los índices de audiencia' (102).[10] Curiously, other recreations of the past have sometimes

7 For instance, the death of Francisco Franco does not become 'real' until it is seen on television by the family, in the very well-known archival footage of Carlos Arias Navarro announcing the demise of the Caudillo.

8 The 'experience' of television shapes what goes on in real life—in this case, the gradually increasing resemblance of Antonio Alcántara to Adolfo Suárez.

9 Silverstone's *Television and Everyday Life* examines the notion of home and the persistence of television as a material object in the household that family members experience every day (as part the furniture, the decor, etc.). These ideas offer a useful insight into Samuel's relationship with the TV set in the series.

10 As an example, Díez describes how the TVE miniseries *Un día volveré* (1991), based on a novel by Juan Marsé about an anarchist gunfighter in Barcelona in the 1950s, was kept under wraps until it aired in the early hours in 1993. He writes: 'Y si esto sucede cuando TVE es gobernada por el PSOE, más reticencias aún se producen bajo los gobiernos del Partido Popular' (102).

had a lukewarm reception; the success of *Cuéntame* is unprecedented. The treatment of the past in this series has proved decidedly attractive to audiences. The success of the show must thus be sought, not in *what* it tells about the past, but in *the way in which* historical events are related to the present of the (Spanish) viewer.[11]

Edgerton argues that stylistic and technical features play an important role in shaping historical representation on television. Because of the intimacy and immediacy of the TV screen, the stories prepared for this medium tend to personalise all social, cultural, and historical phenomena. This personalisation is accomplished through well-constructed plot structures and the use of intimate shots (close-ups and medium shots) that fill the TV screen and allow history to be portrayed as personal drama or melodrama (Edgerton: 2–3). More importantly, given the difficulty faced by both TV and film in expressing temporal dimensions, the 'presentism' of TV history is valuable for its ability to project current concerns and priorities onto past events. Television programmes show more interest in emphasising what is relevant and engaging to current audiences than in offering factually accurate depictions. The past, in this context, is a useful tool *'to clarify the present and discover the future'* (Edgerton: 4, emphasis original).[12]

This is certainly the case in *Cuéntame*, where the voice-over narration continually links the past of the series to the present of the narrator, comparing cultural practices and generational differences. It also communicates dissatisfaction about the present state of affairs and asks how this situation will evolve in the future. The clear desire of *Cuéntame*'s narrator to return to an irretrievable past strongly intimates his negative view of both the present and the future. Indeed, it is the narrator's constant referencing of the future, rather than his obvious nostalgia for the past, that is of note here, since part of the goal of reflecting on the past is to try to improve future conditions, or at least to foresee potential shortcomings. In *Cuéntame*, the recreation of past events goes hand in hand with the unfolding of present-day current events. As Díez observes, '[h]ay un subtexto en constante referencia a la España de siglo XXI, desde la que, por otra parte, se realiza una interpretación de la

11 The manner in which the stories are told is important because the narrator of *Cuéntame* remembers them from the present. The audience is expected to clearly identify with the narrator's present-day experiences.

12 While the notion of 'presentism' (and indeed, the question of whether or not history is even knowable beyond the subjectivity of the present) has been challenged, Edgerton argues that a presentist position is deeply engrained in the TV universe: '[programmes] tacitly embrace presentism through the back door by concentrating only on those people, events, and issues that are most relevant to themselves and their target audiences' (3).

Transición' (103).[13] This relationship between past, present, and the personal speaks to the idea that television history becomes *an experience* in which our personal identification with the lives of historical characters shapes our understanding of the past. As shows like *Cuéntame* illustrate, this process occurs not only with recreations of 'true' historical characters, but also with fictional characters placed in historically accurate contexts.

The process of memory formation is directly connected to the process by which we understand the experiences of the past. Edgerton points to the tension between the work of historians and standard historical representations on TV, suggesting a tacit recognition of the role that the latter plays in forming collective memory (5).[14] While the tasks of an historian and a TV writer/director are clearly different, if we consider the more recent scholarship that focuses on the shared, collective nature of memory (its formation and preservation), we can see how both history and popular culture can contribute to memory production. Edgerton, for instance, invites us to look at 'true' history and history as represented on TV as aspects of the same continuum; to ask ourselves why a particular version of the past is being constructed at a given time (6).

Seen in this light, popular memory is not an act of remembering, precisely, but rather a kind of communal, mythic response to controversies, issues, and challenges. This type of constructed memory is incompatible with the 'pastism' practised by scholars who set themselves up as 'historian-cops' and perceive the past as off limits to those not trained in its academic study (Edgerton: 6-8). Moving away from an oppositional relationship between history and popular culture helps to shift the discussion away from the veracity of the latter's stories and its methods of narration. Indeed, to think of 'TV as historian' is not to allocate a new authority to offer a credible version of the past, but to recognise that 'unprecedentedly large audiences can become increasingly aware of and captivated by the stories and figures of the past, spurring some viewers to pursue their newfound historical interests beyond the screen and into other forms of popular and professional history' (Edgerton: 9).

In this approach, it is important to examine the formal narrative and

13 Díez recognises that, even though he does not have the evidence to prove it, there seems to be a clear correlation between the plotline of the series and current news: 'no cabe duda de que los guiones se han visto afectados por la confrontación política del último año. Existe como un miedo a que el público pueda establecer una relación entre lo que se cuenta del pasado y lo que sucede en el presente. Me refiero, por ejemplo, al hecho de que no deja de ser chocante que la subtrama de la mili haya desaparecido coincidiendo con la segunda Guerra del Golfo' (103).

14 Concerning television and history, see O'Connor (1990) and Sobchack (1996).

visual structures used to maintain the relevance of past experiences to the present. My intention here is not to criticise the lack of a critical historical approach in *Cuéntame*, but to understand how viewers relate to the stories told in the series. We can reflect, for instance, on how the show's episodes tend to become repetitive in certain years, depending on the historical event being treated. Special instalments are employed to wrap up certain seasons, to explain in detail special topics covered by the series, and to offer documentary-like content, featuring interviews and testimonies from journalists, historians, writers, artists, politicians, lawyers, and regular folk who share their personal memories about a particular cultural practice or an important political event. These extra programmes strengthen the show's connection with the audience and offer enriched testimony about the events it covers.[15] Beginning with the fourteenth season, the official DVD release is subdivided even further, each episode complemented by three additional clips. The first contains a commentary by the writers, directors, or producers about the making of the episode; the second informs the audience about a piece of (real) news related to the fictional world of *Cuéntame*; the third presents a clip entitled *El diario de San Genaro*, where the *kioskera* Sagrario (Amparo Pacheco) talks about the Spain portrayed in the series and comments on the lives of the Alcántaras and their neighbours.[16]

The development and multiplication of the series's historical narration reveals a commercial marketing approach that perceives the past as a commodity for consumption. The DVD extras are produced with the single objective of selling the show's narrative; however, the proliferation of this supplemental content is symptomatic of a particular relationship with the past as well as a marketing strategy to prolong the life of the series. Indeed, I contend that the reproductive nature of the show reflects its growing status as a 'memory project'. In *Cuéntame*, the past is meticulously recreated to accommodate a personalised experience; once again, preferences affect over factuality, disrupting the present with its unrelenting need to recreate historical detail. Affect is not a cognitive gesture but what Eugenie Brinkema characterises as an *insistence*, a force that makes us realise 'that play, the unexpected, and the unthought can always be brought back' (xii). Affect's negation of formal structure does not mean an escape from signification; rather, it reinforces the necessity of reading its specificities (Brinkema: xv).

---

15 These testimonies always corroborate the stories told in the series.

16 These shorts were presented as webisodes on RTVE.es during the fourteenth season of the series (2013). Amparo Pacheco is an actress with a long career, as documented in this promotional presentation of the webisodes: http://www.rtve.es/television/20130104/diario-san-genaro-webserie-cuentame-como-paso/595043.shtml.

The interest in memory in contemporary Spain provides an opportunity to examine the production of affect as a disruptive force that challenges the present. The series *Cuéntame* and *La chica* can be examined as instances of memory-as-affect for each perpetuates a relationship with an apparently unresolvable past. The relationship with the past is not cognitive, but intuitive; it embodies the potential for generating new ways of examining the country's sociocultural dynamics in the context of its post-war, post-dictatorship, and post-transitional legacies.

If establishing a relationship between history and television (and the experience of its viewers) is useful in discussing the series *Cuéntame* and *La chica*, it is equally indispensable in addressing the connection between television and memory. Neiger, Meyers, and Zanberg introduce the term 'media memory' to describe this link, which they view as a theoretical and analytical concept rather than a channel or a process (1–2). Incorporating the senses of both 'media' (as in mass media) and 'mediation', the term 'media memory' speaks to exploration of collective pasts that are narrated through popular forms of communication such as newspapers, television, radio, etc. This term gives us a tool for examining the *way* the media perform this communicative role, rather than focusing on the particular *contents* of their productions. In other words, we can see the media as 'memory agents' and question the versions of the past that they shape locally and globally, as well as on commercial and public networks. The term also creates awareness about the access audiences have to media texts within a geography of technology that encompasses an intertwined infrastructure of national and international media conglomerates.

In tracing the connection between collective memory and media memory, we can uncover how the past is shaped and reshaped within the context of public articulation. The merger of collective memory and media is a logical response to the omnipresent dominance of mass media in everyday life and its decisive role in shaping current collective recollections. Considering these concepts in tandem provides new perspectives and new questions 'regarding the interrelations between the shaping of collective memories and the role of mass media in changing cultural, political, and technological contexts' (Neiger, Meyers, and Zanberg: 4).[17] The 'mediation' of memory by the media influences the construction of past events and the way they are perceived (and consumed) by the public. Considering that the media's

17 For more on the relationship between collective memory and media, see Kitch (2002) and Zelizer (1995).

commitment to the representation of the past differs from that of less commercial institutions, such as academia and (historical) museums, it is important to seriously examine the impetus behind the multiplicity of its accounts of the past (Neiger, Meyers, and Zanberg: 7).[18] It is also important to take into account the varying truth-values of the historical fiction-dramas, documentaries, news, and docudramas it produces.[19]

Talking about the media as a memory agent brings up the question of authority: who has the right to narrate collective stories about the past? Although the academy and the state have traditionally been the arbiters of historical credibility, this position is being challenged by the media, which has progressively positioned itself as narrator and interpreter of different readings of a communal past. The question of personal and private memory versus collective and shared memory requires re-examination in this new age, as the media comes to serve 'as the vessel for shared recollections, their distributor, and the "place"—virtual or concrete, in the public arena or in the private domain—where the social ritual of remembering is performed' (Neiger, Meyers, and Zanberg: 13).[20] This intersection highlights the connections between personal and mediated memories in terms of their (in)authenticity.[21] Attention should also be paid to the context in which these accounts are placed: whether they are published for commemorative purposes, whether they are disseminated through old or new media, whether they are marketed through popular or elite outlets, what their intended audiences are, etc.

In his discussion of Spanish media consumption, Paul Julian Smith

---

18 In the case of *Cuéntame*, the episodes are re-run on Spanish television and are also available online. The same is true of *La chica*, available through the Atresplayer application (with a subscription) on tablets and smartphones. In addition to this multiplication of avenues for access, the available avenues for the selection, construction, and shaping of collective memory have also expanded. Mariita Sturken argues in *Tangled Memories* that these differences depend on a specific political, cultural, and sociological context (3–6).

19 Further discussion of the relationship between film and history can be found in Rosenstone (1994). Looking at the 'truth-value' is not the same as opposing 'true' history to history represented on TV. The relationship between these two concepts is discussed above.

20 Another consequence is that globalised outlets and formats are causing national memories to dwindle. The turn to 'cosmopolitanism' means that global concerns are becoming part of everyday local experiences. For a discussion of the role of media and collective recollection, and the distinction between 'memory' and 'recollection', see Huyssen (2000).

21 Here, we can talk about authentic and inauthentic memories. See, for instance, Hoskins's discussion of 'flashbulb memories' (147–50).

points out the disparity between the incidence of newspaper reading and film-going in the country. In particular, he notes that men read newspapers at a far higher rate than women (49% versus 29.6%), while 10% of men report going to the cinema, compared to 8.7% of women. These numbers become most significant when compared to those for television, which is shown to be the medium favoured by both genders: '[b]y far the most balanced medium for all three categories is television, with near equal proportions of men and women, young and old, rich and poor, tuning in every day (there is a slight dip in the 20s which coincides with peak filmgoing years)' (Smith 2007: 6).

According to Smith, despite the popular perception that Spanish television is 'trash', *telebasura*, Spaniards 'are amongst the most avid consumers of television in Europe, watching some four hours daily' (2006: 1). In fact, in respect to the quality of its production, Spanish television has held its own, with dramas such as TVE's *Cuéntame cómo pasó* or Antena 3's *Aquí no hay quien viva* reaching 'a bigger audience in a single night than all Spanish feature film production in a year' (Smith 2006: 1).[22] Smith stresses the popularity, and thus importance, of television in Spain. He has written extensively on contemporary Spanish television programmes and series and has encouraged other scholars to follow suit. However, as Smith himself points out, studies of Spanish TV have their own particular set of problems: not only is there no easy access to archives (while those that are accessible remain uncatalogued), but research into television has generally been limited to the Spanish government's influence on (public) broadcasting (2006: 8).

Historically speaking, a much-remarked-upon facet of Spanish television has been the role it was required to play during the *Transición*. As already documented by Manuel Palacio in his seminal *Historia de la televisión en España* (2001), the relationship between television and politics in Spain was established early on, as TV programmes participated in the establishment of political narratives and the unification of different social sectors in the country. This connection has clearly influenced the didactic nature of Spanish television since its start in the 1960s. Critics like Rueda Laffond and Coronado Ruiz have recognised, for instance, a type of historical fiction, created by Television Española, that began under the dictatorship and persisted into Spain's democracy; they show that the creative direction

---

22 Smith goes on to write that 'a day's broadcasting of the five channels of national reach (public Televisión Española or TVE 1 and 2, private Antena 3 and Tele5, and the regional consortium known as FORTA) offers more hours of content than a year's feature film production' (2006: 1). Given this data, Smith argues that television should be of concern to those interested in Spanish culture and society.

of this programming was influenced by both Francoism and the political transition (18).

Palacio, too, has remarked on the role played by visual media in promoting a break with past ideology and creating the conditions for the production of collective memory (64). The iconic images that are now part of the memory of the *Transición*—the footage of Carlos Arias Navarro announcing the death of Franco, the failed coup of the 23-F, etc.—attest to the capacity for the audiovisual medium to aid historical memory (Palacio: 78). Palacio emphasises the importance of the political transition as part of the current debate about memory in Spain, pointing out that this period saw an unprecedented amount of media censorship (78–79).

The truth is that the years of the *Transición* cannot be understood or remembered separately from the context of Spanish television. Following the early work of Palacio, José María Álvarez Monzoncillo and Juan Menor Sendra argue that television during this period was a space where the symbolic value placed on political change forced it to become a reality. They document how TV was used to project an image of modernity in Spain while it underwent its political transformation (193). The unspoken objective of public television was to firmly establish the narrative of the political transition being engineered by the political elite. It became essential to 'afrontar esos momentos difíciles y para "vender" a la sociedad las soluciones que desde la cúpula del sistema se estaban improvisando' (Álvarez Monzoncillo and Menor Sendra: 193). Television was also where the narration of a new socio-historical timeline was being constructed, one full of 'ilusiones y expectativas colectivas, pero también, como simbolizaban los rostros compungidos de los presentadores de los Telediarios ante los atentados o los actos de violencia, lleno de miedos e incertidumbre' (Álvarez Monzoncillo and Menor Sendra: 194).

Rueda Laffond and Coronado Ruiz likewise point to this time as a seminal moment in which television helped to define terms like 'nation', 'citizenship', 'liberalism', or even 'class warfare'. More importantly, television was used to facilitate the abrupt shift in social structure that Spain needed to achieve democracy, 'en la coyuntura de tiempo presente de la transición caracterizada por la necesidad urgente de socializar prácticas y semánticas democráticas' (67). The 'televised' construction of a new Spain during the transition would become '[un] relato catalizador que dará sentido a un futuro incierto y el que proporcionará un alto grado de integración institucional, cavando con el anterior mito de las dos Españas' (Álvarez Monzoncillo and Menor Sendra: 194).[23] In examining the role of Spanish television more than three

23 The work of integration was carried out earlier, too. Spanish television

decades later, these critics expose how the perception (and memory) of the transition has shifted. If it was once believed that the political change in Spain in the later seventies was an inevitable result of the country's economic modernisation, or that it came about through well-conceived political plan, the present view of the *Transición* is very different. It is now understood as a period marked by uncertainty and political improvisation (Álvarez Monzoncillo and Menor Sendra: 183).

The construction of historical narratives taking place in the media also signals a shift in the spatial and temporal dislocations of memory. Technology, in this case film and television, has the capacity to move viewers through time and space. The question is: how do these technologies affect our understanding of individual and collective memory? What does the concept of 'the experiential' mean in the context of visualising and reliving the past? Alison Landsberg argues that it is modernity itself that makes new forms of public cultural memory possible and even necessary. She uses the term 'prosthetic memory' to identify the memory that 'emerges at the interface between a person and a historical narrative about the past, at an experiential site such as a movie theatre or museum' (2). One is able to retrieve an intimate and deeply felt recollection that, though it is not one's own, shapes one's subjectivity and political view. Rather than examining how these prosthetic memories are formed in terms of authenticity or historical veracity, Landsberg focuses instead on their power and political potential. Within the current excess of cultural technologies, she identifies an enabler of memory projects: 'the construction of prosthetic memories might serve as the grounds for unexpected alliances across chasms of difference' (3).

Given the public role of cultural memory, it seems inappropriate to ascribe 'exclusive' owners to it; cultural memory does not 'naturally' belong to anybody, but to everybody.[24] Taking a cue from Landsberg's effort to eschew

programmes contributed to the 'sedimentación socioterritorial en España', which in the late sixties meant the consolidation of 'la socialización del medio en el espacio urbano' and 'la vertebración histórica de una televisión popular, emplazada entre las directrices del oficialismo gubernamental, el entretenimiento como vector dominante y la capacidad para proyectar valores socioculturales y consultivos masivos' (Rueda Laffond and Coronado Ruiz: 63).

24 I expand the definition of collective memory beyond what is understood in social structures such as laws, statues, or commemorations, in the manner theorised by Pierre Nora's *lieux de mémoire*, or Maurice Halbwachs's idea of memories passed from generation to generation through social and cultural practices. I focus on the public aspect of these memories that circulate through widely available visual and written media.

the familiar paradigm of oppositionality when talking about memory (i.e., social construction vs. essentialism), I shift my attention away from qualitative judgements of memories (i.e., good/bad; authentic/fictional) to examine their mediated nature. In this way, I am able to analyse how public (or collective) memories can be privately felt and later constituted as prosthetic memories, as a person's own recollection melds with mass cultural representations of the past (Landsberg: 19).[25]

Landsberg's theorisation is useful here because it casts mass culture, not in negative terms as a site of domination, deception, and brainwashing, but rather in positive terms as a locus of shared experience. Understanding Spain's many (popular, widely available) historical television programmes as examples of collective experiences changes our discussion of them. The notion of shared experience through popular media persists even if the prosthetic memories that are created are not identical for 'commodified images are not capsules of meaning that spectators swallow wholesale but are the grounds on which social meanings are negotiated, contested, and sometimes, constructed' (Landsberg: 21).[26] The cultural industrial model provides a space where we can examine the circulation of mass cultural representations to trace how they become sources of both memory and meaning.

Considering the sheer number of works related to the Spanish Civil War, the Franco dictatorship, and the *Transición* that popular culture has made available, there is enormous potential in examining how these works are received and how their meaning is constructed from a collective practice. In the case of works on the Spanish transition, part of this collective practice is generational. Looking for meaning in the past is about trying to define one's identity, but also about discovering how the past is still very much connected to the political and social crises of the present. Shared memories are not uniform or simple, but layered and traumatic. Sometimes, more than memories, they are fantasies about a lost time. Most importantly, they

25 These memories are prosthetic because they are not natural; they are derived from mediated representations—in film, museums, television miniseries—and are actually worn on the body like artificial limbs. They are 'sensuous memories produced by an experience of mass-mediated representations, as a "limb" also "marks" a trauma' and they can be useful, interchanged and exchanged underscoring their commodified form (Landsberg: 20–21).

26 The availability of TV series on tablets and mobile devices also means that audiences beyond domestic borders now have almost immediate access to programmes, making this shared experience global. Even when channels and distributors decide to curtail this online access in order to capitalise on a series's growing success, DVDs quickly become available for international purchase.

expose the urge to obsessively examine a past that continues to affect the present and can possibly shape the future.

Cuéntame cómo pasó, currently in its fifteenth season and with no end in sight, has been recognised as one of the most successful television series in Televisión Española's historical drama franchise. After more than a decade, the series still occupies a primetime slot in the TVE scheduling and its triumph in the ratings since its first season in 2001 has been widely examined.[27] Critics have pointed to the show's easy nostalgia and the high quality of its production when emphasising its unique appeal to the Spanish audience. The success of this show has also been explained by its large cast of characters and its sentimental recreation of the past. Although it is most favoured by audiences of 65 years and older, the show has also been successful with viewers of other age groups, although different generations have different perceptions of it. The older generation sees the show as a way to remember a better time, while the middle-aged sector regards it with suspicion because of its fictionalisation of past events. The younger audience has a more simple outlook; for these viewers, the past of the Franco dictatorship is seen as a strange and distant world (Rueda Laffond and Coronado Ruiz: 103–04).

One explanation for the series's ability to reach across generations is the sheer length of its run. The long timespan covered by the programme has given its writers the opportunity to structure a narrative coherence and a temporal organisation that appeal to the audience's memory. Indeed, Rueda Laffond and Coronado Ruiz argue explicitly that TVE's publicity campaign for the series is based on a 'sentimental memory'. Following Martín Barbero's critical reading of the show, they have also remarked on *Cuéntame*'s connection to the debate about historical and collective memory in Spain (106–07).[28] The link between the appeal of the series and the

27 Although the show's ratings can be found online, a good supplement for understanding its performance is the summary by Rueda Laffond and Coronado Ruiz (104). The show has come under fire recently for its labour practices. Actress Pilar Pinzano, who portrayed the daughter of the Alcántaras from 2010, took to Facebook to reveal her dissatisfaction with the way she was fired from the show. She revealed a negative atmosphere on the set and denounced the producer (and husband of actress Ana Duato, who plays the role of the mother) for financially exploiting the show. She also criticised Imanol Arias for his behaviour towards other (female) actors and his lack of support. A brief review of the problems on the set of *Cuéntame* can be found at http://cultura.elpais.com/cultura/2015/09/07/television/1441659259_121132.html.

28 Paul Julian Smith also notes the parallel between *Cuéntame* and the collective interest in history in Spain, which is reflected in diverse cultural phenomena such

ongoing debate about memory in Spanish society highlights the intersection between collective memory and television.

By emphasising the idea of a family and a close-knit community that survive a difficult period, *Cuéntame* projects a view of the passage of time that is always positive, both personally and financially. Similarly, the notion that the family is able to remain united despite the challenges (and changes) it experiences has proved especially appealing to the Spanish audience. These characteristics create and solidify the three foundations of the series: 'la persistencia de un grupo protagonista, la formulación de efectos realistas, y la proposición de una mirada edulcorada, y de nostalgia de un tiempo pasado básicamente feliz' (Rueda Laffond and Coronado Ruiz: 109). The synthesis of these narrative pillars translates into a semantic overload that advances a tightly controlled version of the past. This overload of signification and control is evinced by the historicity of the series and the extensive behind-the-scenes work that goes into producing a credible recreation of the past (Rueda Laffond and Coronado Ruiz: 110). The show never loses its focus on the Alcántara family, although its members go through distinct phases when confronted with increasing political and social change. These transformations are first resisted, then celebrated, and, finally, the present-time narrator expresses ambivalence about their unwanted consequences. The doubt contained in the present-tense off-screen narration establishes the nostalgic tone of the series.

The effort to build a realistic account of the past, in this case as a way of drawing connections with the present by being 'pedagógica, testificadora y presentista', relates to the earlier didactic role that television played in Spain (Rueda Laffond and Coronado Ruiz: 111). The connection with the present through off-screen narration connects the past and the 'televised' memory to the individual recollection of each spectator. Although he, too, is a fictional character, the voice of the series becomes almost the omniscient voice of a documentary narrator, whose version of the past is totalising and irrefutable. It also carries out the essential task of reminding us about how past events connect, or are relevant, to the present. While this voice has been criticised for its idealised representation of the past, it is important to remember that the narrator effectively maintains a relationship between present and past by emphasising his own experience and that of his family. I will return to this point later.

Moving beyond the formal features of the series, Paul Julian Smith focuses on its emotional aspects and how the programme 'exploits the

as 'the recent exhibition on the Spanish exile community and the continued search for war burial sites' (2004: 371).

unique temporal and spatial matrix of TV to show that it is only by passing through the private (passionate) sphere that we can come to know the public (dispassionate) history of the nation' (2004: 364). Following the idea that emotion is also a form of cognition, Smith examines the domestic period drama through the lens of television's role in providing both information and entertainment (2004: 370). In his discussion of the series's American inspirations, *The Wonder Years* and *Forrest Gump*, Smith notes that the Spanish audience does not seem to be bothered by the influence of these 'US nostalgia feasts' and comments on the 'quality' of the series, its casting of well-known actors, its cinematography, and its use of a type of art design still rare in Spain (2004: 371).[29] Smith argues that, because *Cuéntame* is targeted at a Spanish audience, we must consider the centrality of television in the country's emotional history:

> the publicity still that graces the soundtrack CD (music is vital to the show's sentimental appeal) shows the family grouped around their period TV set. Frequent meal shots reveal the regular cast enacting the change in family communication effected by television: they sit around three sides of the table with the father facing the camera, where the new television is also placed. (2004: 371)

But the omnipresent television is not the only element that elicits or points to the emotional quality of this show. Smith remarks on its privileging of the emotional over the social or the political. The melodramatic nature of the series invites us to engage 'in a non-linguistic amorous intelligence or emotional cognition which ... transcends plot and dialogue' (Smith 2004: 372). However, the appeal of the show cannot be explained by its facile nostalgia alone. The coexistence of fictional time and real time (despite the limiting structure of TV scheduling) allows audience members to follow the development of the stories and the characters (Smith 2004: 372–73). Smith elaborates on Martha Nussbaum's theorisation of knowledge and feeling by suggesting that, even when Spanish viewers may not be able to correctly identify the historical setting of *Cuéntame* (or the political events it narrates), they can nevertheless relate to the human relationships and everyday objects depicted in the stories. In this way, the series itself, like the Alcántara family's television set, becomes an emotional object.

---

29 As Smith states, this show 'prides itself on the authenticity of its studio-shot interiors, crammed with original artefacts' (2004: 371). In fact, more than its narrative, viewers have noted the series's production design, items like the sewing machines or the record player, calling the show a 'museum of memory' (Smith 2004: 371).

Likewise, the series's historically accurate and detailed art design helps emotional attachment.[30] This attachment, however, is driven by loss. Smith calls it an 'anticipated mourning' that 'can only be understood when we (when the child) have [sic] grown into that present position from which we watch the show' (2004: 373). To have a relationship with the past is inherently to acknowledge a loss. Recreating a former time and filling its space with period artefacts is an act of mourning those objects' current absence. But the process of grieving also opens up a deeper connection with the past and a greater insight into its experiences. It is from this perspective that culture teaches us a lesson. Smith borrows Martha Nussbaum's words to remind us that through the world of television, 'viewers can receive an education for compassionate citizenship' that goes beyond consciousness or words (qtd. in Smith 2004: 374). In arguing for emotion to be valued as a form of cognition, Smith stresses the importance of paying attention to the way objects aid in the flow of sentimentality. In *Cuéntame*, for instance, objects acquire special importance as they play a significant role in shaping the consciousness of Spanish viewers (Smith 2004: 374).

Nostalgia should not be viewed exclusively with suspicion. Ana Corbalán suggests that the nostalgic recollection of the past in *Cuéntame* should be recognised for its critical potential. Following Svetlana Boym's definition of reflexive nostalgia, Corbalán argues that affective memories do not erase a critical understanding of the past (Corbalán: 341–42; Boym 2001: 49–50). She further suggests that the excellent art and set design of *Cuéntame* directly aid the series's viewers in forming cultural memory (342), permitting television to serve as a conduit through which to establish a connection and a dialogue with the past.[31] The potential for entering into this dialogue is contingent upon the formation and sustenance of collective memory. As Maurice Halbwachs has theorised, memory is by definition a social construct, and requires a social infrastructure to survive. Television and television viewing can be understood as part of a social context that encourages the creation and preservation of collective memory. In *Cuéntame*, the many moments in which the audience participates in the Alcántara family's television viewing can be considered moments of a collective act of remembering.

Corbalán explores this active audience participation using a survey of her own design, distributed among her family and friends, which asks

---

30 Smith emphasises the mixed feelings Spaniards have towards television, as an object that inspires 'as much rage as love', noting how 'some viewers clearly fear even a fiction apparently benign as *Cuéntame*' (2004: 373–74). This apprehension, for Smith, is indicative of an ambivalent relationship with the past.

31 Corbalán follows Anderson (2001).

viewers how they interact with the show. Her group of viewers, ranging from 25 to 75 years old, comment on how the show helps them remember their own youth or childhood—a finding that, according to Corbalán, demonstrates the strength of their emotional attachment to the programme (346–48). Here, Corbalán's assessment parts ways with Isabel Estrada's critical reading of the show. Estrada focuses on how the series shares the state's ideological position, which favours forgetting Spain's conflictive past (Corbalán: 350; Estrada: 562). In contrast, Corbalán emphasises how the story of the Alcántara family exposes the social injustices of the dictatorship. She explains that, while this criticism may not be overt given the intended audience of the show, a political commitment can be seen in the script and the extra material prepared for the show in terms of interviews, behind-the-scenes stories, etc. (350–51). More importantly, she argues that the objective of the series is not built around the task to 'crear una visión consensual del pasado español, sino en evocar una sucesión de memorias y emociones en la memoria cultural que inciten a incrementar el pensamiento crítico y la nostalgia reflexiva' (351). Rather, the aesthetics of the show contributes to the task of creating a collective memory in which 'los telespectadores pueden reescribir su historia personal y cultural, autodefiniéndose y adoptando sentimientos nostálgicos y reflexivos de identificación con las vivencias experimentadas por los protagonistas de la serie, sin olvidar la actitud crítica y comprometida que se transmite en boca de algunos personajes' (354).

In her reading of the series, Corbalán establishes a connection between the moment in which the viewers identify with the characters of the show and the moment in which they form a critical view (and memory) of the past. Throughout the series, the past is recreated through the easily recognisable format of a family drama, from which the audience is encouraged to retrieve elements of set and artistic design to effectively produce and preserve a visual and cultural memory of the past. In this context of 'making memory', it is important to note how each member of the Alcántara family is directly linked to the historical events referenced in the series; indeed, each historical incident involves a varying degree of physical or emotional involvement from each family member as well as their friends and relatives. The use of TVE's own archival material to establish these relationships is crucial. For instance, not only does *Cuéntame*'s plot line establish a physical proximity of the family members to key events (e.g., the assassination of Carrero Blanco), but actors re-enact some of these historical episodes through digital placement into very well-known footage of the period.

This practice has already been seen in films like *Forrest Gump* (Dir. Robert Zemeckis, 1994), where CGI techniques were used to allow the main character to interact with already deceased historical figures. In *Cuéntame*, this placement brings to the forefront the tantalising idea of physically bonding with the past. The identification of the audience with the characters and the art design of the show, conveyed through the 'direct' link of the Alcántaras with key historical events, reflects a need to make the past relevant to the present and the audience's immediate lives. It is the physical connection of the characters that mediates a better understanding of the past. In turn, this 'physical' link, mediated by television, helps the viewer achieve a personal connection with the past. In the subjective view of the past, what is at stake is not cognition or the desire to find an accurate representation of history, but an emotional imprint that can only be grasped with hindsight and mediated by affect. The past acquires importance because of the emotional (and physical) experience it produces.

Misha Kavka writes about the affective power of the mediated image and its ability to generate feeling (1), focusing on the 'connection between media and the *feeling* of proximity—between (im)mediacy and intimacy' (2). In the debate between real and mediated spaces, she argues that the former are typically favoured, while the latter are devalued as 'illusory' or 'deceptive'; Kavka herself, however, rejects this value-laden distinction. Instead, she follows Todd Gitlin's theorisation to bring the concepts of real and mediated spaces together, describing mediated spaces as those that saturate 'our way of life with a promise of feeling, even if we may not know exactly how we feel about one or another batch of images except that they are *there*' (Gitlin 2002: 6, qtd in Kavka 2008: 3). For Kavka, '*feeling* is crucial to maintaining a working knowledge of the media/reality distinction'; it is important to pay attention to how it 'operates like sonar for traces of the real within media (re)presentations' (4). Opposing the view that television creates false consciousness, she argues that television's presence is related to affective productivity, where domestic space becomes a zone of intimacy and 'representation a mode of "presence"' (5). Television draws viewers close because of its affective elements: intersubjectivity, privacy, and presentism (Kavka: 5). This closeness translates into temporal immediacy and the re-experiencing of an event that has already taken place (Kavka: 6).

This notion of 'closeness' is an important participatory aspect of *Cuéntame*. The storylines that link each member of the Alcántara family with specific historical or political events allow the spectator to connect with these characters' experience. This connection grows stronger as viewers become engaged with the storyline of each episode, moving beyond mere emotional identification with historical objects that are depicted on the show. Television's unique ability to establish an intimate connection between audience and story creates a strong sense of reality. Kavka argues that this intimacy 'cohabits with a sense of presence, which in turn supports the mediated delivery of actuality as reality' (11).[32] The easily recognisable family drama, the intimate shots of the main characters and their daily experience, creates a sense of history that is not only personal, but also has real material and current presence.

As an example, consider how *Cuéntame* develops its storyline about the legacy of the Spanish Civil War. During the third season of the series, Antonio and his family return to his home village of Sagrillas, where his mother, Pura (Terele Pávez), is ill. While there, Antonio is summoned by Don Mauro (Walter Vidarte), one of the *caciques* of his town and a man known to have sided with the fascists during the war. Antonio brings his son Toni along, thinking that Don Mauro might be interested in the small land owned by his family; instead, he is forced to hear a terrible confession. On his deathbed, the old man reveals that during the war, he ordered soldiers to execute Antonio's father, not because of politics but because he was in love with Pura. Don Mauro's admission is part of a larger, well-documented historical narrative in which crimes committed during the Spanish Civil War were often related to private affairs settled between neighbours. For Antonio, this declaration brings the history of the war into his life and, literally, into his present.

The confession of Don Mauro marks an important turn in the narrative of the series. Up to this moment, the memories and references to the war have been indirect—revealed, for example, in the constant fear of Herminia, the grandmother, or through the experience of other distant relatives. In episode 15, season 1, 'Pretérito imperfecto', it transpires that Uncle Teodoro (Agustín González) spent thirty years in hiding after the end of the war, throughout the Francoist repression; Teodoro's story becomes an excuse to revisit the past. It is during this story arc that the child Carlitos, along with the viewers, first learns how his own grandfather was killed at the beginning of the war for his union membership.

In the discussion of the fate of Antonio's father and that of Uncle Teodoro, the family members bring up how everyone in Spain is 'amnésico'. As we have seen in previous chapters, a term that relates to the amnesia mentioned during the debate on historical memory in Spain.[33] Herminia declares that she has been silent too long, and that a person needs to know about her

---

32 Kavka talks about this experience in the context of watching reality television, but the connection she identifies and the 'sense' of reality she describes can equally be applied to the context of watching different types of television programme.

33 The show references the 1969 Amnesty Law and calls attention to the war crimes committed in villages, which resulted in the deaths of many innocents. Its narrative echoes the later amnesty law of 1976, which freed political and criminal prisoners alike, as though they were equally guilty.

own past. Her statement echoes the sentiment expressed in the title of the series, demanding and needing to know 'how it happened'.[34] In this episode, Antonio also rethinks his own attitude about the past, even though his fear (and that of his family) ultimately trumps any ethical impulse behind his desire to remember. His aversion to the past only disappears when history becomes personal and emotional in later seasons.

From this perspective, the revelation of the real, personal reason behind the execution of Antonio's father is significant for two reasons. First, since his death can now be mourned as a private (and local) tragedy, the ideological implications of the recreation of this past can be avoided. Second, the identification of the father's death as part of a private family drama rather than a political one makes it easier for the viewers to empathise with the pain that Antonio experiences. Even when Toni lashes out against Don Mauro for his fascist past, this political characterisation loses significance when compared with the renewed pain felt by the Alcántara patriarch. The tragedy separates from its own historicity and becomes depoliticised—while what remain, stronger than ever, are Antonio's raw emotion and the pain felt by the rest of his family. The memory of the past matters because of its capacity to produce affect—an affect that can transform the world view of a subject.

Once the secret of his father is revealed and his mother is dead, Antonio's relationship with the past is changed. His view of history takes on a personal significance, and it is through his own experience that he begins to understand the historical events recreated in *Cuéntame*. This sort of personal process is precisely what foments an intimate connection between a show's characters and its audience. Another example of this type of experience can be found in episode 80, season 5, when Antonio accompanies his old boss Don Pablo (José Sancho) to the Soviet Union. This business trip allows the screenwriters to touch on the topic of the Spanish children sent to the USSR during the war.[35] Enrique Villar (Carlos Iglesias), the translator and the

34 It is noteworthy that the title of the show does not demand to know 'what' happened but '*how*' it happened. Perhaps the nuanced question speaks to the fact that many of the stories told in the series are well known. Trying to understand 'how' demands a greater personal engagement with and empathy for what happened in the past.

35 It is difficult to ignore the correlation between *Cuéntame* and other TV programmes dealing with forgotten memories of the dictatorship and the Civil War. The episode about the Spanish children sent to the Soviet Union aired in May 2004. Two years earlier, a much talked-about two-part documentary by Montse Armengou and Ricard Belis, entitled *Els nens perduts del franquisme*, aired on Catalonia's TV3, and in 2003 *Los niños perdidos del franquismo* was published by historian Ricard Vinyes, in

guide for the trip, turns out to be one of these children, sent by his parents during the war and never able to return. The tragic story he recounts later manifests itself in Antonio's subconscious as a nightmare.

Dream sequences are frequently used in *Cuéntame* for two purposes: first, to explore the subconscious of the characters by visualising their anxieties and, second, to allow the characters to experience historical events. Even if the device of the dream sequence means that the experience never actually took place, the characters wake up feeling that they have physically lived through the event in question, and their actions upon waking follow as direct consequences of their dreams.

In the same manner, the Alcántara family's corporeal connection with the political events of their time and the past is emphasised repeatedly over the seasons of the show. Each family member is frequently inserted into archival TVE footage. This visual effect is employed extensively in *Cuéntame* to establish an indisputable, direct connection between this family and Spain's past. The physicality of this link gains significance in light of the argument explored in this book: that the past only becomes comprehensible through its affect. Although the main aim of using stock footage is to create historical authenticity, the importance of this footage to *Cuéntame* lies primarily in how the characters' 'presence' in these historical images (no matter how digitally manipulated) establishes a personal, physical contact with the past. It is this contact that produces the emotions experienced by the members of the Alcántara family. These feelings are relevant to their daily lives and shape their thoughts, decisions, and actions. In turn, viewers can identify with these emotions more easily than with facts about the past.[36]

While the episode about the Soviet Union ultimately reads as a criticism of the country's totalitarian regime and a lament over its citizens' lack of freedom, Antonio's empathy for Enrique is what dominates the storyline. The repetition of the guide's account in Antonio's dream signifies that the story of the Spanish children is now part of his own experience and memory. Enrique's story becomes part of Antonio's own narrative. A final parallel is established between these two characters at the end of the episode: Enrique

collaboration with Armengou and Belis. The subject was later made into a feature film, *Ispansi!* (2010), by the same actor who appeared in the *Cuéntame* episode, Carlos Iglesias, who also starred in it.

36 The idea of proximity and the physical reaction to an historical event is clearly expressed in the episode where Carrero Blanco's vehicle is blown up by the Basque terrorist group ETA in the year 1973. The Alcántara family is driving down the same street when the bomb goes off and they are stuck in traffic until they figure out what has happened.

is arrested at the end of the trip and Antonio gets into trouble with the customs official when he returns to Spain. Ironically, the officer is not concerned about the forbidden book Antonio is smuggling for his son, but rather the music box he is bringing his wife, which happens to play the melody of the *Internationale*.

The brutality of the Spanish police portrayed in the show pales in comparison with what this episode suggests about the institutional violence that takes place behind the Iron Curtain. Nevertheless, the parallel scenes draw a link between the characters through the fear felt by both Antonio and Enrique when confronted with the officials. What remains between them is a deep emotional experience. Antonio is profoundly affected by his incapacity to give Enrique the piece of *chorizo* he so longed for, the taste of which would remind him of his many losses: his childhood, his parents, and his homeland. Once again, Enrique's story acquires importance because of its emotional appeal. Antonio is able to empathise and connect with him because of the loss of his own father, his own fatherhood, and his appreciation of a good *chorizo* (which his mother-in-law had forced into his suitcase despite his protests). The personal dimension of these elements is what gives meaning to the experience and legacy of the Spanish Civil War.

In his own writing on the relationship between affect and television, Lawrence Grossberg explores the viewer's desire (or even need) to *feel* (141). However, Grossberg does not believe that this aspect permits signification to sidestep the debate about representations of reality, forms of cognition, or the ideology portrayed on television. As explained by Kavka, a refusal of signification does not imply indifference or a lack of meaning, but rather an opportunity to examine how television works as an affective calling. Viewers are able to identify with an affective situation which is '*not* a secondary, imitative or vicarious feeling, but rather an affective reality, something we are given to feel, which arises from the resonances played out across and through the television screen' (Kavka: 27).

Affect has a material presence and is capable of embodiment and action: '[w]e *feel* in some sense because affect moves through and across us, in palpably material form, resonating across divides that may otherwise be blocked by cognition or representation' (Kavka: 33). Kavka's reading of affect, and her emphasis on its materiality, stresses that affect should be seen primarily as a social relation. What takes place in television is 'the mattering of matter, a doubling which involves the evacuation and refilling of a material object with the "material" of feeling that is and is not my own' (Kavka: 34). The object here may literally be the television set itself; regardless, what Kavka describes is a process by which an audience voids a televised episode of its original meaning and fills it with their own feelings (which may derive from viewers personally or arise as a consequence of the show). Affect can thus be understood as a social relation enabled by television. In the case of *Cuéntame*, the object of the show is the past—a past that is emptied out and refilled with the meaning and feeling that emanate from the present. The affective connection to this past is what makes its memory relevant and enduring.

While Kavka focuses on the use of affect in reality television, her observations can be extended to fictional programmes like *Cuéntame*. Despite the didactic expansion of the series, what remains consistent is the wealth of feeling that it continues to inspire in its audience.[37] In a special programme aired at the end of the first season, as if it were another episode of the series, journalist Victoria Prego explains the success of the show by pointing out how it has motivated viewers to turn to their fathers and other older relatives to hear more stories about the past, to demand 'cuéntame más'.[38] What is stressed is the affective connection between generations, rather than the transmission of actual knowledge.

Prego's interviews with the entire cast of the show reflect this perspective. The main actor of the show, Imanol Arias, who plays Antonio, for instance, remarks on how the show is mainly a tribute to the older generation, and that this is what makes it such a big success.[39] Even if the later seasons display

---

37 The didactic intention of the show is clear. The special episodes with journalist Victoria Prego and the documentary-style programmes with real interviews that are incorporated when the show covers an important historical moment (like the death of Franco's political heir, Admiral Carrero Blanco) attest to a clear desire to educate the audience and to help them remember their own experiences. Other moments portrayed in the show in which members of the Alcántara clan are physically present or involved include the ETA bombing of Cafetería Rolando in 1974, the toxic oil scandal in 1981, and the 23-F (Toni is present as a journalist in the Spanish Congress). While the historical explanation offered by the special episodes reinforces the official narration of political change in Spain, it is important to note the affective weight that these recollections carry. These special episodes, which are actually special programmes about the series, are aired during the regular season at the slotted time for the show. In the later DVD packages they are numbered and titled as the other episodes. The unified way in which they are presented create a seamless narrative that links the fictional with the real.

38 The title of the special episode, '33. Episodio Especial: Háblame de ti', is telling because of the personal connection it establishes between the television series and its viewers.

39 In a special episode after the first season, the actors of the show are interviewed about their thoughts and experiences while making the series. Sánchez-Biosca has commented on the generational aspect of the show: '*Cuéntame* se propone, pues, restablecer un diálogo generacional; así lo han declarado los actores y autores y así ha sido recibido por su público' (69).

a more educational intention and a clear message about the importance of preserving the memory of the country's recent past, the narratives of the earlier episodes privilege an affective approach rather than an historical one. When asked about the research they have done for their roles, the actors playing Toni Alcántara (Pablo Rivero) and Marta Altamira (Anna Allen) tell Prego about the difficulty they have had in imagining what it would have been like to be a young person during that time. Both actors were compelled to turn to their parents and grandparents to capture the world view of the period, and both express their gratitude for this opportunity to form a new emotional connection with their relatives.

Meanwhile, when talking with the child actors of the show, Ricardo Gómez (Carlitos), Santiago Crespo (Josete), and Manuel Dios (Luis), Prego speaks about the dictator as if he were part of a fairy tale ('Hacía muchíiiiiiiisimos años había un señor que se llamaba Franco ...'). The past is presented to them as something far away and unattached to their reality. For these children, the past becomes 'real' as they 'live' through their fictional characters. Prego's statement about the show underlines this position and emphasises the importance of a physical connection to the past:

La España que se describe aquí no tiene nada que ver, es más que evidente, con la España actual. La España de esta serie es una España que los jóvenes están descubriendo ahora y que los mayores recuerdan perfectamente y reconocen. Por eso participan y se identifican con los personajes de la serie.

Ironically, Prego establishes a clean break between the present and the past even as she admits that the memories of the past still live with the older generation. Her words imply a need to connect the past to the present, and it is in this mediation of history and memory that the link to the intimate 'now' of the family drama is recovered.

In another special programme about the show, included as part of the regular episodes of the series, Imanol Arias (Antonio) reflects on his personal experience playing his character. Entitled 'Pasen y vean', this episode was aired in January 2007 during the show's eighth season, set between 1974 and 1975. In this programme, viewers were invited to see how each episode was prepared and filmed. Actors and writers, technicians and other team members are seen performing their tasks or talking about their craft. In Arias's interview, he discusses how, after eight years of doing the show, his own memories have become intertwined with those of his character, Antonio Alcántara. In discussing how he learns from Antonio's experience and vice versa, Arias describes the relationship between the show and Spain's 'memoria histórica'.[40] Arias also draws a parallel between his own experiences and the plot of the show during the eighth season which follows the unfair incarceration of the Alcántaras' daughter Inés (Irene Visedo) after the police find political flyers belonging to her roommate in her flat.[41] Arias recollects a time when he himself was interrogated by the police and remarks on the show's effort to offer a faithful account of the reality of the time. However, what these testimonies from the actors and producers truly reveal is the fact that the real appeal of the programme is not the historical accuracy of its storylines, but the pleasure it gives its viewers ('se divierten mucho') by helping them to remember their own stories. Many of the writers interviewed in 'Pasen y vean', for instance, mention that they were born around the same time as Carlitos, the Alcántaras' youngest son, and that they appreciate working on the show because they see it as an opportunity to tell their own personal stories.

The subjective perspective of history enabled by television is what creates and promotes affective relationships with the past. Even if *Cuéntame* plays a very clear role in providing official historical narratives of a critical period in Spanish history, these stories ultimately succeed by providing frameworks within which the audience can fit their own personal and intimate experiences. In episode 40, season 9, 'Un año para la Historia', viewers are presented with a political and social re-evaluation of Spain before Franco's death. The stories that take place in the time leading up to this, starting with the year 1968, are presented as a chain of events that could only result in the arrival of democracy in Spain. In this episode, Victoria Prego, the voice of authority outside the fictional world of San Genaro, recounts the realities of the time. The episode draws a parallel between the political changes of this period and the two historic soccer matches played between Atlético de Madrid and Germany's Bayern Munich for the European Cup Final in 1974. In this version of the past, the loss suffered by the beloved underdog Atleti embodies the political frustration felt by the

40 As explained in Chapter 2, this much-debated term was introduced to refer to the law concerning the legacy of the Spanish Civil War, passed by José Luis Rodríguez Zapatero's Socialist government in 2007.

41 This prolonged incarceration is used as an opportunity to tell the story of women prisoners during the dictatorship, a topic that resonates with two popular works in recent years: Dulce Chacón's novel *La voz dormida* (2002), adapted into a film in 2011 by director Benito Zambrano, and the story of 'Las Trece Rosas', about which Jesús Ferrero wrote the novel *Las Trece Rosas* in 2003. This story of 13 innocent young women executed after the war was also recreated and remembered in a documentary, a non-fiction book, and a feature film directed by Emilio Martínez-Lázaro in 2007.

Spanish populace under the dictatorship.[42] In a tale of what could have been but never was, both personally and collectively, the episode remarks on the harsh political reality of that time. In describing an 'España sobrecogida', Prego pinpoints the fear that everyone experienced after the death of the dictator and the anxiety they felt about the future: 'Franco enfermó y toda España se hospitalizó'. Although this historical framework helps to further several plotlines developed to narrate Franco's death, the comparison of the political situation with Spain's most cherished and painful soccer memory functions, once again, to situate history within the structure of a personal memory.

I have suggested that the special episodes and documentary-style programmes produced for *Cuéntame* are intended for educational purposes. The format of these episodes confirms this characterisation; the speakers in these programmes are journalists, academics, politicians, and regular folk who recount their own experiences. The information and narration provided in these episodes clearly communicates a *way to talk about the past*. In some ways, the memories and thoughts expressed mirror Manuel Vázquez Montalbán's chronicles about everyday experiences during the years of the dictatorship and the transition; like Vázquez Montalbán's work, the special episodes of *Cuéntame* function as part of Spain's 'educación sentimental'[43]— an education that relies on personal recollections and the reliving of fears and moments of joy rather than political facts or historical data. It is only through affect that the past becomes accessible and teachable.

The connection between the political and the personal in *Cuéntame* is especially clear in the series's depiction of the early years of the *Transición*. As I have already mentioned, in addition to the special episodes of the show, the characters are given opportunities to participate, physically and emotionally, in important political and cultural events taking place within the show's historical scope. This connection rarely becomes as literal as when Antonio Alcántara starts displaying a physical resemblance to a politician of the time, Adolfo Suárez. The audience first witnesses this physical transformation at the beginning of season 10, which covers the year 1976 (episode 168, 'El coche nuevo del emperador'). We hear the off-screen narrator commenting on the news programme his father is watching, a clip about a politician who has quickly risen through the ranks on his way to becoming the most

42 The love for this team is also political; the other team from the capital, Real Madrid, has always been seen as the team that was favoured by the Franco regime. This privilege was reflected, according to soccer fans, in the way their matches were refereed.

43 The titles of these works are *Crónica sentimental de España* (1971) and *Crónica sentimental de la transición* (1985).

Figure 4.1   The news clip that the narrator, the adult Carlitos, reflects on; he reminisces about the ongoing changes and notes how everyone is trying to emulate the persona of the politician Adolfo Suárez. *Cuéntame cómo pasó* (TVE, 2001–)

powerful man in the country and whose face we see in a close-up on the TV screen. The man in question, Adolfo Suárez, again becomes the topic of the news (this time a radio show) while Antonio is getting dressed for an important business dinner, causing the latter to ponder the difficulties one must face as 'presidente'. From this close-up, we move on to the family room, where Carlitos is setting up for Josete's farewell party—and again, we see Adolfo Suárez on the TV set. As the narrator talks about the politician and how he represents a new time of change, the juxtaposition of the scenes clearly establishes a physical resemblance between the Alcántara patriarch and the politician (Figs 4.1 and 4.2).

As the audience visually connects these two characters, the narrator explains how everyone at the time wanted to be like Suárez; he goes on to draw a comparison between the politician and his own father. Suárez is presented as the most popular figure of the time among the Alcántara family. His youth signalled the dawn of a shifting era, his political success represented new possibilities, and his promise to bring change (while maintaining the status quo) was irresistible.

In the episodes that follow this first overt parallel, we see how Antonio Alcántara, like many other Spaniards, is seduced by this politician and his project for the future. The patriarch's resemblance to Suárez becomes complete when Antonio runs for office in the president's party, the UCD

Figure 4.2   Antonio dresses as he listens to a radio show about Adolfo Suárez and his rapid ascent in Spanish politics. *Cuéntame cómo pasó* (TVE, 2001–)

(Unión de Centro Democrático). His defeat in the polls leads, later, to the consolation prize of the position of Director General in the Ministry of Agriculture—a department in which Antonio used to work as an 'office boy' in the early seasons of the show. His success is short-lived, however, and Antonio is eventually forced to resign amid political scandal. Both Antonio's short political career and the nature of his demise resonate with those of Suárez, who rose from rather obscure beginnings (as a member of the Falangist party), began by occupying entry-level positions, and was ultimately abandoned by his own party and defeated by the Socialists in the 1982 elections. While the title of this episode—which references Hans Christian Andersen's fairy tale the 'Emperor's New Clothes'—refers to Antonio, it can also be applied to Suárez, thus cementing the link between them. The easy connection drawn for viewers between the two men (one fictional and the other real) reinforces the practice of understanding history (and politics) through a personal experience. The lack of distance between the history recreated in the show and its viewership in the present intensifies the series's affective turn towards the past.

At first glance, the political and financial crises of the late 1970s portrayed in *Cuéntame* seem to contradict the official narrative of a successful *Transición*. Yet the temporal progression of the series yields an understanding that the future will always be better. Even if this perspective is at odds with the nostalgic tone of the narrator, the cumulative experience of the series intimates that each event and change that takes place leads inevitably to Spain's democratic present. As the years pass, *Cuéntame* continues to be, above all, a narrative in which history is mediated through *a personal situation*.

This pattern continues in episodes 182 and 183 (season 11), which share the title 'Cambia, todo cambia'. In this pair of episodes, we follow the Communist Party's path to legalisation through the story of Antonio's brother, Miguel (Juan Echanove), who has been a member since his days in France. Suárez is once again a major focus of these episodes. The personalised view of this public figure (which mirrors the way that Javier Cercas writes about him in *Anatomía de un instante*) is justified by the off-screen narrator, who states that during that time 'todos los españoles se ven reflejados en Suárez'. The politician's every move is closely followed because his actions embody those of the collective. These two episodes also mark the official politicisation of Antonio, who in subsequent instalments strives to become identical to Suárez. According to the narrator of the show, Antonio tried to emulate the 'hero' of the transition by acting and speaking like him.

The interpretation of the title shared by these two episodes is ambiguous. 'Cambia, todo cambia' is the name of a song written by the Chilean Julio Numhauser (b. 1940) and popularised by the Argentinian Mercedes Sosa (1935–2009) in the early 1980s. Written in exile during the dictatorship of Pinochet, this piece is clearly tied to left-wing ideology and has been interpreted as a symbol of political resistance, especially as part of Mercedes Sosa's repertoire. Given this context, at first, the use of this song's title in *Cuéntame* appears to pay homage to the Communist Party and the suffering of its many members who, like the fictional Miguel Alcántara, were persecuted and exiled during the dictatorship. But we soon realise that it also applies to Suárez, whose political orientation and accomplishments, after all these years, are no longer significant because of their ideological bent, but because of the way he is remembered, as part of Spaniards' own experience.

While it would be easy to criticise this nostalgic view of history and to question how the narrative framework of the family is used to shade over the mistakes of the past, I suggest that the perspective adopted in *Cuéntame* is consistent with the way the history of the *Transición* is currently viewed in Spain. Recent criticisms of this historical period—which, as evidenced by the recent work of people like Gregorio Morán, Pilar Urbano, Torcuato Fernández Miranda, and Fernando Ónega, have begun to focus on the individual political players of the time, such as Adolfo Suárez and King Juan Carlos—

are reflective of a symptomatic tendency to establish a particular relationship between the past and the present.[44] This insistence on remembering the names of once-important figures has gradually transformed the recent past into a memory project in which no amount of detail is deemed excessive (the sheer length of these narratives attests to this view) and history only acquires meaning through a personalised relationship.

In *Cuéntame*, it is the focus on the subjective and the physical that produces an affect—an emotional resonance—that the audience recognises and incorporates into their reality. The past becomes meaningful when it is 'embodied' in concrete events experienced personally; its importance lies in this intimate connection. Television, and the media in general, plays an important role in helping us visualise how experiences of the past, mediated through the immediacy and concreteness of the present, become memory and *archive*, in Michel Foucault's sense of a series of discursive practices that are more than a static system of storage: 'a practice that causes a multiplicity of statements to emerge' (Foucault: 129–30).

The notion of archive-as-practice also helps us better understand Jacques Derrida's theorisation about the relationship of the archive to the future. Derrida questions the relationship between the archive and memory, pointing out that the former never closes, and furthermore opens to the future through repetition (68). More than repetition, however, the act of archiving is a pursuit of the ineffable—of what cannot be fully grasped—and therein lies its compulsion, its repetitiveness, its nostalgic desire (Derrida: 91). The mediated memories of *Cuéntame* reflect this repetitiveness and the desire to uncover a trace of the past, yet the production of this nostalgic recreation only leaves a stronger desire for more. It is not surprising that the characters on the show also engage in the production and consumption of memory, as in the case of the 8 mm home movies in which Carlitos documents life in his neighbourhood, in the same episode (168) where the resemblance between Suárez and Antonio is first suggested. These homemade films of the series's own past are later screened as part of a send-off for one of the family's friends (Fig. 4.3).

In this meta-moment, memories relating to both the real past and the series's own fictional history are mixed and recreated. What they preserve

44 Morán followed his early biography, *Adolfo Suárez: historia de una ambición* (1979), with the more recent *Adolfo Suárez: ambición y destino* (2009). Pilar Urbano's *La gran desmemoria* (2014) is the latest addition to the list of critical publications centred on politicians of the *Transición*. The strongest criticism of the political and public figures of the time has been offered by Gregorio Morán, who in an interview from 2013 characterises them as an embarrassment. Available at http://www.jotdown.es/2013/12/gregorio-moran-los-padres-de-la-transicion-eran-absolutamente-impresentables/.

Figure 4.3 Carlitos makes an 8 mm film of the neighbourhood for Josete (Santiago Crespo) to remember the family by when he moves away. *Cuéntame cómo pasó* (TVE, 2001–)

is, above all, an emotional connection between the two times. This mix of times is also what entices the viewer's nostalgia for the series itself.

The same idea of an intimate connection between past and present is also explored in the Spanish adaptation of the critically acclaimed British TV series *Life on Mars* (BBC 1, 2006–07), Antena 3's *La chica de ayer* (2009). The show tells the story of a modern-day cop, Samuel Santos (Ernesto Alterio), who finds himself transported to 1977 in the aftermath of a car accident. Living in the past, Samuel fights against a backward and brutal police force while working on cases with his new colleagues. He also realises that he now has the opportunity to solve a mystery from his own childhood: the absence of his father. In the original British series, protagonist Sam Tyler (John Simm) returns to the year 1973; this timeline was changed in the Spanish version to accommodate the show's storylines—it would have been impossible to keep plotlines involving homosexuality or divorce during the dictatorship. The success of the British show, which had 6.8 million viewers during its first season and 7.1 million in its second (28% of the country's market share) did not translate to the Spanish reproduction, which was cancelled after its first season. Despite its commercial failure, the Spanish remake has garnered critical interest because of its treatment of the past, the legislative context in which it was produced, and the adaptation process it underwent for the Spanish market.

Paul Julian Smith has thoroughly documented the boom in the production of television series in Spain, arguing strongly for the popularity and importance of this medium. He contends that, while legislation and funding have played a role in production figures and audience shares, the issue of seriality is also important to measuring viewership statistics. Relative to other European countries, Spain has a higher 'seriality index', meaning that it produces a larger number of episodes within a smaller number of shows; additionally, primetime slots are held by domestic programmes while foreign shows are relegated to less-prized times (Smith 2009: 13). The increase in Spanish TV production can be attributed to a piece of legislation, introduced in 2001 and reinforced in 2007, which dictated that 5% of the earnings of private television stations must go towards the production of film and domestic television (Cascajosa: 263; Smith 2012: 54).[45] Following this legislation, private channels like Antena 3 tried to maximise their investment by producing miniseries, and others quickly followed suit. As both Cascajosa and Smith document, private and public channels were soon busy producing series that focused on historical periods, events, or public figures from the country's recent past. The list of programmes produced under this legislation is long and includes biopics of politicians and members of the royal family (*Adolfo Suárez, el presidente* [Antena 3, 2010], *Alfonso, el príncipe maldito* [Telecinco, 2010]) and historical dramas (*23-F: el día más difícil del Rey* [TVE/TV3, 2009], *23-F, historia de una traición* [Antena 3, 2009]) (Cascajosa: 263).[46]

As Smith describes, the legislation has had a number of unintended consequences, including the resurgence of the television series and a newfound proclivity for engrossing serialised dramas that guarantee the allegiance of a weekly audience (2012: 54). The most successful of these serialised dramas in the Spanish market, with both a lasting audience and continued profitability, is of course *Cuéntame cómo pasó* (TVE). Cascajosa suggests that the production of *La chica* was strongly influenced by *Cuéntame*, both in terms of the period covered and the focus on family issues. The two shows even worked as a tag team, in a sense: *La chica* aired between the eleventh and twelfth season of *Cuéntame* (2008–09) and concentrated on the same year—1977 (Cascajosa: 266). While the two shows' coverage of that year

45 As noted by Cascajosa, film production legislation is not a new phenomenon in Spain. While the ultimate consequences of the Ley Miró passed in the 1980s are still being debated, the legislature's involvement in Spanish filmmaking and the television industry is not novel (263, 273).

46 The list of titles that can be connected to this legislation is long; examples can be found in Cascajosa (2012), Rueda Laffond and Coronado Ruiz (2009), and Smith (2009, 2012).

differ (one centred on a serial murder case investigated by an antiquated police force and the other centred on the political developments of that year), the multiple recreations of this period reflect a collective interest in the *Transición*.

The original British series *Life on Mars* is an innovative spin on the generic cop show. It traces Sam's adventures and his attempts to make sense of his new time and place while constantly drawing parallels with modern crime-solving procedurals; references to personal computers, mobile phones, and DNA testing abound. The show also deals with issues like sexism in the workplace, racism, hooliganism, police brutality, and corruption, from the vantage point of the 'post-feminist, multicultural, and liberal-bureaucratic twenty-first century' (Frosh: 118). According to Paul Frosh, the 'presentism' of the show is valuable because it allows Sam to encounter 'the racism, sexism, and injustice of the past in the program's discursive "now"' (123). The possibility of experiencing past situations in the present permits a confrontation with 'the moment of their becoming and challengeability, seeing that things can be otherwise' (Frosh: 123). In other words, the opportunity to look at past problems from an informed present offers a useful tool for considering alternative outcomes of those historical conditions (Frosh: 123). Though the future need not necessarily be better by definition, this sort of framing does provide an awareness of social and cultural dynamics otherwise made invisible by a normalised view of our reality.

The show's engagement with the past is embedded in a critical understanding that media and memory can be flexible. Here, again, memory is understood as a social construct, in terms of both its formation and its preservation. Moreover, memory is in constant symbolic composition, intersecting with different narratives including illusion, storytelling, spectacle, fabrication, and art (Frosh: 117). The media, especially, offer a vessel through which memory can be reconstructed. Frosh argues that our theorisation of memory needs to be connected with imagination in order for us to move beyond the negative connotation of its illusionary nature and ideological motivation. Mass media should be recognised as central to 'the performance and explicit thematising of the intersection between memory and imagination, for enabling (and constraining) the imagination of memory' (Frosh: 117). Frosh also argues that the process of fact-checking memory (or its representation in the media) is unproductive, since the media explicitly offer an imaginary space that creates 'historically specific concretizations of shared temporality, spatial orientation, and social agency' (118).

The treatment of the past in the Spanish adaptation of *Life on Mars* has been criticised for its failure to capture the violence and the important political events of 1977. Rueda Laffond and Coronado Ruiz document how the writers (Darío Madrona, Agustín Martínez, and Susana López Rubio) and the production company (Ida y Vuelta) adapted the British version to make it relevant to Spain. They report that, according to Madrona, the Spanish version promised to be better because 'Inglaterra en el setenta y tres es un país atrasado, pero España en los setenta es un país diferente. Es una cosa que no tiene nada que ver, es un momento político muy fuerte dramáticamente para meter a alguien del futuro ahí' (Rueda Laffond and Coronado Ruiz: 295). While the series did indeed address social issues including gender inequality and the impossibility of divorce during that period (which, incidentally, required rewriting the leading female role), the programme did not deal concretely with historical events of that time. Concepción Cascajosa goes so far as to dismiss both the British and Spanish versions as nothing more than psychoanalytic exercises about missing fathers.

Nevertheless, both series provide glimpses into a tumultuous political moment in history with faithfully recreated sets, a viewpoint tinged with nostalgia, and a satirical tone that exposes the problems of the time (Cascajosa: 266). In the British show, the audience is confronted with urban degradation, inflation, strikes, unemployment, police corruption, and the violence unleashed by the situation in Northern Ireland. In Spain, the same decade (both before and after Franco's death) was a time of uncertainty, political violence, and financial crisis (Cascajosa: 266). Yet, ultimately, the memory of the *Transición* in *La chica* is optimistic. The year 1977 is presented as a moment when dialogue was possible and compromise was frequent in the political sphere (Cascajosa: 266).

The show's glossed-over version of the past focuses on the popular culture of the time instead of its violence. Cascajosa reminds us of how critical 1977 was to the process of the *Transición* and of the unprecedented violence unleashed at the beginning of that year. January 1977 was the bloodiest month since the process of political transformation began; it saw the deaths of protesting students Arturo Ruiz and Mari Luz Nájera, the kidnapping of General Lieutenant Villaescusa by the antifascist terrorist group GRAPO, the massacre on *calle* Atocha in Madrid—where labour lawyers Enrique Valdevira, Luis Javier Benavides, and Francisco Javier Sauquillo were killed alongside the student Serafín Holgado and the administrative assistant Ángel Rodríguez—and the assassination of two policemen and a Guardia Civil by GRAPO (Cascajosa: 267–68). Cascajosa questions the show's silence regarding these deaths and goes so far as to wonder whether the historical setting for the series was nothing but material for its plotline, drawing attention to the comedic tone and the way the treatment of the past is often rudimentary and simplified.

Examples of this light, jovial attitude abound: when Samuel jumps to the past, the first thing he asks for in both versions of the series is his mobile; in the final episode of the Spanish series, the underground movement la Movida is treated lightly, almost mockingly, by Samuel: 'menos mal que pronto viene la Movida y vamos a poder ir al *Rock-Ola*'. That this is the only aspect of the movement highlighted is ideologically troubling, and the treatment of other political issues is equally problematic. As examples, Cascajosa mentions the third and seventh episodes of the series, where a labour union leader and an old communist are portrayed negatively. In 'Llega el inspector Quintana', the murder of a labour union member is only treated as meaningful for the light it sheds on a troubled relationship between a father and son, where 'la actividad criminal se presenta como la consecuencia [de] un padre ausente cuya actividad sindical no solo es inútil, sino que seguramente ha provocado la caída en desgracia de su díscolo hijo' (Cascajosa: 271–72). Meanwhile, in 'El abandono', an old communist is freed from jail thanks to the amnesty law, but becomes a common criminal when he kills the police informant who put him in prison in the first place.

Perhaps the expectation that *La chica* would be faithful to the political moment in which it was set stemmed from the fact that it shared air space with other historically oriented programmes on Spanish television. Indeed, the critical reading of the show—exemplified in the quotes from Cascajosa above—derives largely from the perspective that, by definition, the treatment of the past in Spain has been problematic. Embracing viewpoints from indifference to politically motivated nostalgia, the relationship between contemporary Spanish society and its recent history has been one of conflict, in which the legacy of the Spanish Civil War, the abuses of the Franco dictatorship, and the unfulfilled promises of the country's political transition to democracy are still being disputed. Despite the abundance of both fictional and historiographical works about this history, the enduring impression is that this period is still not fully known or understood. It is within this context that recent criticisms about works on the political transition must be read. Historian Carme Molinero's definition of the period captures this viewpoint perfectly:

> resulta sorprendente que, en el contexto de relecturas de la transición de la dictadura a la democracia que se están haciendo en España, no es puesta de relieve por la izquierda la tergiversación que hace la derecha española ... Es una prueba más de la paradoja constatable desde hace más de una década según la cual, en la actualidad, reivindican la Transición una parte de los que se resistieron al cambio político. (35)

The contestation of what took place during the *Transición* provides a critical framework within which to examine recent recreations of this period.

Historiographical accuracy is important to the act of remembering; ideological manipulation is frequent in representations of the past. Yet the current recreation of historical events in Spanish television series challenges us to reimagine the connection between popular culture, history, and the factors that shape our world views. Recreations of the past that do not rely on direct referential relationships with historical events can be understood as part of a *spectrum of possible representations of past experiences*, each of which may have its own 'truth'. If we theorise memory in connection to imagination, as Frosh suggests, such variant representations need not carry negative connotations; we can find new paradigms to help us to move past the fact-checking of popular accounts (Frosh: 117). In the case of *La chica*, the omission of the violent incidents of 1977 need not be understood solely as a vote in favour of forgetting this bloody past. If we step back to consider how experience is mediated by television, we may conclude that the show's writers made a deliberate choice to exclude certain historiographical details in order to explore different memories and connections to the past. As Agustín Martínez explains, '[p]ara el contexto, nos interesaban cosas que pudiéramos recordar, como la matanza de Atocha, porque el espectador también podía recordarlas. Pero no queríamos meternos en concreto en ese día, en qué pasó eso exactamente. Nos daba igual' (Rueda Laffond and Coronado Ruiz: 299–300). In contrast to the detailed accounts of this period provided by Cercas's narrative or *Cuéntame*, *La chica de ayer* approaches the past through an indirect lens, one which uses history as a context for storytelling rather than a narrative end in and of itself.

In the previous chapter, I highlighted the possibility that a referential index might become a pure signifier, acquiring signification not because of its referentiality but because of the aesthetic strategies at play. This form of signification can help us analyse the popular recreation of the *Transición* presented in *La chica de ayer* and the ways in which such recreations create new meanings for the past. Above all the historical context of *La chica de ayer* exposes a need for a different way of knowing. When Samuel talks about his current and past experience of 1977, historical significance is lost in favour of personal memory. Here, the experience of Spain in this tumultuous year is explored through the everyday, dispersed through the social practices of the time. The series invites us to look into the past in a diffused manner.

While the approach taken by *La chica de ayer* may be deemed ideologically problematic, it does reveal a particular way of relating to previous experiences. In the opening sequence of each episode, we hear Samuel's voice telling the audience about the past:

> Dicen que 1977 fue un gran año. Bueno, es cierto que no existían los teléfonos móviles ni los MP3. ... Pero ese año se celebraron las primeras elecciones democráticas. ... El Betis ganó la primer Copa del Rey, que antes se llamaba del Generalísimo. Ese año se estrenó *La guerra de las galaxias* y en todas las emisoras de radio se escuchaba 'Gavilán o paloma'.

Television here provides a space where these events can be imagined, mediated, or remembered through everyday experiences. The constant presence of the TV set helps Samuel to remain connected to the present and to access his memories; his experience reflects the same connection between history and the present that the viewers experience when watching the show.

In the early scenes of the first episode of *La chica*, while Samuel is still in the present, his girlfriend Sonia (Marta Solaz) tells him that she is leaving him. She suggests that he needs to 'feel', not just 'think'. Samuel's time travel crucially allows him to follow his emotions and to understand his obsession with solving crimes—an interest that is intimately connected to the mystery of his own family. By trying to make sense of his father's absence, Samuel discovers the moment at which he lost touch with his emotions. The importance of affective connection is enforced from the very beginning of the series, when Samuel's only contact with the present is hearing Sonia's voice on the radio.

Samuel's struggle to 'feel' becomes part of his experience in the past, a period which only becomes comprehensible once he lets go of his of future self. This shift means, for instance, that despite his strong sense of integrity and duty, Samuel acts unethically, creating a situation in which his boss, Inspector Quin Gallardo (Antonio Garrido), kills a suspect who would otherwise have become a serial killer. While this unexpected consequence is a troubling 'reward' for Samuel's emotional transformation, the situation makes him aware of his own limitations and those of the time he currently inhabits. Ultimately, this situation helps him understand that the imperfections he observes will continue into the future and he must therefore be constantly attuned to these shortcomings.

La chica portrays the past through a physical relationship with the present. Even if Samuel's search for the reason behind his father's absence does not result in any life-changing insight about his own history, his physical relationship with the past that surrounds him contributes to the

Figure 4.4   Opening car chase against Madrid's futuristic skyline. *La chica de ayer* (Antena 3, 2009)

significance of the moment at which he arrived during his accidental time travel.[47] In the British version of the show, Sam's jump from a building in the series finale signals a clear separation of past and present;[48] in the Spanish version, however, the time-travelling device is used to establish a physical contiguity between the two times. The opening shots of the series capture the most modern, futuristic skyline of Madrid, represented by the four towers of Torre Caja Madrid, Torre PwC, Torre de Cristal, and Torre Espacio. It is against this backdrop that the series's opening scene—police cars racing to arrest a suspect—unfolds, and it is in this area that Samuel's time travel occurs (Fig. 4.4). This modern road leads to a tunnel from which Samuel emerges to the past (Fig. 4.5).

The opening scenes of *La chica* feature police driving to the residence of a man they believe to be a serial killer. These scenes revolve around the four towers in the background; they constantly shift in and out of the shot as the camera follows the police cars. The visual contrast between the hyper-modern towers and the 1970s Madrid into which Samuel emerges drives home for viewers the significance of the development that has taken

47 It could be argued that, because the series was cancelled after only one season, the storylines had to be resolved more quickly, leading to hurried narrations that did not fully explore Samuel's experience as a child or the fate of his father.

48 Sam's jump is alluded to as suicide in the first episode of *Ashes to Ashes*, the sequel to *Life on Mars*.

Figure 4.5   Samuel jumps through time in the same tunnel the police cars drive through in the opening scenes of the show. *La chica de ayer* (Antena 3, 2009)

place between these two periods. The disparity is emphasised not only by the physical absence of the modern buildings, but also by the manipulation of colour. From a bright, steel-coloured Madrid, we transition to a street shot in warmer tones, filled with people and small shops. In this visual juxtaposition, the viewer recognises the urban transformation and the real estate boom that is about to hit the city. While this contrast may invoke a nostalgic view of the past, it can also be read as a criticism of the neoliberal transformation of the Spanish capital and a lament for the loss of small neighbourhoods with tight-knit communities. This criticism is timely, as the contrast between the two scenes establishes a concrete link between Spain's recent crisis and the mad real estate boom that started in the 1970s. I suggest that, rather than being suspicious of the wistfulness we experience when faced with the nostalgically tinged past in which Samuel finds himself, we should focus on exploring how this visually quaint past connects to the present through its criticism of Spain's current financial reality.

The time travel sequence in the first episode of *La chica* offers a good example of how the viewer is invited to make a critical connection between past and present. As Samuel is hit by a car and knocked into the past, we hear 'Bohemian Rhapsody' by the British rock band Queen blasting on the radio.[49]

---

49 Unlike the British show, which takes its title from the popular David Bowie song that also serves as the soundtrack of the series, the Spanish adaptation borrows its title from a popular Nacha Pop song, though it is not used in the programme.

Just as the moment of time travel occurs, the song reaches its climax in which the singer calls for his mother and confesses to a murder. The singer's lament that he is 'just a poor boy' and uncertainty about distinguishing between 'real life and fantasy' resonate with the plotline of the miniseries. The sense of loss expressed in the lyrics foreshadows the search that will occupy Samuel during his time in the past. Most importantly, the last two lines of the initial stanza, 'caught in a landslide / no escape from reality' acquire meaning as Samuel's involuntary time travel throws him into the past without any means of escape.

Samuel must face the reality of the past to survive his experience. His final decision to remain in the past—despite his realisation that the present is accessible on the other side of the tunnel—suggests two interpretations. First, it emphasises the physical connection between past and present that is embodied in the character himself. Second, it offers the possibility and promise of a different future: one in which Samuel faces his emotional reality. The representation of the past now shifts to emphasise its connection to the present, while the role of imagination becomes productive in its projection of the future. In the context of the ongoing debate over the conflictive relationship between past and present in Spain, what this recreation reinforces is the inevitability of the connection of the two periods, both intimately and ideologically. While the nature of this connection remains flexible and ever-changing, it is precisely this flexibility that demands our critical attention.

Linda Williams explores the nature of TV serials in her study of the lauded American series *The Wire*. Her work invites us to consider the physical (and aesthetic) possibilities of TV series, their dramatic resonance, and their potential for expressing interconnected truths through interconnected events. Discussing the possibility of a visual 'history' (or a visual 'novel', as she characterises *The Wire*), Williams remarks on the complex narrative universe allowed by the medium of the TV series, mostly due to the resource of abundant time (210). The evolution from soaps to cop series to cumulative serials such as *Cuéntame* is a perfect example of the complexity of narration. Williams invites us to value the possibility of assembling different parts of a story (or, indeed, a history) into a whole narrative. The medium of television enables the process of building a complex story with its 'world enough and time' (213). Long-format series allow viewers to follow timelines, stories, and the developments—emotional, intellectual, political, financial—of each character through his or her familiar (and social) role.

Series like *Cuéntame* and *La chica* create universes of experiences that provides new forms of cognition by intercutting from one character (and his or her social space) to another, with the aid of the voice-over narration that frames each episode. One aspect of this process, as I have mentioned, is the digital insertion of fictional characters into archival material, where they are exposed to many objects from the past. In their melodramatic rewriting of history, these shows do not depend on abstract ideas or concepts to explain the political, economic, and social reality of the time. Their conditions (both in terms of potential and limitations) are designed to be understood in a concrete and accessible form that refers to everyday experiences and implies connections with the outside world.

Time is an important element in this process: it is used to build a character, to develop the story, to unfold the plot's many complexities, and to give meaning to the process by which each character finds his or her place in the world. It is *time*, argues Williams, that should be valued in this new kind of television, which serves as 'serial melodrama, that can juxtapose dramatic situations over time, allowing situations to ripen, characters to change, history to unfold' (221). Long-format storytelling that incorporates the passage of time also necessarily recovers a sense of past time. It takes time to transform social types into credible subjects that, in turn, enable the creation of a 'world' capable of (re)producing the sociopolitical context of a moment far more effectively than our imagination can. An enormous amount of time is spent on developing the idea of change in a series like *Cuéntame*. The passing of time, both within the series and in watching the episodes, establishes a strong connection between the show and the physical world. While Toni belongs to the generation that is currently 'remembering' the transitional period, it is Carlitos's experience of growing up during the 15 years of the series that makes this historical period more real. Coming-of-age tales play an important role in connecting the experience of the past to the present day; the inherent introspection involved in tracing a child's growth produces a strong awareness of one's current circumstances.

Early in this chapter, I talked about mediation and its relationship with (prosthetic) memory-making. As Frosh indicates, if we think of television in terms of its connectivity rather than just as a representational device, we understand that the experience of watching television is not simply characterised by exposure to particular programmes, but more fundamentally by the routine, domesticated potential for mass connectivity.[50] It is within this context that we should consider memory, imagined and performed

---

50 Frosh follows J. Meyrowitz's thinking about place and television here, 'even when there are no programs being transmitted, the television signifies our perpetual connection with an outside world that is separate from us' (qtd. in Frosh: 128).

through a social nucleus—a 'shared audio-visual simulacrum, collected and unfolding in a synchronous now, via a central spatial location that is connected to everyone' (Frosh: 129). In other words, as it pertains to the worlds of both *Life on Mars* and *La chica*:

> Television *re-collects* as a working spatial assemblage both memory objects from the 1970s (clothes, décor, cars, offices, hairstyles, etc.) and mediated-memory sequences from the 1970s (music, cultural icons, narrative scripts familiar form the period's television programming), ransacking its own institutional history and back-catalog of programs in order to gather and renew the collective past at the social centre. At the same time television *re-collects* its audience as participants in this act of synchronous remembering, gathering them together as a collective in the reimagining of a past shared in and through television. (Frosh: 129)

Writing about the relationship of contemporary Spanish fiction and film to the past, Jo Labanyi shares a personal anecdote: '[w]hen teaching adult Spanish students who grew up under Francoism, I have frequently been struck by the fact that the only historical knowledge they had about Spain's immediate past was transmitted to them by their families (and "family" here means a collective, extended family network)' (2000: 67). As this story suggests, the family unit has been and continues to be a useful frame through which to mediate and connect narratives. It is not surprising, then, that in the series *Cuéntame cómo pasó*, the Alcántaras offer a perfect model for exploring kinship as a vehicle of narration for the past. Even the broken family in *La chica* plays a similar role.

While this transmission format may be questionable because of its informal connection to the past, one must bear in mind that this 'family'-style method of historical transmission is itself yet another social and political consequence of Spain's past. Labanyi sees the reliance on family lore for transmitting memory as an outcome of the country's oppression under various power structures:

> What is so striking here [talking about the erasure of memory in South America, specifically of Argentina and the history of its 'desaparecidos'] is that the casualty of this suppression of all forms of collective discourse should have been private memories. For popular memory— relying on oral rather than written transmission—requires some kind of collective space, even if it be reduced to that of the family (which is never a purely private sphere). (2000: 67)

The fact that television has become a space for these narratives is a testament to the usefulness of visual media in facilitating the narration of the past. Writing about the possibility of world-building in television, Jeffrey Sconce argues that whatever TV 'lacks in spectacle and narrative constraints, it makes up for in depth and duration of character relations, diegetic expansion, and audience investment' (95). The notion of 'cumulative narrative', as it has been termed by Horace Newcomb, describes a new narrative mode that 'balances episodic treatments of a program's story world with larger arcs of long-term narrative progression' (Sconce: 97–98). Perhaps it is in this way that series like *Cuéntame* mediate Spain's relationship with the past. By considering the ways in which they both create and mediate memories, we can explore how the continued presence of these programmes and their recollections keeps audiences coming back for new ways to understand the past.

Alison Landsberg has argued that cinema and mass cultural technology are the tools in our time with which we can create 'imagined communities' (to borrow Benedict Anderson's term) that are no longer bounded geographically or nationally; the ability of audiovisual media to serve in this capacity derives from their ability to create 'shared social frameworks for people who inhabit, literally and figuratively, different social spaces, practices, and beliefs' (8). Commodified mass culture offers the possibility for people who have little in common to share concrete memories. Recall that the value of these prosthetic memories does not lie in their authenticity, their ownership, or their capacity to change existing memories. They are important because they encourage 'ethical thinking': '[o]ne's engagement with them begins from a position of difference, with the recognition that these images and narratives concerning the past are not one's "heritage" in any simple sense' (Landsberg: 9).

Despite understanding this difference, people are inspired to connect to others through prosthetic memory and thus become aware of differences, of the experience of the 'other'. Prosthetic memory is positive in this sense, because it allows the movement and coexistence of different recollections. *Cuéntame* does this, working with its viewers to blend personal and fictional experience. Its rich visual documentation of Spain's recent past, thanks to TVE's abundant archives, creates a space where individual memories come in contact with created material to build an understanding of the past.[51]

51 In a Q&A session during the 2014 Kentucky Foreign Language and Literatures Conference in Lexington, Jorge Marí pointed out that, in a way, incorporating these archives into the series signifies that the memories being created are TVE's own memories. While I agree with this statement, I also think that these memories lose the imprint of ownership as they become part of a fluid circulation of visual memories (and recollections) from the past.

Moreover, it is not only Spanish audiences that access these memories, as confirmed by the series's international appeal. The fact that this storyline can be adapted to fit other national histories is evidence that the creation and representation of memories is fluid, and that their circulation engenders a collective interest and investment in the past.

The shared qualities that Landsberg detects in prosthetic memory are also explored in José van Dijck's discussion of mediated memories and the process by which objects from the past come to signal our autobiographical and cultural identities.[52] As she writes, 'collections of mediated memories raise interesting questions about a person's identity in a specific culture at a certain moment in time' (1). Van Dijck's explanation of our relationship with the past as mediated by technology moves us away from the antagonistic positioning that often limits critical discussion of popular representations:

> Media technologies and objects, far from being external instruments for 'holding' versions of the past, help constitute a sense of the past—both in terms of our private lives and of history at large. Memory and media have both been referred to metaphorically as reservoirs, holding our past experiences and knowledge for future use. But neither memories nor media are passive go-betweens: their mediation intrinsically shapes the way we build up and retain a sense of individuality and community, of identity and history. ... As private collections, mediated memories form sites where the personal and the collective meet, interact, and clash; from these encounters we may derive important cultural knowledge about the construction of historical and contemporaneous selves in the course of time: How do our media tools mould our process of remembering and vice versa? How does remembrance affect the way we deploy media devices? (2)

When examining memory production about the *Transición*, it is important that we ask how remembering is moulded both privately and collectively, and how we influence and 'consume' memory via popular culture.[53] These recreations are important for how they encourage us to think, to

52 Unlike Landsberg's 'prosthetic' memories, mediated memories are not prostheses of the mind. They are not wholly located in the brain or outside, but 'exist in both concurrently, for they are manifestations of a complex interaction between brain, material objects, and the cultural matrix from which they arise' (van Dijck: 28). The emphasis on this connection—or the interaction, per se—is crucial, as it allows us to break away from the binary structures to talk about memory and cultural objects (and the biases we expose in our discussions).

53 Andrew Hoskins discusses our relationship with the past in terms of mediation/ remediation in a global context (333–46).

remember, and to engage with this historical experience, rather than for their relationship with the past.

By adopting a purely critical stance and focusing only on how these widely popular recreations promote a nostalgic view of the past, we prevent ourselves from delving into the question of how these memories are mediated and maintained, preserved and multiplied. Ultimately, we are unable to see how this experience affects individuals—or, to use Margaret Wetherell's explanation of affect as embodiment, 'to understand how people are moved, and what attracts them, to an emphasis on repetition, pains and pleasures, feelings and memories' (2). Wetherell borrows the social science perspective on 'affect' to examine the emotional in social life, trying to find 'shifting, flexible and often over-determined figurations rather than simple lines of causation, character types and neat emotion categories' (4). Here, affect should be understood as 'embodied meaning-making', a flowing activity, a pattern or a habit that relates to power value and capital, 'always "turned on" and "simmering," moving along, since social action is continually embodied' (Wetherell: 12).

As the past becomes 'embodied' through concrete events in *Cuéntame*, characters and audience members alike are able to share the emotions produced by these recreations. When we talk about our personal and collective memories of the Spanish Civil War and the *Transición*, it is important to consider their affective pull: the context in which they are created and the way in which they acquire social, cultural, and political meaning. Considering the production of such works more generally, we can understand 'affective practices' as those that 'unfurl, become organized, and effloresce with particular rhythms' (Wetherell: 12). Understanding this pattern is vital, given that affect is about 'sense as well as sensibility'; it 'gets patterned together with feelings and thoughts, interaction patterns and relationships, narratives and interpretative repertoires, social relations, personal histories, and ways of life' (Wetherell: 13–14). In other words, by reading these memories as a social practice, even as a way of life, we open up yet another context in which to consider the recreations of the Spanish *Transición*.

As we weigh the ongoing debate between media recreations and memory formation, on the one hand, and the historical credibility of these constructs, on the other, it is important not to subscribe to fallacious binary and hierarchical structures. Rather, as suggested by van Dijck, the essential point is to acknowledge how historical memory and mediated memory transform each other. In fact, changing technologies (in this case, digital) and objects reflect (and embody) changing memories: '[t]he term "mediation of memory," if we attend to its conceptual flaws, may be rearticulated as "mediated memories," a concept that may add to a better understanding of the mutual shaping of memory and media' (van Dijck: 21). By acknowledging this relationship, we can accept that these memories are not static objects or repositories, but fluid vessels that draw connections between the self and the other, the private and the public, the individual and the collective, and past and future through our present.

Van Dijck organises memory along two axes: the horizontal, expressing relational identity, and the vertical, articulating time. Considering memory in this way provides us with a conceptual tool to analyse complex cases of memory formation and transformation (21). To describe this functionality, van Dijck introduces the example of a personal shoebox, the contents of which can become culturally relevant without displacing their psychological weight of personal or cultural memory, or the historian's notion of collective or cultural memory (22). This organisation of memory is useful in the Spanish case. The juxtaposition of a proliferation of cultural artefacts relating to the past against an increasing academic and popular acknowledgement of a collective amnesia presents a challenging cultural paradox. The concept of 'memoria histórica' deserves reconsideration in the context of the multiplicity of these cultural objects and not only as a symptom of a crisis of memory. To deny the role these artefacts play in the transmission and formation of memories is to ignore their presence and significance, and to hold a limited view of how the past (and its experiences and memories) can interact with the present through transmission and recollection.

Finally, the notion of mediated or prosthetic memories is similar to that of 'tangled memories' articulated by Marita Sturken. However, Sturken's reading differs from the one developed above in that her analysis focuses exclusively on the collective realm, while van Dijck also valorises private memory objects, regardless of whether they have gained public recognition (23). Subjective experience can complement the historical, political, and cultural dimensions of memory; we cannot separate these features but 'should integrate psychological and cognitive perspective into cultural theory' (van Dijck: 23).[54] This perspective allows us to take into consideration the dynamic, continuously changing memory artefacts and items of mediated culture (van Dijck: 24).

The notion of change can be used as a tool to examine the ways in which memory work has developed in contemporary discourse in Spain. As the inquiry into this past continues, the significance of past events enters a state

54 In the case of Spain, the individual is no longer the direct victim of a traumatic event. The historical trauma that an individual experiences affects his or her memory and relationship with the past, but the personal recollection of events related to this past and the individual's subjective experience are added to the memory of this time.

of constant transformation. Both *Cuéntame* and Cercas's *Anatomía* show clearly how relationships and recollections of the past affect individuals as they change and evolve. The continuous reshaping of memories can be understood as a relational act; collections of mediated objects provide connection between generations amid changing perceptions of family and self. At the same time, public projects absorb these objects, producing social and cultural transformations and adding to a shared experience of remembering. Therefore, far from being fixed articles, 'mediated memories never remain the same in the course of time but are constantly prone to the vagaries of time and changing relations between self and others' (van Dijck: 24).

This idea of change is important in the case of Spain, especially considering the evolution of cultural artefacts narrating the past. Popular discussion of trauma has expanded beyond the memories of the Spanish Civil War to include the succeeding dictatorship and now the post-dictatorial years. It is in this shifting of the past towards the present that memory transforms the experience of temporal distance. The memories of the *Transición* have become part of the Spanish 'cultural memory', close in conceptual terms to Williams's 'structure of feeling'; as such, they embody change. It is the notion of cultural connectivity, based on shared memories and experiences (bridged by cultural artefacts that connect private and public memories, prosthetic, mediated, and tangled memories), that affects our understanding of the past—an understanding that implies a view of the future, as I will discuss in the conclusion. By shifting the focus from collective memory to private memory, attention can be directed to the private *objects* of memory while continuing to gauge the individual by the collective.[55] It is the relationship between the individual and the collective that is enforced again and again in the works I analyse in this book. In this particular case, that relationship is enabled by the experience of watching television. The linkage between the private and the public leads to a collective experience of memory, solidified by affect.

---

55 Van Dijck argues that the content of shoeboxes should not only be interesting in hindsight, after history has decided the value of its content. She encourages us to think about the importance of shoebox creation as a cultural act, and to consider how artefacts teach us the ways in which we 'deploy media technologies to situate ourselves in contemporary and past cultures and how we store and reshape our images of self, family, and community in the course of living' (25).

CHAPTER FIVE

Transitional Stories

¿Transición? ¿La transición española? ¿Transiciones democráticas?
¿Transiciones, de dónde a dónde? ¿De qué a qué? ¿Un concepto
sociológico de transiciones? ¿Un simulacro?
Eduardo Subirats, *Intransiciones*, 13

In 2011, four novels connected with the years of the *Transición* were published in Spain. Their authors, all born between 1960 and 1963, were clearly shaped by the experience and memory of this period. Ignacio Martínez de Pisón (b. 1960), Rafael Reig (b. 1963), Antonio Orejudo (b. 1963), and Benjamín Prado (b. 1961) were born under Franco's dictatorship and were young men during the gradual easing of his regime and the arrival of democracy. Their literary education took place to a world dominated by the narrative of the country's successful democratisation, and their present work is cognisant yet critical of the changes that took place during those years. In this final chapter, I examine how Spain's political transition is recreated and remembered in Prado's *Operación Gladio* (2011), Reig's *Todo está perdonado* (2011), Orejudo's *Un momento de descanso* (2011), and Martínez de Pisón's *El día de mañana* (2011). While the stories told in these novels are not always directly connected to the politics of the late 1970s, the world and the characters portrayed in their narratives are unmistakably marked by the events of this period. More importantly, each novel emphasises that the *Transición* cannot be read as a 'break' from the past, that the latter should be examined for its endurance and its continued ability to affect the present. In Martínez de Pisón's narrative, for example, as the later years of Francoism blend into the early days of the political transition, change pervades the characters' everyday lives—a change that is imperceptible until reflected upon from a temporal distance. In these authors' novels, the intimate and physical connections the characters make to the years of the *Transición* are varied and unexpected; each novel revisits this period with an obsession that reflects what we have seen in the other works analysed in this book. In a close reading of these authors' works, I highlight the impulse exhibited by both characters and authors to connect their present lives to the past through narration, and tie this process of remembering to the debate about historical memory in Spain. On the one hand, these works help to perpetuate the popular interest in this memory; on the other, the writers themselves are shaped by the political impasse that surrounds any discussion about the past.

The novels analysed in this chapter differ from both the works about the 23-F and the television series discussed in the previous chapter in offering a more directly critical response to the official version of the political transition in Spain. These works openly question Spain's democratic transformation, reveal the many ways in which the power structure of the dictatorship was never dismantled, and challenge the rhetoric of successful change that has permeated Spain's political and cultural discourse since the later days of the Franco regime. At the same time, all four novels display narrative features already discussed in this book, such as the favouring of first-person accounts and emphasis on physical and emotional connection to the past.

In each of the novels, it is the narrator's intimate link to previous events that solidifies his account of the political and cultural history in Spain. This 'burden of the past' is often presented as an obstacle in the current life of the narrator, and this tension lends a sense of urgency to the act of remembering and examining what took place during this time. The credibility of the narrator is established through bearing witness: each narrator was present during important events of the past and is directly affected by them in the present. This authority is not challenged, even when narrators describe surreal and absurd situations, as they do in the novels by Orejudo and Reig. In these narratives, the past acquires meaning through its ability to shape daily concerns; ultimately, the historical events of the time can only be understood as accumulations of everyday experiences. The 'I's in all of these narratives are insistent about the importance of their own personal experience in understanding and mediating the past. Ironically, the emphasis on the personal in these novels is counterbalanced by large amounts of historical and journalistic research that often blurs the distinction between creative and historiographical work.

Recent scholarship on contemporary Spanish fiction has focused on the connection between literature and history, examining how writers blend imagination with collective and historical memory. Christian von Tschilschke and Dagmar Schmelzer employ the media studies term 'docufiction' to describe this hybridisation of genres, which they term a 'rhetoric of anti-fictionality' (13). Docufiction, as they use it, describes a mode of representation that goes beyond the traditional parameters of media and the literary genre to blend documentary and fictional elements through a range of different narrative techniques and strategies. Docufiction functions to deconstruct the boundary that separates fact from fiction; the resulting uncertainty can cause either acceptance of a new epistemological experience in the reader/viewer or a normalised state of continued confusion. According to von Tschilschke and Schmelzer, 'la conciencia de la ficcionalidad y la construcción mediática de la realidad se han convertido desde hace mucho en un patrón teórico interpretativo conocido y en un punto de referencia estable de la experiencia cotidiana' (19). When writers are continually exposed to this mode of representation in their everyday experience, it shapes the world views expressed in their fiction as well.

Other studies on contemporary Spanish fiction have examined the intersection between memory and literature and the role of history in fiction. The subtitles to the two-volume work *La memoria novelada* (2012) capture the themes of this narrative: *Hibridización de géneros y metaficción en la novela española sobre la guerra civil y el franquismo (2000–2010)* and *Ficcionalización, documentalismo y lugares de memoria en la narrativa memorialista española*.[1] An earlier volume by Javier Gómez-Montero bears the title *Memoria literaria de la Transición española* (2007). Hibridisation, metafiction, fictionalisation, 'documentalism', and memory are key words used to describe the blended narrative present in contemporary fiction.

These studies also point to an ongoing interest in the memory and legacy of the Spanish Civil War, the Franco dictatorship, and the *Transición*. Gómez-Montero has argued that the structure of literature makes it the ideal vehicle for constructing memory ('la memoria histórica se forja ... a base de narrativización e imaginación') and historical discourse ('la lógica autónoma de su discurso ... que permite reenfocar el subconsciente colectivo, lo privado o públicamente reprimido (su amnesia), así como analizar las prácticas sociales y las construcciones históricas correspondientes con los recursos de la fabulación ficcional') (8). Fiction may also be seen as a possible tool with which to intervene in current political issues: '[l]a literatura, como discurso social, lógicamente ha venido acompañando este mismo proceso, al ir señalando, desde el terreno de la ficción, aquellos asuntos que convenía recordar a fin [de] contribuir a la plasmación de una verdadera justicia social' (Cruz Suárez and Hansen: 11).

---

1 The first volume was edited by Hans Lauge Hansen and Juan Carlos Cruz Suárez, the second by the same Juan Carlos Cruz Suárez and Diana González Martín. Both were published in 2012.

The long list of writers studied and mentioned in the two volumes of *La memoria novelada* and *Memoria literaria* unmistakably identify a tendency in contemporary Spanish narrative to make a fundamental connection between literature and current social issues. While this connection of contemporary literature to politics is not the same as the politically committed social realism of the 1950s, it does share a similar vision of a fiction defined by pragmatics. The underlying assumption here is that literature is capable of social and political intervention. Juan Carlos Cruz Suárez and Diana González Martín articulate this position when they link the so-called 'novela memorialista' to social action: 'apela a unos interlocutores concretos: aquéllos que, de varias formas (nostálgica, empática, crítica, desmitificadora o utópica), se involucran en lo que leen y, trascendiendo el tiempo efímero de la experiencia estética, saben reflejarlo y hacer intervenir en sus vidas' (12–13). Narratives that blend fiction, history, and memory represent different ways of looking into the past and making it relevant to the present.

In the context of the *Transición*, critics have argued that docufiction plays a valuable role in challenging the official version of what took place after the end of the Franco dictatorship. Yet, as I have already pointed out, this narrative of Spain's successful transition has been challenged from the beginning. Thus, in this chapter, rather than focusing on the novelty of this criticism or a lack of 'true change' in Spain and the country's amnesia about its violent past (which we have established already exists in abundance), I examine the *conditions* that reinforce this critical position and guarantee its persistence in literature.[2]

In pursuing this discussion, I consider Gómez-Montero's notion of a 'periodisation' of fiction related to the Spanish transition: it may be *of* the time, produced *during* the time, or be *about* the time itself (13). This flexible categorisation, according to Gómez-Montero, reflects the changing nature of this fiction and its versatile relationship with the time of the transition—the result of an 'experiencia generacional' that soon acquired a foundational status in all political, cultural, and literary discourses in contemporary Spain (Gómez-Montero: 9). In the recent debate about collective and historical memory, however, the *Transición* has become an

2　Among the early critics of the *Transición* were Teresa Vilarós, Eduardo Subirats, and Joan Ramon Resina, who questioned the change that took place in Spain after the death of Franco and the new democratic government's failure to deal with the legacies of the Civil War and the dictatorship. Critics of this period belong to many different fields and are too numerous to list here. I mention the works of these three specialists in particular because they have shaped the study of this period from the perspective of literary and cultural studies as practised outside of Spain.

'asignatura pendiente', a period in need of narratives that can explain the country's past (Gómez-Montero: 15).

In the volume *Memoria literaria de la Transición española*, the temporal arc within which this historical experience is examined is extended to include the years between the late 1970s and the terrorist attack that occurred at Madrid's Atocha Station on 11 March 2004. Gómez-Montero sees this incident as a symptom of a sociopolitical moment in Spain that demanded a cultural and regional reorganisation under a single unified state; such a unification, in turn, required that conflicting historical memories be rejected or resolved (Gómez-Montero: 15). I suggest that this temporal arc can be extended further, to encompass the debate on the Law of Historical Memory in 2007, the financial crisis that started in 2008 and continues to this day, the 15-M movement, the emergence of the populist left-wing party Podemos in the elections of 2014, and the 2014 and 2015 Catalan referenda on independence. The flexibility of the periodisation of the *Transición* speaks to the popular perception of Spain's process of democratisation as 'unfinished business'.

The works of the authors I study in this book could be classified into many of the categories mentioned above. Javier Cercas's *Anatomía de un instante* and Benjamín Prado's novel about the disappearance of a journalist looking into the 1977 Atocha murders are texts that blend documentation with fiction. Rafael Reig's dystopian narrative is written as a detective novel, a mixed literary genre that recalls the 1950s and the *Transición* in detail. In a surreal narration, it depicts Madrid, its roads replaced with water to aid navigation after an oil crisis, amid the final match of the Spanish soccer team in the 2008 European Cup. History is also the backbone of Ignacio Martínez de Pisón's novel, which deploys a choral voice to narrate the life of Justo Gil Tello from the late 1960s to the early 1980s. Finally, in Orejudo's absurd pseudo-campus novel, the narrator uses real academic publications to relate a fictional account of the adventures of a failed academic who returns to Spain after living in the US.

While these stories expose familiar criticisms about the *Transición*, their world view reveals a specific way in which the narrators have internalised the past. The authors situate these novels within affective structures where the characters live an existence of unfulfilled desires. They are found in a moment of impasse that links their current lives with the past, in which their previous experience (or action) is perceived as an obstacle for their future. Imagination, history, and memory intersect in these narratives to reveal a past that insists on shaping the present while interfering with any attempt at imagining a future. Indeed, at times these novels seem to be even more obsessively occupied with the future than they are with the past.

I focus on the novels of Prado, Reig, Orejudo, and Martínez de Pisón because these authors have been identified in the press as part of a generational group expressing a shared interest in and critical stance towards the *Transición*.[3] I look into this characterisation not as a way to generalise the experience of a group (which is undoubtedly exclusionary by definition), but to articulate the perception implicit in this classification. On the one hand, this generational grouping conveys the notion of a critical juncture in the production of memory works in contemporary Spanish narrative; on the other, it establishes a basis of similarity between the narratives produced by these authors. It also evokes the idea, discussed earlier in this book, of a generational response that embodies Raymond Williams's notion of a 'structure of feeling'. I have referred to the temporal quality of this phrase and the use of the term 'feeling' as part of a 'practical consciousness of a present kind' (132). It is important to pay attention to the language used to encode a social experience that is still in process, especially in connection to the memory work about the *Transición*. To consider these novels as examples of a generational response allows us to look into the connections between the narratives and a specific historical and political moment.

As observed by historian Pablo Sánchez León, the generation who lived during the transition have much to tell us about their experience through their generational identity and collective visibility (165–66). If we consider Prado, Reig, Orejudo, and Martínez de Pisón as exemplars of this generation, it is clear that their identity is intimately connected to broadly circulating feelings about Spain's troubled past. Kathleen Stewart's notion of 'ordinary affects' comes back into play here to characterise this public feeling and its usefulness in detecting the manifestations of an unresolved history. As Stewart theorises, the significance of ordinary affects lies 'in the intensities they build and in what thoughts and feelings they make possible' (3).

What I explore in these narratives is the way these emotions move between present and past—sometimes strengthening the intimate or historical ties between the two, at other times weakening or even severing this connection. These writers and their work ensure the continuity of this unresolved past while simultaneously being sustained by it. Lauren Berlant's definition of 'cruel optimism' captures the paradox between the desire that propels a fiction and the social and political context that enables it. Her discussion

3 In an article in *El País* on 31 March 2011, Tereixa Constenla identifies this group of writers (along with Javier Cercas) as part of the 'generation of the sixties' whose work narrates Spain's process of democratisation without the usual complacency. Even if this label is simply a marketing ploy that bookstores and blogs have used to promote these four writers and their novels, the group does have a generational imprint in their relationship with the *Transición*.

of affect applies to the world(s) described in these novels, to the social structures and dynamics experienced by their characters, and to the authors themselves, caught in a generational moment that confronts them with the past. Berlant's work discusses the ways in which individuals deal with the deterioration of everyday myths that sustain daily living. While her focus is on the US in the present day, I contend that the 'negotiation of fantasies' to make one's current existence bearable is a concept that applies equally well to other national contexts and time periods. After all, what always makes the present tolerable is the belief that one's prospects are better and that change can and will happen in the future.

'Cruel optimism' is, according to Berlant, 'the condition of maintaining an attachment to a problematic object *in advance* of its loss' (2010: 94 , emphasis original). The cruelty of this situation lies in how it affects the subject with the attachment, 'because whatever the *content* of the attachment is, the continuity of the form of it provides something of the continuity of the subject's sense of what it means to keep on living and to look forward in the world' (Berlant 2010: 94). This characterisation is useful when considering the meaning of a generational experience, since it not only produces a particular view of reality, but also reveals the ways in which one is bound by that perception. In the case of the generation focused on in this book, what has shaped their world view is the belief that Spain's conflictive past has yet to be solved. The optimism implied in this attachment lies in the effort to recreate and recover this past—an effort that relies on the assumption that the situation can be, if not fully settled, at least properly and politically addressed. The cruelty, in turn, has to do with the realisation that the attachment to the object is, as Berlant explains, '*im*possible, sheer fantasy, or *too* possible and toxic' (2010: 94). How the subject endures the affective structure of this attachment can help us to understand, for instance, the relationship between the generation of writers examined in this chapter and the unrelenting production of memory works in present-day Spain.

Berlant discusses 'cruel optimism' in terms of the fraying of the fantasies of the 'good life'. She reads this unravelling in the 'scene of neoliberal restructuring within the ordinary' and looks for 'the fantasmatic, affective, and physical adjustments' that allows the survival of fantasy in the impasse of the present (2011: 15). Luisa Elena Delgado cleverly deploys Berlant's theorisation about national fantasies to examine Spain's nationalist discourse in the context of the current financial and political crisis; she provides a perfect case for Berlant's explanation of cruel optimism and its affective structures by showing how the narrative about Spanish exceptionalism and quality of life persists in the face of the suffering of the nation's citizens (2014: 282). In Delgado's discussion of present-day Spain, the increasing

disconnect between the hardships of everyday life and the state's intention
to stay its course is clear:

> si algo caracteriza la España del apogeo de la crisis (2011–2013) es la
> insistencia en presentar el interés común como estático e incuestionable
> … En nombre de la defensa de ese bien común, las respuestas oficiales
> a todos los retos, escándalos, iniciativas fallidas y fracasos políticos
> estrepitosos es, precisamente, por un lado la negación de la legitimidad
> de los afectos que movilizan a los ciudadanos (la ira, la indignación) y
> la promoción de otros que los paralizan (el miedo), por otro. (2014: 260)

Faced with this political practice, Delgado argues that, instead of selling the
idea of Spain as an all-encompassing fantasy, it would be more productive
to do the opposite: 'enfrentarse a las fantasías que sostienen la identidad
nacional en su versión hegemónica' (2014: 298).

Delgado's suggestions about Spain's *future* can equally be applied to
discussions of its *past*. The ongoing debate about memory and legacies of
conflict in Spain is itself a catalyst for fantasy. The public sentiment that
Berlant and Delgado point to is couched in the stories we tell ourselves to
make our realities more bearable—and these stories are about both the
present and the past. In Spain, the narrative about the past is one of success:
a difficult situation (civil war, dictatorship) was overcome and, therefore,
can be suitably forgotten. The memory of this success is only deployed as a
paralysing measure when a threat to the status quo is perceived.[4] Despite
this triumphant rhetoric, however, we have seen throughout this book
that there has been a steady production of critical (and political) discourse
that challenges the standard assessment. In its persistent reiteration of
scepticism, this discourse has become less an ideological position and
more a cultural condition. The fantasy that feeds the perpetuation of both
the triumphant and the critical discourses can be read as the enactment of
cruel optimism—especially because of the social and political toll that this
deadlock entails.

Berlant's thinking describes a fantasy scenario in which sustaining an
ideal requires constant adjustment, ultimately pushing the situation to a
stalemate. Her theorisation recognises an essential relationship between the

---

4 A good example of this rhetoric is the discourse concerning the Spanish
Constitution of 1978, as I discuss it in 'La producció del patriotisme constitucional'
(2003) and 'El patriotismo constitucional o la dimensión mnemotécnica de una
nación' (2005). While consensus about the Constitution and the need to re-evaluate
it have changed recently, the symbolic status of this document persists, especially
for the Spanish government and its politicians.

eventual impasse and the historical moment in which it takes place. Examining the affective structure of this situation can give us better insight into the time during which the negotiation of the fantasy takes place. In the context of my discussion of recent recreations of the *Transición* and their relationship to the memory and legacy of the Franco dictatorship and the Spanish Civil War, 'cruel optimism' explains why each event of the past that we recreate or remember is only ever represented in terms of its direct relationship to the present. For instance, the events of the past that are narrated in the novels examined in this chapter only acquire meaning once they are linked to the 'present' of the plotline. The present is perceived affectively because it 'is what makes itself present to us before it becomes anything else, such as an orchestrated collective event or an epoch on which we can look back' (Berlant 2011: 4). Moreover, the present is sensed affectively and is in constant revision; it is 'a temporal genre whose conventions emerge from the personal and public filtering of the situations and events that are happening in an extended now whose very parameters (when did "the present" begin?) are also always there for debate' (Berlant 2011: 4).

I suggest that affective mediation is also applied to the past. In the case of contemporary Spain, the experience of the present and the memory of the past are saturated with each other, wrapped up in an ongoing and unending debate about the past. The constant narration and revision of this history means that the contours of the memory work on Spain's past are continuously changing too.[5] The parameters of inquiry into the past seem to continually shift over the years, as more events and years are understood to be relevant to the present. Along this temporal continuum, the distinction between past and present becomes increasingly blurred as more current political and social conflicts acquire historical significance. The works of Prado, Orejudo, Martínez de Pisón, and Reig display this temporal blending, with past and present events often sharing the same implications. Berlant suggests that we should ask how 'aesthetically mediated affective responses exemplify a shared *historical sense*' in order to capably describe 'the activity of being reflective about a contemporary historicity as one lives it' (2011: 3, 5). The historical sense that appears in these novels reveals the persistence of a narrative about the past that makes it impossible to imagine a future.

Brian Massumi has argued that affect is the key to our understanding of how master narratives have foundered in our information- and image-based late capitalist culture (27). Though affect and emotion are often treated synonymously, Massumi argues that the two terms belong to different

---

5　Colmeiro talks about this blending of times in his *Memoria histórica e identidad cultural* (2005).

orders. If 'emotion' has a subjective content and is defined as personal, then 'affect', as a qualified emotion, differs in its intensity. Affect is recognised by its intensity, not by its meaning. The intensity can be felt in 'semantically and semiotically formed progressions, into narrativisable action-reaction circuits, into function and meaning' (Massumi: 28).

Massumi's definition of affect has been criticised for its ontological perspective that rejects meaning. He considers 'form/content of conventional discourse as constituting a separate stratum running counter to the full registering of affect and its affirmation' and understands affect solely for 'its expression and for itself' (28). While I do not entirely agree with Massumi's notion of affect, his explanation is useful for its recognition of affect as a valid form of cognition. Identifying the intensity involved in the circulation and production of affect is also valuable, as it allows for a better understanding of how affect works. The force with which affect is injected into narratives and conventional discourse derails meaning and creates situations that challenge us to seek new forms of understanding. The works of fiction analysed in this chapter display moments of intensity whose meaning lies beyond the story that is being told. Keeping an eye on these moments is important in these texts, which narrate, once again, the all-too-familiar stories of Spain's troubled past. Historical events that are rehashed repeatedly seem to lose meaning through repetition, but the affect present in these narratives invites the reader to examine them anew.

Berlant's work teaches us to pay attention to sets of processes that, although not world-shifting, may nonetheless be identified as emerging events. She describes the start of such a process as 'the becoming-event of something' which involves 'questions about ideology, normativity, affective adjustment, improvisation, and the conversion of singular to general or exemplary experience' (2011: 6). In her discussion of the process by which affective events become history, Berlant, too, follows Raymond William's suggestion 'to think about the present as a process of emergence' (Berlant 2011: 7). According to this discipline, to pay attention to 'cruel optimism' is to enter the 'ordinary from the vantage point of an ongoing crisis': it is in the affective scenarios that 'we can discern claims about the situation of contemporary life' (Berlant 2011: 8). Indeed, the retelling of the past that repeatedly takes place in the novels of Prado, Orejudo, Reig, and Martínez de Pisón traces an emerging realisation that has more to do with the situation in which the storytelling takes place than with the story itself.

Finally, it is important to note that Berlant's work moves us away from the discourse of trauma. Berlant believes that most events that change people are better described as systemic crises accompanied by an affective impact. For her, '[c]risis is not exceptional to history or consciousness but a process embedded in the ordinary that unfolds in stories about navigating what's overwhelming' (2011: 10). The novels of Prado, Reig, Orejudo, and Martínez de Pisón describe the trauma of the Spanish Civil War and the dictatorship, but they are so far removed from these events that their relationship with this past is much better understood in Berlant's terms: as embedded in the ordinary, shaped and mediated by affect. In these works, trauma is no longer the only mode to comprehend the legacy of Spain's conflictive past.

The literary pieces examined in this chapter can be characterised as 'memory projects' together with the other works analysed in this book. Again, we see the urge to narrate the past pressing on these authors, as though the task had yet to be accomplished.[6] These writers delve into the past with a determination to recreate a past experience accurately and in detail—but the significance of their labour lies in the affect produced through their writing, rather than the factually accurate stories they narrate.[7] My focus throughout the chapter is on the impulse behind these authors' stringent research and their desire to find a narrative capable of settling the past 'once and for all'. This obsession blurs the line between fiction and history so forcefully that sometimes it is difficult to classify their fiction exclusively as a creative work or an historical archive. Ultimately, however, their efforts only reveal the impossibility of their task. This incapacity, in their fiction, points to the political impasse that pits the present against the past. And in this confrontation, what is at stake is the future. Narratives about the past may be constantly challenged in these novels, but the present is also complicit in them. In each novel, the characters are ultimately incapable of foreseeing or imagining a future free of the burden of past and present.

Benjamín Prado's *Operación Gladio* narrates an investigation of the 1977 Atocha murders, delving into the questions that remain today concerning the many violent incidents that took place during the *Transición* in the late

---

6 Samuel Amago identifies this urge as an 'archaeological impulse' and uses Benjamín Prado's *Mala gente que camina* as a paradigmatic example to theorise 'how discourses of memory, the archive, and the uses of archaeology as motif function together to generate a kind of manifesto for the ethical responsibility of the writer to engage with his or her political and cultural milieu' (330). The notion of using the archive and archaeology to talk about contemporary Spanish culture and its accelerated fossilisation is also found in Silvia Bermúdez's writing on Alaska and la Movida (293).

7 Here I depart from the traditional interpretation of these works as ethical contributions to current discourses on historical and collective memories, as evinced in the footnote above.

1970s. The violence unleashed during the last years of the dictatorship and during the early years of the transition has since been eclipsed or forgotten, giving way to the narration of the country's successful democratisation. Looking back on those years, Prado reveals a period full of fear, insecurity, and violence that, when looked at closely, exposes too many unanswered questions. Finding the clues to answer these questions proves to be a dangerous affair, as past violence remains intimately linked to the present. As time passes, the need to protect and shield those responsible for earlier crimes only grows greater.

Prado's previous novel, *Mala gente que camina* (2006), also inquires into the period of the Spanish Civil War and the Franco dictatorship. That novel's main character, Juan Urbano, a high school teacher who discovers a secret episode of the war, returns in *Operación Gladio* to learn about the violence of the *Transición*. Prado's *Mala gente* revealed the fictional biography of a right-wing writer whose story intersected with the tragic (true) story of the Republican children stolen during the Civil War. *Operación Gladio* picks up this theme with an investigation that intersects with the true search for victims of the Spanish Civil War and the Franco dictatorship. The demands of family members to obtain permission to exhume the remains of their relatives from the Valle de los Caídos still provoke an ongoing debate in Spanish society.[8]

Carmen de Urioste has described the physical contiguity between private/family space and the civil/public sphere that exists in Prado's earlier novel *No solo el fuego* (1999); she shows how the multiple crises experienced by the family in that novel serve as a metonymy for different historical and political moments in contemporary Spain (130–31). A similar relationship between fiction and reality can be found in Prado's novels about the Spanish Civil War and the *Transición*. A recurrent theme throughout Prado's fiction is a concern for the future. Urioste identifies Prado's fiction as heir to the 'tremendismo' aesthetics of the 1940s, which sought to reveal the decomposition of the individual and, by extension, of society (141). The possibility of his failure affects the future of the social and political structure that sustains him.

The intimate connection between the individual and society in Prado's work is further emphasised by Sara Santamaría Colmenero, who describes his work as part of the recent fiction about the Spanish Civil War that

8 The quest of families trying to recover the remains of their relatives buried in *El Valle de los Caídos* was made into a documentary by Montse Armengou and Ricard Belis (*Avi, et trauré d'aquí!*, 2013). For a good genealogy on the exhumations that have taken place in Spain since 2000, see Francisco Ferrándiz's *El pasado bajo tierra. Exhumaciones contemporáneas de la Guerra Civil* (2014).

deploys witnesses and researchers to recover the memory of the past (55). In the form of historical narration she describes, testimony, memory, and the experiences of witnesses are revalued through fiction in order to establish the 'truth' about the past. Fictional first-person accounts stand on equal footing with historiographical or political discourse. This is certainly true for the self-reflective narrator in Prado's story, who does not consider the pitfalls of interpreting or remembering the past but instead offers what he believes to be unquestionable truth, established through his own experience and account.

In Prado's narrative, as well as the others analysed here, historical veracity is not as important as the impulse that moves the characters to engage with the past. The need to fully understand what took place is made urgent by the characters' drive to disentangle their current lives. In this context, the *Transición* is a period full of questions whose answers are needed for the characters' present to make sense. As Santamaría observes, '[e]l cuestionamiento de la Transición como momento fundacional de la nación española democrática tiene por objeto realizar una relectura de la identidad nacional en la que la República y los valores de la izquierda ocupan un lugar preponderante' (65). In Prado's novel, questioning a foundational moment in the nation's history also involves the self-examination of the narrator. The weighing of the protagonist's current life through the forgotten values of the Spanish Republic can be seen as an exercise in optimism, allowing one's identity and connection with the past to be firmly established. This is the reason why the 'I' in Prado's narrative is essential, as it is in the other novels. The narrator is the only one able to serve as a mediator for the past from the present moment of his narration.

In *Operación Gladio*, narrator Juan Urbano alternates between first- and third-person narration to tell the story of Alicia Durán, his journalist girlfriend who vanishes in the present day during an investigation. At the moment of her disappearance, Alicia is researching the violence that took place during a week in 1977 known as the 'Semana Negra'. As Concepción Cascajosa has reminded us, the list of violent acts during those seven days is striking, although in its aftermath the string of incidents was quickly forgotten, giving way to the idea of a peaceful political transition. Cascajosa reminds us of the murders of students and police officers, the kidnappings, and finally the murder of the labour lawyers in their office on Atocha Street (267–68). Alicia, Juan tells the readers, has published in her newspaper a series of interviews related to this period and has been asked by a publisher to produce a book. She is trying to find out more about the lawyers' murders in order to finish her manuscript when she goes missing (Prado: 11). While working on her project, she also comes into contact with members of a volunteer organisation, the real-life ARMH (Asociación para la Recuperación de la Memoria Histórica), which helps family members search for the remains of relatives who perished during the war and under the Franco regime.

The narrator of *Operación Gladio* establishes the veracity of his account by offering transcriptions of the work done by his girlfriend, which he is reading alongside the readers. These excerpts consist of extensive interviews carried out by Alicia with different characters that are somehow connected to the events of the Semana Negra of 1977. The killing of the labour lawyers in their offices on Atocha Street that year is presented here as a mystery in need of solving. Alicia's curiosity about this crime and the way it was never quite resolved leads her to dig deeper into the past. The comprehensive interviews that she conducts and that Juan Urbano reads and transcribes uncover a very troubled time in post-Franco Spain and trace the many connections that exist between the often violent political events of that period and the present day.

As Amago noted of Prado's earlier novels, the work of this writer 'forces the reader to experience at least two temporalities simultaneously, and thus to think about how the past inhabits or inflects the present' (334). The interview transcriptions are exposés of a time ignored by some and forgotten by others. Alicia's interviews appear throughout the novel separated by bold-typed headlines, introducing each new character alongside an intriguing quote. For her interview with Judge Baresi, for instance, she chose the title 'Pier Luigi Berasi: "Los asesinos de la calle de Atocha trabajaban para la CIA, aunque tal vez no lo supieran"' (Prado: 148). Each of her pieces begins with an introduction that sets the context for the interviewee, often connecting it to the reader's experience in the past. Her use of the informal 'tú' in addressing each interviewee and her colloquial tone and clarity help the reader to quickly comprehend the purpose of her piece. In the interview mentioned above, Alicia's text starts the following way: 'Si alguien te dijera qué tienen en común los malhechores más peligrosos de Italia y respondes que [*sic*] al juez Baresi, podrán pensar que exageras pero no que desvarías' (Prado: 148). This introduction urges the reader to pay close attention to the interviewee's words to see what will be revealed about the past. In this particular exchange, Alicia's investigation leads her to take a closer look into the international connections to the Semana Negra, not only widening the scope of her project but also the critical nature of her work. What starts as a local mystery develops into a story with transnational repercussions. Meanwhile, the parallel story of a small-scale search for the remains of relatives lost during the war becomes connected to national human rights issues with international implications. The fact that neither of these stories finds a satisfying ending in the novel is significant within the context of the discussion of memory and the legacy of the past in Spanish society.

The documentation of Alicia's work in the pages of *Operación* serves, on the one hand, to provide information about her investigation and, on the other, to preserve her work for posterity. At the beginning of the novel, Juan explains how Alicia's work had caught the attention of a publishing house, who wanted to print her interviews in the form of a book. This proposition both surprises and scares his girlfriend, who is accustomed to her work as a journalist—a day job in which writing is transient and cruelly subjected to time, the unending avalanche of events, print space, and the whims of an authoritarian editor: 'Pueden ocurrir mil cosas distintas, pero el resultado es siempre el mismo: has corrido mucho y no has avanzado nada, y te sientes igual que si una ola se hubiera llevado de repente todo lo que habías escrito sobre la arena' (Prado: 14). But here Alicia's journalistic writing does not disappear in the wave of up-to-the-minute news or under the restrictions of an editor, it is preserved in the novel we are reading. Alicia's disappearance shows that digging into the past is dangerous work, so the idea of fiction as a 'safe place' is important. What is critical is not the information she is able to piece together about the *past*, but the meaning of that information for the *present*. The silence preserved around the period of the *Transición*, allowing the violence inflicted and suffered during these years to remain forgotten, parallels the silence that surrounds the search for victims of the Spanish Civil War and the dictatorship. The task of families trying to recover the remains of their loved ones is fraught with difficulties. The connection between these two searches—laden with ominous overtones in light of Alicia's own disappearance—also points to the open-ended nature of both efforts.

Writing, in this context, should be read as a form of affect. What matters is not the substance of the writing but the physical act itself: '[a]ffect as promise' that 'increases in capacities to act (expansions in affectability: both to affect and to be affected)' (Gregg and Seigworth: 12). If affect can be understood as a 'leading visceral indicator of potent threat' (Gregg and Seigworth: 13), then the physical act of writing can emphasise what lies beneath, for instance, the successful and peaceful narration of the *Transición*.

In Prado's fiction, the idea of seeking safety in literature goes beyond the preservation of information. As readers, we realise that Alicia's work can be more easily appreciated and more effectively preserved within the context of a novel, where it is not confined by the limitations of space or buried under the avalanche of daily news. The case for literature, repeatedly made throughout Prado's novel, serves as a metaliterary gesture pointing to the actual pages of the *Operación Gladio*. Juan's tracing of Alicia's whereabouts, along with her work, uncovers a material trail that we, too, discover as we read the novel: we remember not only the story of Alicia's disappearance, but also the information she has uncovered. Literature thus serves as a protected medium within which stories about the past can be safely narrated. In the earlier companion novel *Mala gente*, Juan freely searches the past for clues to narrate, if not a factual story, then at least one that captures a realistic account of historical events. Within the safe confines of fiction, historical speculation is not merely allowed, but encouraged.

This cocoon of safety also applies to memory. Prado highlights fiction's capacity to sidestep the power struggles that lead to the suppression of historical and political events. Under the Franco regime, when writers experienced harsh censorship, literature was used as a vehicle for resistance and political opposition. Given the current institutional silence regarding the remaining legacies of the Spanish Civil War and the dictatorship, literature is seen, once again, as a space from which to remember and engage with both fictional and historical recreations of the past. Creative thinking, combined with an ethical positioning about the past, resonates with the earlier politically committed literature of the 1950s and the experimental work of the 1960s and 1970s. Although Prado's work does not exhibit the same political ideology, his novels nevertheless invite us to reconsider the connection between fiction and politics. The notion of a politically committed literature that worked in opposition to a dominant regime is no longer relevant. In Prado's fiction, there is no clear political target. Instead, we identify writing, not as the expression of a political belief, but rather as a political *process*. Writing as affect underscores the latter's capacity for expressing in-between-ness: '*a form of relations* as a rhythm, a fold, a timing, a habit, a contour, or a shape ... to mark the passages of intensities' (Gregg and Seigworth: 13). It is this relationship that remains when fixed meaning and political positioning are stripped away.

The politics criticised in Prado's novel (and in the other novels analysed in this chapter) belong to both right- and left-wing ideologies; all politicians are seen as responsible for the transitional politics that fostered the current relationship between Spanish society and its past. Literature represents a space where writers can freely pursue their own research about the past, obsessively document historical and political events, and attempt to correct and supplement what we remember about past experiences. This obsession is embodied in Prado's literary characters too. They engage in Berlant's notion of 'cruel optimism', which is ambitious, and its feelings mixed: 'at any moment it might feel like anything ... the whole gamut from the sly neutrality to browsing the aisles to excitement at the prospect of "the change that's gonna come". Or the change that is "not" going to come ...' (2011: 2).

The possibility of change drives the action of all the characters in *Operación* and urges them to engage with the past.

The obsession shared by the narrator and the other characters reveals the affective structure that enables their action and pushes them to take risks. Berlant says that this structure 'involves a sustaining inclination to return to the scene of fantasy that enables you to expect that *this* time, nearness to *this* thing will help you or a world to become different in just the right way' (2011: 2). Both Juan Urbano and Alicia Durán feel this inclination, and while the latter vanishes in her quest to find the 'truth', Juan remains behind, writing and hoping for a better outcome 'next time'.

Affective structure is also about indirection. Writing expands in rhetorical moves intended, not to provide ultimate meanings (or versions) of the past, but simply to serve as a condition or a practice, productive because of its repetition. Berlant relies on Barbara Johnson's work on apostrophe and free indirect discourse to explain the poetics of indirection: 'each of these rhetorical modes is shaped by the ways a writing subjectivity conjures other ones so that, in a performance of fantasmatic intersubjectivity, the writer gains superhuman observational authority, enabling a performance of being made possible by the proximity of the object' (2010: 95). Writing affects Prado and his fictional characters equally. Despite the clarity expressed in Prado's stories about the right and wrongs of the past, they (and his narrator) fail to make a difference. Their narration is better understood as a performance, or as a condition created by an unresolved past.

From the beginning of *Operación Gladio*, it is clear that the central research on the violence of 1977 has already been completed, and what we are reading is mainly the transcription of Alicia's previous work. While the individuals she interviews are fictional, they often answer in the words of actual politicians and other historical figures involved in the process of Spain's political transition. Alicia's inquiry is sparked by her interest in assessing the *Transición* from the present; as her investigation gains momentum, she identifies the murder of the labour lawyers in 1977 on Atocha Street as the key to answering all of her questions about the period. Following a trail of violence that connects many of the incidents that shook Spain in the 1970s and 1980s, Alicia vanishes when her trail leads her to Italy and what appears to be an international political conspiracy centred about 'Operazione Gladio', a clandestine Cold War operation tied to right-wing terrorist attacks in Europe.[9] The novel offers no clear answers

9 In *The Italian Revolution*, Mark Gilbert explains the origins of Gladio, a stay-behind operation plotted by the CIA and right-wing activists to subvert any legitimately elected Communist government (109). Later, the code name Operazione

to the questions raised by Alicia's research about the murders of the Atocha Street lawyers and the putative involvement of the CIA in sponsoring Gladio; however, it does succeed in raising important questions about the violence unleashed during the *Transición* and establishes a connection between this past and the current search for victims of the Spanish Civil War and the Franco dictatorship. Alicia's investigative journalism and Juan's involvement in her search uncover a hidden, forgotten aspect of the history of Spain's political transition.

Rather than simply telling a story, what Prado's novel accomplishes is the creation of a space in which Alicia's work can be recovered and preserved. The novel can also be understood as a gesture: a promise to provide answers to unresolved questions. I argue that it is precisely this promise that underlies most recent recollections of the *Transición*. Ironically, the unresolved disappearance of Alicia at the end of the novel echoes the open-endedness of the discussion of these memories. This ending also underlines the fact that the past narrated in *Operación Gladio* is most important for its effect on the present. The fact that the reader, like the characters in the novel, will never fully know what took place during those years finds a parallel in the lack of resolution surrounding Alicia's disappearance. It is precisely this lack of resolution that keeps the reader's interest alive and susceptible to the many questions raised in Alicia's interviews and Juan's reflections during his search. Berlant's work suggests that these questions are part of the costly adjustments that we must make to our expectations in order to maintain optimism—to be able to keep on digging in the face of so many unanswered questions. The open-ended story offered by Prado in his novel can be understood in part as a reference to the ongoing discussion about how to resolve the country's conflictive past. That discussion, which shifted briefly from the private to the public sphere during the debate on the Law on Historical Memory, has since been redefined as a private matter. In the foreseeable future, therefore, we can expect no official answer to how these matters should or will be addressed in Spain.

The narrator of *Operación Gladio* recounts how Alicia struggled to shape her work into a book; he reports that she felt as though something important was missing from her writing. Though being approached by a publisher was flattering, she did not consider her interviews to be book-worthy material. When Alicia realises that the missing element is the connection between her research and the present, her writing and investigation take off at an almost

---

Gladio was used to refer to any covert, stay-behind operation. In the context of the Spanish transition, Gladio is connected to the violence perpetrated by right-wing groups in the 1970s.

dizzying speed as she begins to comprehend just how deeply related is her current inquiry to the recovery of the victims of Spain's violent past and its troubled legacy in the present day. The implied danger of understanding this connection is manifested in her own disappearance, which follows quickly on the heels of her discovery. As the novel progresses, it becomes clear that Juan is more interested in Alicia's journalistic work than in trying to find her. Ultimately, the ending of the novel—where Juan walks towards the morgue to view a dead body matching Alicia's description, found by the Italian authorities—constitutes a refusal to close the discussion on the investigation that took place in *Operación Gladio*. The last words of the novel are Juan's plea: 'Que siga desaparecida ... Que no sea ella, por favor' (Prado: 380). The imploration stems from the narrator's hope for Alicia's safety, but also his deep awareness that there are questions remaining to be answered and work that needs to be done:

> tratar de entrevistar a los supervivientes del crimen de la calle de Atocha, sobre todo a la enigmática Dolores González; y verse con el inspector Medina; y quizá también con algún antiguo miembro de los GRAPO, para preguntarle, entre otras cosas, de dónde habían sacado las armas del ejército de Tierra que usaron en el secuestro de los presidentes del Consejo de Estado y el Consejo Supremo de Justicia Militar que el último declaró recordar perfectamente, durante el juicio celebrado tras su liberación: 'Las que han quedado en mi retina han sido las dos pistolas Star con las que me apuntaban' (Prado: 379–80)

Ultimately, Juan wishes to finish this work (either with Alicia, once she is found, or on her behalf) so that he himself can heal and get on with his life: 'Y seguir adelante, curtido por el dolor: con el tiempo, las heridas se juntan como gotas de mercurio y forman un armadura' (Prado: 380). In order for this healing to occur, the past, with its questions and remnants of conflict, needs to be resolved.

Alicia Durán's investigative report supplies the reader of *Operación Gladio* with more than enough information about the *Transición*. However, the focus of the novel remains on the search for more clues—a process that, ultimately, raises more questions than it answers. Juan emphasises at the beginning of the novel that the journalist's job should not be to look for answers: 'Alicia sabe que su trabajo no consiste en dar respuestas, sino solo en buscarlas, porque un buen periodista no tiene que orquestar las cosas, sino oír su sonido y silbárselo a los lectores. Nada más que eso' (Prado: 15). Despite this injunction, however, Alicia, captivated by the story and its connection to the present, develops a strong—perhaps ultimately fatal—desire to tell the truth (Prado: 15). Her attachment to this story reminds us how cruel optimism is. As Berlant tells us, this cruelty manifests itself when we realise that 'the object/scene that ignites a sense of possibility actually makes it impossible to attain' (2011: 2).

Alicia's search for answers is complemented by Juan's narration. Unlike his girlfriend, Juan is free to comment on the journalistic pieces she has written. He imagines alternative scenarios, entertains conspiratorial explanations, and offers possible interpretations in order to provide a comprehensive narration of the past that does not obsess over historical accuracy. The plausible scenarios he describes turn Alicia's interviews into compelling stories. Juan enjoys his omniscient position as narrator, commenting on the feelings and thoughts of his girlfriend and offering his own insights as he reads her personal notes. It is this emotional investment in his reading process that makes Alicia's investigation relevant, yet, at the same time, Juan's words are marked by impotence, as his writing and his search for his girlfriend only express what Berlant calls 'the conditions of projected possibility' (2010: 95).

As the novel becomes increasingly focused on Juan's rather than Alicia's quest, what pervades is a feeling of unresolvedness. Both searches wrench open and keep open the trail of violence started in the past. According to Cristina Moreiras-Menor's reading of post-Franco Spain, violence originates from the erasure of memory. She expounds on this erasure, arguing that it is in the traces remaining from these deletions that the past becomes manifest for generations that did not live it (17). In Prado's novel, the interruption in Juan and Alicia's life is connected with the forgotten violence of Spain's recent past. Alicia's inquiry into the political transition reveals to the reader the hidden linkage between the crimes of 1977 and the legacies of both the war and the Franco regime.

As I conclude my reading of Prado's work, I return to the beginning of *Operación Gladio* to trace the affective (and social) structure that sets up the story of Alicia and Juan. The first pages of the novel open with a description of Alicia Durán as she takes notes about the people in attendance during the removal of a statue of Franco. The quick characterisations she jots down in her notebook capture the very different reactions of people who otherwise do not seem particularly dissimilar from each other. Alicia describes a man who reminds her of a scavenger bird, 'tan majestuosa mientras están en las Alturas y tan repulsivas cuando se posan en el suelo' (Prado: 10–11). The immediate dislike she feels for this man contrasts with her impression of a woman whose eyes express 'una paz exótica en aquel lugar e incongruente con aquella situación' (Prado: 11). The disparity in these descriptions parallels Spaniards' different reactions to the past. This scene is directly connected to the aftermath of the 2007 'Law of Historical Memory', which mandated the removal of Francoist symbols from public spaces; furthermore, it is here that Alicia first encounters the group of volunteers working with the ARMH. This encounter advances the plot of the novel in two important ways: first, the journalist finds the missing link between her investigation of the *Transición* and the present that will make her work relevant; second, it initiates the secondary plot of the novel, focused on the search for victims of the war and the dictatorship. Juan Urbano's own search for his missing girlfriend collides with this pursuit. As he becomes increasingly intimately involved with this second search, he develops a physical relationship with Mónica Grandes, the archaeologist who works with the ARMH to help the families searching for their missing relatives.

As Alicia takes note of the people attending the removal of the statue and later engages them with questions, the narrator explains her presence there. He describes her ongoing investigation of the Semana Negra of 1977 and how she was not fully convinced about the work she is doing. She is looking for something that will give her a sense of what she is trying to accomplish. Her uncertainty contrasts with the very clear questions she has been able to articulate about her research. The importance of finding the answers to these questions lies in the present. Alicia's questions, which also become Juan's questions, point to the many unknowns of the *Transición*:

¿Qué papel jugó el espionaje norteamericano en esos instantes? ¿Qué y quiénes estaban detrás de los GRAPO, un supuesto grupo maoísta que, sin embargo, parecía más interesado que nadie en una nueva rebelión militar y que un ex agente de los servicios secretos de Estados Unidos, llamado Philip Agee, afirma que fue manejado por la CIA? ¿Qué precio pagaron los comunistas por su legalización? ¿Por qué se impidió que los jueces llegaran hasta los auténticos inspiradores de la célebre matanza de la calle Atocha, en la que se mató a varios abogados laboralistas? ¿Por qué se abandonó, en ese caso, la pista que hablaba de organizaciones de ultraderecha italianas como Ordine Nuovo y de la red paramilitar Gladio? ¿Tal vez porque la última de ellas estaba controlada por la inteligencia norteamericana? (Prado: 11–12)

Together, these detailed questions describe a conspiratorial reading of a time when most events were presented from the domestic perspective of political accomplishment. Prado himself has discussed these questions and his interest in the role of the CIA in post-dictatorial Spain and other parts of the world.[10] His reading of this political period from an outside perspective

10 Prado has described the CIA's covert operations in Europe as a 'portable dictatorship' and has talked about their participation in the Spanish transition.

represents a break from previous interpretations of the *Transición*, which mainly focused on its ramifications as a domestic affair. Again, the unclear nature of this period is evident, as new explanations introduce parallels to the unfinished search for the victims of the Franco dictatorship and the Spanish Civil War.

The individuals who attend the removal of the Franco statue and who provide Alicia with the missing link to her book are people for whom the past is not settled. Mónica Grandes, the archaeologist and ARMH member, Dolores Silva and her husband Paulino, who are seeking permission to retrieve the body of Dolores's father, Salvador Silva, and Bárbara Valdéz, the judge considering their petition, are all people affected by the past. It is the story of their lives that provides Alicia with the context necessary for both her newspaper report and her book. All these people are missing something in their current lives, and all are about to be profoundly shaken by their contact with the past. Alicia is able to use their stories because of their emotions:

> y un matrimonio que estaba en primera línea, ella con un chándal verde oscuro y él con una camisa a cuadros; ella llorando sin estridencias, tal vez con lágrimas que venían de una tristeza muy antigua que fue pasando con el tiempo del dolor a la amargura y de la amargura a la resignación como lava que se enfría, y él más exaltado, hasta el punto de que en un momento llegó a gritarles algo a los que defendían la estatua, algo dicho con rabia contenida, sin poderse reprimir pero a la vez queriendo sujetarse: sinvergüenzas, canallas, indecentes ... (Prado: 15–16)

The scenario described here reminds the reader of articles published in the (real) Spanish press about the removal of Francoist objects and the exhumation of mass graves from the Spanish Civil War. Alicia's presence in this scene in one sense offers a thinly veiled account of the real events that took place during the discussion about historical memory in Spain. But the kind of work she undertakes does not fully address the affective dimension of the loss. The narrator explains the way Alicia works and how she herself understands her duties: 'ése es su trabajo, resumir, condensar, hacer que lo más grande quepa dentro de lo más pequeño' (Prado: 11). Alicia's work is clearly different from that of Juan, whose narration works in the opposite

See 'Benjamín Prado relata en *Operación Gladio* la "dictadura portátil" de la CIA llevada a cabo en la Transición española' (http://www.europapress.es/andalucia/ sevilla-00357/noticia-benjamin-prado-relata-operacion-gladio-dictadura-portatil- cia-llevada-cabo-transicion-espanola-20110426173015.html).

way: his interest in the story is expansive, repetitive, and exhaustive. The detailed nature of this account bloats the novel to almost 400 pages, in sharp contrast to the succinct narrative style of his journalist girlfriend. Even if part of this extension can be attributed to the length of Alicia's interviews for her book, the actual plot of the novel consists of Juan's approach to this material, his contact with the relatives searching for their loved ones, and his constant reflection on his own life and experiences. The way this situation affects Juan is symptomatic of the generational interest in the *Transición*.

As part of his explanation of his girlfriend's journalistic report, Juan describes Alicia generationally, emphasising her chronological and political distance from the event: 'por otro lado le dio pereza ponerse a investigar aquella época que para ella resultaba bastante indefinida, porque es demasiado joven: tiene treinta y cinco años y cuando murió el dictador tenía dos' (Prado: 12). It is Alicia's irreverent style that inspires her editor to give her the assignment in the first place, and her subsequent investigation opens up the *Transición* to a new, younger generation of readers. In fact, her style, 'tan controvertido, tan espontáneo y tan personal', is the reason why she is asked to write an entire book about this period (Prado: 13). However, as Juan explains, Alicia struggles with her book, finding herself in a situation where she seems to have the answer, but does not understand the question. Alicia finds the key to her book in an unexpected place:

> Encontró la salida del laberinto aquella noche en la plaza de la que se llevaban la estatua del dictador, mientras observaba a las personas que se habían reunido allí, y al verlas se dio cuenta de que también era necesario contar su historia para que el círculo se cerrase y la realidad quedara atrapada en su interior. (Prado: 14-15)

Concerning Alicia's determination to follow the story, Juan concludes:

> ¿Qué fue, entonces? ¿Un presentimiento? Yo diría que más bien fue la suma de una sospecha y una certeza, porque después de haberse dedicado muchas horas a estudiar el asunto que la ocupaba, había concluido, y así lo escribió en la última línea de su última entrevista, que 'la Transición fue un triunfo de todos que también tuvo sus perdedores', y estuvo segura de que ellos también tendrían que estar presentes en su libro si quería contar en él la verdad. (Prado: 15)

Alicia's desire to 'tell the truth' goes beyond her journalistic duty to report all sides of the story and reflects a personal investment that allows her to probe further into the past. Her work, and that of Juan, offers a promise: to dig deeper, even if there seems to be no end. Their work forces the reader to

take notice of the moment when, as Berlant would say, 'the subject can no
longer take his continuity in history for granted but feels full of *something*
ineloquently promising, a something that reveals, at the same time, a
trenchant *nothing* general' (2010: 105). The absence of an answer and the lack
of a resolution are negative spaces of attachment where the object of desire
must be absent despite its proximity to the subject, forcing the reader 'to
transact a different, more open relation of unfolding to what she is reading,
judging, being, and thinking she understands' (Berlant 2010: 96). This is
ultimately what is laid bare by the relationship between Alicia's quest, Juan's
uncertainty, and the unfulfilled wish of Dolores and Paulino:

> No iban a hacer nada. ... Así que el Valle de los Caídos seguiría en su
> lugar, con su cruz diabólica, sus evangelistas y sus virtudes teologales,
> la Fortaleza, la Justicia, la Templanza y la Prudencia conmemorando
> la sanguinaria epopeya del dictador que lo hizo construir; y aunque
> tal vez él y el jefe de la Falange terminaran por ser trasladados a
> un cementerio normal, Salvador Silva y otras decenas de miles de
> republicanos seguiría allí por toda la eternidad, porque liberarlos de
> su última prisión resultaba complejo, problemático y muy costoso, y ese
> punto era tan importante que bastaba con mirar las cifras para darse
> cuenta del poco interés que tenía el Gobierno en el asunto y del carácter
> retórico de su Ley de Memoria Histórica, a la que había asignado un
> presupuesto de sesenta mil euros cuando el precio de un solo análisis
> de ADN con garantías judiciales era de quinientos. (Prado: 311)

It is useful to think about the motives that propel these stories and
these recurrent memories of the past. Berlant has suggested that '[p]olitical
depression persists in affective judgments of the world's intractability—
evidenced in affectlessness, apathy, coolness, cynicism, and so on—modes of
what might be called detachment that are really not detached at all but constitute
ongoing relations of sociality' (2010: 97). The idea, first, that sociality is what
sustains an affective work like Juan's (and, by extension, Prado's) and, second,
that collectively shared public feeling insists on an optimistic attachment,
explains the continued production of memory works in contemporary Spain.
Part of this attachment includes the persistent examination of the *Transición*,
which continues to represent a key moment in confronting the legacy of the
Franco dictatorship and the Spanish Civil War. But, as the above quote from
Prado's novel reveals, this inquiry exposes an impasse, an unsurmountable
obstacle that stands in the way of resolution. This impasse also implies
the impossibility of a true future; like Juan, we must put our lives on hold
until we are able to solve this open-ended mystery—in Spain's case, the
mystery of a troubled past in need of critical intervention. The possibility

of addressing this need is what motivates the ongoing literary recreation of the Spanish transition. At the same time, however, works that engage in this recreation also speak to the difficulty of the task: it is impossible to imagine how past conflicts can be resolved after the passage of so much time and the entrenchment of such antipathetic political positions.

Giving up this attachment, however, would signify the loss of a narrative that is required in the present to explain Spain's grim political and financial situation. Perhaps it is this impasse that makes it necessary to carry out 'affective bargains about the costliness of one's attachments, usually unconscious ones, most of which keep one in proximity to the scene of desire or attrition' (Berlant 2010: 94). As Berlant explains, 'if the cruelty of an attachment *is* experienced by someone or some group, even in disavowed fashion, the fear is that the loss of the object or scene of promising itself will defeat the capacity to have any hope about anything' (2010: 94). Keeping abjection at bay means maintaining hope, which in turn requires that we preserve the conditions under which narrators like Juan Urbano engage with the past, hoping for a better outcome but exposing, in the process, the emotional cost of sustaining this fantasy.

In *El día de mañana* (2011), Ignacio Martínez de Pisón captures the world view of a small section of Barcelona society as it experiences the later years of the Franco dictatorship and the early years of the *Transición*. The novel follows the story of Justo Gil Tello, who arrives in the city with his invalid mother. In the process of trying hard to find a cure for his mother and to get ahead in his new life both financially and socially, Justo ends up becoming an informant for the Franco police. After the death of the dictator, his life is affected by the tumultuous changes of the years of political transition. Finally, he is murdered by a group of right-wing terrorists. Justo's adventures, or perhaps misadventures, are told by a choral narrative of 14 separate characters. These narrators are the relatives, failed business partners, acquaintances, and friends of Justo, as well as, finally, the police. What the first-person narration of all of these characters has in common is an incomplete knowledge of Justo's life story. Even though the memories they offer of Justo span almost two decades, his life remains shrouded in mystery; we only ever receive glimpses of the reasons behind his behaviour or the aspirations that drive his life. The narration offered by these multiple voices is, in a sense, more about their own lives than that of the main character. Their stories about Justo seem almost accidental, as if mentioning him is only useful because it helps them remember a particular period in their own lives, their jobs, or the activities they were engaged in when they came into contact with Justo.

Through the everyday stories of these 14 different voices, the reader is able to identify every key political or cultural event that took place in the late seventies and early eighties. *El día de mañana* is, in a way, a novel about the passing of time, and Justo is the link that ties together the different narrative strands that together offer a comprehensive sense of an historical period. The multiple voices weave together a collective memory captured by the ordinary events of everyday life. The difficulty of articulating this fleeting experience in words parallels the elusiveness of Justo's character and the many versions of his life we read in the novel.

A prolific writer, Ignacio Martínez de Pisón has published more than 15 books, among them *Carreteras secundarias* (1996), *María bonita* (2001), *El tiempo de las mujeres* (2003), *Dientes de leche* (2008), and *Enterrar a los muertos* (2005). This last title concerns José Robles Pazos, the translator and friend of John Dos Passos, killed in 1936 by the Soviet secret service. Robles, a faculty member at Johns Hopkins University, was in Spain the summer the Civil War broke out, and decided to remain in the peninsula and join the Republican side of the conflict. A blend between historical novel and essay, *Enterrar a los muertos* came about as a result of Martínez de Pisón's investigation in the archives of Johns Hopkins University and Robles's personal files, to which he had access through a daughter living in Seville (Fernández Zaurín: 34). The mix of historiographic research and literary speculation Martínez de Pisón offers in his narration of the forgotten episodes of the Spanish Civil War has been identified as part of a narrative trend in contemporary Spanish literature. María-Teresa Ibáñez, for instance, borrows José-Carlos Mainer's term 'novelas a noticia' to discuss Martínez de Pisón's work, describing a form of fiction containing real events narrated from 'un mundo que nos llega a través de la información cotidiana' (qtd. in Ibáñez-Ehrlich: 265). The narrative's obvious privileging of personal memory is made clear by the physical presence of the writer in the text. As Ibáñez observes, 'la necesidad personal que los propios autores parecen sentir de formar parte de la ficción no sólo para opinar críticamente sobre ella, sino también para que su peso como voces sociales sea eficiente y relevante' (267). The weight of this subjective memory, the authority of the physically present narrator, and the information that comes from the everyday are features that are constantly found in this author's narratives.

In his award-winning *El día de mañana*, Martínez de Pisón deploys multiple first-person narrations that not only recount past events but also evoke the emotions of the period in question.[11] The physical presence of the narrators

---

11 The novel won the Premio de la Crítica de la narrativa castellana and the Premio Hislibris for best writer in 2011, and the Premio Ciutat Barcelona in 2012.

in each of the novel's historical moments allows them, on the one hand, to describe the social and political context of the time and, on the other, to offer an intimate recollection of a moment of personal significance to their lives. While Justo is the excuse for these recollections, he also functions as a moving target for the novel's narrators, who must constantly locate him geographically and temporally. Justo occupies multiple spaces in the city of Barcelona and frequents different social classes, including the upper middle class to which he aspires. As the narrators explain their respective relationships with Justo, they reveal an awareness of the need to situate the reader (or listener) in the social milieu of the character in order for their story to acquire meaning. When Justo consorts with people above his station, for instance, the narrator always provides a detailed description of why he stands out and why he never succeeds in being perceived (or treated) as an equal. The informal tone of these recollections creates the impression of listening to a casual conversation where the speaker feels comfortable enough to confide insights and personal beliefs to his or her interlocutor. From these shared confidences, the reader can arrive at a broad understanding of the period that the narrator is relating. The history produced here is not based on political or cultural incidents, but is instead produced through the accumulation of small stories and intimate experiences that reveal the social structure that sustains larger political or historical events. The fact that the magnitude of these events does not become clear until they are remembered in seemingly everyday stories points to the banality with which we experience history in our daily lives.

Martínez de Pisón has talked about his preference for writing about historical periods he himself has lived through and his interest in narrating the experience of the urban middle class. He believes that his intimate knowledge of this environment enhances his capacity to capture the texture of this world and its time. Most of his stories, therefore, are situated around the period of the late dictatorship and the *Transición*. What he tries to accomplish in these stories is to 'transmitir la atmósfera de una época y de unos lugares determinados, eso me permite transmitir una sensación de realidad' (Fernández Zaurín: 33). With the exception of *Enterrar a los muertos*, Martínez de Pisón generally shies away from writing about the war. He has articulated his belief that many more works will be written about the Spanish Civil War because of its (epic) symbolism, including the idea that it was the 'last romantic war', in which freedom and democracy were defended against fascism. Furthermore, the experience of this war endures in the imagination of writers both at home and abroad thanks to the idealism and generosity demonstrated by the International Brigades and other foreign volunteers. The main reason for this persistence, according to Martínez de Pisón, is that no version of the Civil War exists that can or would be accepted by everyone: '[l]os historiadores hace tiempo que están ofreciendo una lectura imparcial y objetiva de la guerra que podría servir para alcanzar ese consenso, pero esa lectura aún no ha arraigado en la sociedad o no ha sustituido a las visiones parciales anteriores' (Escobedo: 95).

In contrast to the inherent controversy of the Civil War, Martínez de Pisón believes that the opposite effect holds for accounts of the *Transición*. He points out that although there may be many objections and criticisms of this period, there is actually a generalised consensus about it: 'lo cierto es que lo importante se consiguió: se pasó de una dictadura militar de casi cuatro décadas de duración a una democracia homologable con las de nuestros vecinos europeos. Y sobre eso la sociedad española parece estar de acuerdo' (Escobedo: 96). Thus, Martínez de Pisón suggests, writers like himself do not situate their works in these years for political reasons, but rather for personal or aesthetic reasons. In his case, he writes about the Spanish transition 'porque son mis años, los años en que crecí, en que me formé como persona, y porque creo que los novelistas tenemos que transmitir a los lectores futuros el espíritu de nuestra época y de la sociedad que nos ha tocado vivir' (Escobedo: 96).

Reading *El día de mañana* is indeed an exercise in discovering the world of the story. In the narrators' chronicles, which describe the life of Justo almost incidentally, we see an exercise of repetition and a reaffirmation of a vision of the past. Each character tells easy-to-recognise stories about the transition; each account merges into and departs from common points. Despite a strong sense of transformation that runs throughout the stories, there is also a palpable feeling that things are not changing very drastically. Even the eventual downfall of Justo, whose struggle to survive only leads him into deeper trouble with the law and his acquaintances, is not presented as a catastrophic story but rather as a series of small incidents that do not quite achieve a dramatic finale. While Justo's violent end is indeed tragic, there is nothing exceptional about his character. In the end, Justo and his narrators are minor players in a chain of unstoppable events that will constitute an important historical experience only once they are examined in hindsight. What these characters transmit is the social fabric of an era of slow transformation for which the most important element is not ideology or political conviction but *time*. As Mateo Moreno, the police officer under whose supervision Justo becomes an informant, states, '[l] o importante era el tiempo, ¡el tiempo!' (Martínez de Pisón: 123). These words are spoken in connection to the process of dealing with political detainees, but also reflect the changes that take place more broadly in the world of the novel.

Kathleen Stewart has talked about the ordinary as 'a shifting assemblage of practices and practical knowledges, a scene of both liveness and exhaustion, a dream of escape or of the simple life' (1). She uses this idea to detect the elements that give everyday life the quality of continued change: the ordinary affects that happen 'in impulses, sensations, expectations, daydreams, encounters, and habits of relating, in strategies and their failures, in forms of persuasion, contagion, and compulsion, in modes of attention, attachment, and agency, and in publics and social worlds of all kinds that catch people up in something that feels like *something*' (2). In Martínez de Pisón's novel, the stories told by the 14 narrators engage in these affects, which in turn give a sense of what their lives in Barcelona were like. Their personal stories serve as the backbone for the changes experienced by Spanish society during the period of the novel, and their informal version of what took place during those years reveals some of the better known events or practices of that period: the student protests, the police station on Laietana Street where detainees were tortured, the Gauche Divine and their hangout place Bocaccio, the circulation and consumption of drugs like hashish, the gradual sexual liberation of a generation, the (undercover) work of the Franco police, the sit-in at Monserrat Abbey, political theatre and performance art, the persecution suffered by members of the underground Spanish Communist Party, the activities of the Catalonian far right groups, and the Atocha murders of 1977. The personal recounting of these events by these narrators as their lives intersect with that of Justo transforms history into an intimate series of events that are physically and emotionally connected to each of the novel's characters. The personal connection between each character and the political events of the period is especially obvious in the latter part of the book, when Justo becomes most active as an informant for the police and infiltrates different political groups opposed to the dictatorship.

The version of events offered by these narrators is clearly not as triumphant or glamorous as the official version of the *Transición*. The difference can be seen, for instance, in the imprecisions that permeate most of the stories about Justo. This very vagueness works as a counterpoint to the discourse of change that permeates each narrator's version of what took place during those years. Despite the overall attempt of the collaborative narration to present an accurate picture of Justo, the memories produced about this character are anything but definitive. The stories about Justo start *in media res*; their impressions of what takes place are informal, generalised, and, at times, even uncertain. As Pere Riera, one of the earlier narrators, states: 'No sabíamos nada de él: de dónde había salido, si tenía familia o no, si le gustaba el fútbol o la música ... Y lo poco que averiguábamos solía estar equivocado'

(Martínez de Pisón: 25). Even if the reader is able to piece together Justo's life by combining details from these many stories, there remains uncertainty about the protagonist's real motives or aspirations and the actual nature of the activities he participated in with far right groups that ended in his assassination.

Instead of gaining insight into these central points, the reader learns about a series of events that will only later be identified as key historical and political moments that led to the great transformation of Spanish society. The stories told by the narrators are not important for their historical meaning; rather, they are significant because they reveal how the events of this period were experienced personally. Against the official view of the past, the reader encounters many versions and different explanations of what took place during the years of the Spanish transition. For example, the politicisation and activism of some of the characters seems to have stemmed from selfish motivations rather than ideological conviction. What becomes apparent in these stories is the gap between the varied experiences of the people who lived through the *Transición* and the linear account of how Spain accomplished full democratisation after so many years under an authoritarian regime.[12]

At the same time, the recollections we read in Martínez de Pisón's novel seem to reflect what the different narrators tell *themselves* about the past. As they try to recall Justo's life, they are offered the opportunity to revisit their own personal experiences and, in the process, they end up revealing the narratives that they have internalised about this period. Ironically, the reminiscing tone of the narrators' recollections also reflects an awareness of the historical significance of the period they lived through. They repeatedly employ terms that indicate political transformation. This framing of the past indicates an intervention from the present, one that points to a solidified narrative about the *Transición* and reveals the contradiction between what the narrators *say* and the way they instinctively characterise their stories. Each narrator constantly borrows modern terminology and phrasing to narrate their experience of the past.

The tales told by the 14 narrators in Martínez de Pisón's novel remind us of Berlant's discussion of the challenges individuals face when they must continue even when life events are not happening or evolving as expected. The difficulty comes from the phenomenon Berlant terms 'cruel optimism'.

---

12 In this account, history is presented in a naturalised narrative where everything happens for a reason and the present is its only possible and desirable outcome. In the received narrative about the *Transición*, each event can only lead to its success.

I repeat here Berlant's detailed description of the concept as I think it will be useful to refer to in the discussion of the novels to follow:

> [Cruel optimism is] a concept pointing toward a mode of lived imminence, one that grows from a perception about the reasons why people ... choose to ride the wave of the system of attachment that they are used to, to syncopate with it, or to be held in a relation of reciprocity, reconciliation, or resignation that does not mean defeat by it. Or perhaps they move to normative form to get numb with the consensual promise and to misrecognize that promise as an achievement. ... These suspensions open up revelations about the promises that had clustered as people's objects of desire, stage moments of exuberance in the impasse near the normal, and provide tools for suggesting why these exuberant attachments keep ticking not like the time bomb they might be but like a white noise machine that provides assurance that what seems like static really is, after all, a rhythm people can enter into while they're dithering, tottering, bargaining, testing, or otherwise being worn out by the promises that they have attached to in this world. (2010: 97–98)

We can detect this suspension in the repetitive and sometimes circular stories told by the narrators in *El día de mañana*. Their recollections of the past revisit incidents, emotions, and insights; although they try to communicate a sense of progression and change, it becomes obvious that these characters are faced with a lack of alternatives. Given this situation, it is not surprising that none of the characters' own stories has an actual conclusion. While Justo's demise signifies the close of a period directly connected with Francoism, the stories of the narrators are left open. The reader remains wondering about the fate of these narrators who, like Justo, are shaped by the experience of the dictatorship but, unlike him, will have to carry on. In the artificial postponement of their stories' end we can identify the impasse created by the past and see how the characters are constantly required to adjust their expectations.

Nowhere are this impasse and tension more clear than in the case of Carme, perhaps the most significant character in the book after Justo. Carme Román is an orphan of the tragic flooding of the Ripoll River in 1962.[13] While her ostensible importance to the novel lies in her business relationship with Justo, her story offers a glimpse into a world forged within the confines of her uncle's small paper business, where she works. Ultimately, her story's

---

13 More than 1,000 lives were lost during the sudden overflow of the Ripoll River in the El Vallès region in 1962.

importance stems not from Justo's obsession with her, but rather from the stories she tells about herself and her relatives.[14] Carme speaks candidly about her aspirations and hopes, and how things did not work out for her or for her cousin, who ended up committing suicide after losing her fiancé in a tram accident. Carme's eventual involvement in political protests and her own political awakening has, in truth, little to do with ideology. What drives her to political participation is her longing to be part of something collective, to feel that her actions mean something. Her awareness of this situation is apparent in this extended monologue:

> Mi mayor contribución al antifranquismo fue acompañar a Clara a comprar garbanzos. Sé que no es mucho. Nosotras íbamos a la Boquería a comprar garbanzos, y luego otros, durante las manifestaciones, los esparcían por el suelo para que patinaran los caballos de la policía armada ... Ésas eran las armas de los estudiantes, los garbanzos, y con tan poca cosa hicieron mucho por cambiar España. ... Ojalá hubiera tenido yo valor para hacer algo más que ir al mercado ... Pero, en realidad, es que tampoco me sentía muy a gusto con los amigos de Clara. Se reunían con frecuencia para intercambiar libros y listas de libros, siempre libros sobre el marxismo, sobre el Tercer Mundo, sobre el Ché, sobre Cuba, sobre América Latina, y cuando los comentaban me recordaban al cura de religión del colegio de Tarrasa, tan serio, tan solemne, tan ofendido de todo. Una vez, uno de ellos me dijo que lo que yo tenía que hacer era proletarizarme. ... ¿Proletarizarme yo, que había perdido la casa y la familia, que vivía acogida en casa de unos parientes, que no tenía nada? ¿A qué más tendría que renunciar para proletarizarme? (Martínez de Pisón: 290–91)

Carme's account reflects an internalisation of the discourse of political change that characterises the narrative of the late dictatorship and the *Transición*, in which the force of change came to be understood as an unstoppable tide. Carme also demonstrates an awareness of the contradictions of her time. Her reaction to ideological discourse mirrors a broader lack of real connection that people felt between their personal situations and political positions. Carme knows that the political opposition is as incapable as the governing regime of offering her what she needs and desires, yet the rhetoric of change prevails in her own discourse and in those of others.

---

14 The only regret Justo ever shows about his actions concerns his treatment of Carme. Losing her inheritance weighs heavily on his conscience and marks the point at which he loses his innocence. His longing for her can be read as a desire to return to the past.

Mateo Moreno is another example of a narrator who constantly talks about the possibility of change—this time, from the side of the dictatorship: 'Franco ya era un anciano. Podía vivir cuatro, cinco, diez años más ... ¿Y después? Después, los mismos a los que nosotros teníamos que interrogar podrían estar dándonos órdenes desde el ministerio' (Martínez de Pisón: 121). Or: '[e]n jefatura, lo que más preocupaba a unos y a otros era poner el culo a salvo. Por lo que pudiera pasar o, como se decía entonces, por si se daba la vuelta a la tortilla' (Martínez de Pisón: 273). Ultimately, these narratives challenge the idea that change is happening in Spain in any meaningful way during this period. Rather than reflecting contemporary change, these narratives reflect the characters' expectations about a political transformation that has yet to occur.

Carme's insight into the historical moment she has lived through reveals her personal connection to it. Her minimal actions and reactions capture the complexities of history as a lived experience. As Stewart has written:

> To attend to ordinary affects is to trace how the potency of force lies in their immanence to things that are both flighty and hardwired, shifty and unsteady too. At once abstract and concrete, ordinary affects are more directly compelling than ideologies, as well as more fractious, multiplicitous, and unpredictable than symbolic meanings. (3)

While the recollections of the various characters in the novel provide an opportunity to trace the everyday progression of a political period, they also reveal the multiple meanings that this narrative can produce. Even when the personal becomes political in the weaving of the events that organise Justo's life story, it remains uncertain how exactly the social structure that sustained his life has changed. The physical presence of the novel's characters during every political incident recounted in the story establishes a direct and affective relationship between subject and past. This mediated past is constantly present in the physical and emotional burdens borne by the characters, and this connection to their past shapes each of the narrators. In the end, it is the weight of the past that haunts the narrators and their narrations. As Carme Román says, after encountering Justo for the last time in her life: '¡Ay, con qué dureza me estaba tratando la vida! Porque para mí aquello fue como una señal del destino, una señal que el destino me enviaba para decirme que el pasado me perseguiría siempre y que nunca podría desembarazarme de él' (Martínez de Pisón: 303).

Although Justo disappears at the end of the novel, his presence, his desires, and even his work as an informant do not fully fade away. Perhaps the vagueness of his life's meaning and the unclear evolution of his character reflects the nebulosity of an era torn between the need for change and a strong desire to preserve the status quo. The way the voices of multiple narrators are picked up and left in the middle of their narrations provides no closure. Even in the title of the novel, the implied future in the word 'tomorrow' suggests an unfinished project. This uncertainty surrounding Justo's life and death reminds us of Alicia Durán's disappearance in Prado's novel. Both highlight the violence that characterised the years of the *Transición* and that continues to be linked to the present; both stories imply, to different degrees, that the narrative of change and transformation is an unfinished discourse that still shapes the present.

Ultimately, these novels, like the contemporary nationalistic discourses examined by Luisa Elena Delgado, cannot be understood in isolation from the public narrative of change and democratic success. The examination of the political and affective structures that sustain this narrative of transformation remains an important task in contemporary Spain, since it is these structures that expose what Spain's nationalistic rhetoric conceals: a deep-seated fear of an unfinished project, one that still struggles to reconcile the Francoist model of a unified nation, sanctioned by the *Transición*, with the reality of the diversity of its own people.

The past literally catches up to the present in both Antonio Orejudo's *Un momento de descanso* (2011) and Rafael Reig's *Todo está perdonado* (2011). While they are radically different in their treatment of the past, these novels share surrealist and absurdist tendencies that seek to counteract the fantastic story told about the Spanish *Transición*. The connection with this political period is not as clear in Orejudo's novel as in Reig's, but both narratives must be read within the context of Spain's political transformation. These novels reveal the unfulfilled promises of a time of political and cultural change that, instead of dismantling past practices, simply reinforced them. The illogical and bizarre realities presented by the two novels are portrayed as the rational consequences of a time that can only be described by its incongruities.

Antonio Orejudo's *Un momento de descanso* follows the misadventures of the academic Arturo Cifuentes, who moves back to Spain after he is fired from his teaching job at a university in the US. A 'failed campus novel', as its narrator describes it, *Un momento de descanso* offers a plot that crosses the Atlantic, revealing the absurdities and corruption found in institutions of higher education on both sides of the ocean. Author Orejudo shares biographical commonalities with both the eponymous narrator and the character Cifuentes. His familiarity with US academia is clear; the first half of this novel is situated in a southern US university and the entire book is littered with the names of real-life specialists in Hispanic Studies from both sides of the Atlantic. *Un momento*, with its references to both campus life and politics, lends itself to the genre of a campus novel, but Arturo Cifuentes and the narrator Orejudo quickly leave behind the closed universe of academia to tell a wide range of stories, recounting, among other things, a pharmaceutical drug trial under the highly secretive auspices of the US government, Orejudo's desecration of the codices of *El Mio Cid* housed at the Biblioteca Nacional during a romantic encounter with a librarian, the shooting of a porn film, and, finally, the forgotten story of an academic executed under the dictatorship. These different stories are complemented by visual elements such as old photographs, personal documents like death certificates, an image of the *El Mio Cid* manuscript, musical scores, etc. The presence of this visual documentation creates and maintains the illusion of veracity.

A parody with metafictional elements, *Un momento* creates situations in which both humour and absurdity are used to draw attention to the irrational reality we live in and the discourses we create around that reality. Orejudo, the author, is a novelist and academic who continues to work as a university professor in Spain teaching early modern Spanish literature. Cifuentes, the character, is also a specialist in the same field, having earned his degree from the same institution as the author in Buffalo, New York. Orejudo the *narrator*, on the other hand, describes himself as having been unable to finish his PhD at the same institution after participating in what turned out to be a top-secret military drug trial. The new-found powers he obtained from his participation in this trial, including an altered state of consciousness and a ability to randomly 'know' things about people and events, led him to imagine and to invent non-existent works and authors that he then analysed in his essays for his graduate courses. After being asked to leave the doctoral programme, the narrator reports, he decided to return to Spain, where he became a novelist.

Orejudo the *writer* is the author of *Fabulosas narraciones por historias* (1996), *Ventajas de viajar en tren* (2000), and *Reconstrucción* (2005); Orejudo the *narrator* mentions these same novels as his own published works. The conflation between the first-person narrator of the novel and the novel's real-life author creates the impression that the fiction that we are reading contains some truth and is to some extent biographical. As noted above, this feeling is reinforced by the different visual elements included in the book, such as old photographs and pictures of old newspapers. Orejudo also connects the story he is telling with work carried out by real academics, including Jaume Claret Miranda's *El atroz demoche* (2005) and Mercedes del Amo Hernández's *Salvador Vila. El rector fusilado en Víznar* (2005).

Despite this framework of legitimacy, the absurd situations described by the narrator shatter any possibility that the novel is recounting 'true' events.

Instead, what comes to light is the role played by the narrator in retelling a story Cifuentes tells him about their past. This story soon turns into an obsession for the narrator, who spends the rest of the novel checking the truthfulness of his friend's account. This journey results in his recovery of memories of his youth and the uncovering of a hidden, forgotten structure of corruption in Spanish academia—a structure intimately related to the politics of the dictatorship and only reinforced during the *Transición*.

Orejudo's work has been noted for the complexity of its narrative system (Valenzuela: 85). Considered by the Spanish press as one of the most promising writers of the twenty-first century, Orejudo has won various prizes for his earlier novels, and his literary work continues to attract interest from critics, who praise his talent for storytelling and his irreverent sense of humour (Maginn: 541).[15] In her analysis of Orejudo's earlier *Ventajas de viajar en tren*, Alison Maginn shows how the narrative engages in a risky game, 'un juego que seduce y encanta al lector para extraerlo de su propio mundo y hacerlo entrar en un mundo de pura textualidad' (542). Here, 'textuality' refers to a dialogic process in which narrator and reader become complicit in the process of producing meaning from the text.[16] Orejudo follows Cervantes's notion of *tropelía*, a narrative sleight-of-hand where things are not what they appear (Maginn: 543). Both reader and narrator must engage in this game in order to understand the story that is being told. The narrator of *Un momento* engages in the same tactic, requiring the reader to pay constant attention to what is being narrated. Personal memories, retellings of third-party accounts, and archival and research materials blend together to create a narrative in which there is a lingering feeling of disbelief. The narrator makes himself still more unreliable through his admission of his altered state of consciousness and the unbelievable scenarios he describes. While Maginn sees in this narrative complexity a postmodern sensibility, Orejudo's multilayered narration of visual and written material may also be understood as a comment on the difficulties of telling a story about the past (Maginn: 549).

The main narrative of *Un momento* revolves around the secret of an old professor, Augusto Desmoines, whom Cifuentes and the narrator admired and worked with during their university days. Desmoines, as Cifuentes comes to discover, has usurped the life story of Claudio Castillejo: the pre-war founder of the modern Spanish university system who was later betrayed by his own disciple and executed. Both Cifuentes and the narrator

15 Valenzuela notes that Orejudo has been called a 'literary terrorist'. He describes him as 'un tío cachondo' and his literary resources as 'incontables como sus ocurrencias, y no hace una novela lineal y no se conforma con un solo relato central' (85).

16 Maginn draws a parallel between this narrative game and the process of transference that takes place in psychoanalysis (543–44).

recollect Desmoines telling a version of this story as his own, recounting how he had survived his sentence by hiding in a well where he wrote essays, such as his well-known study on 'la otra generación del 27' (which included writers like José María Pemán, Miguel Mihura, Enrique Jardiel Poncela, and Álvaro de la Iglesia) (Orejudo: 100). When Cifuentes tells the narrator about Desmoines's deception, Orejudo confesses that he has always thought it odd that a leader of the Republican cause would spend his time in hiding producing essays about a group of conservative writers. For Cifuentes, the conclusion and the explanation are very simple: 'todo, absolutamente todo lo que nos había contado Desmoines, era falso, una pura mentira que el mundo entero se había tragado de principio a fin' (Orejudo: 105). He soon discovers that Desmoines was in fact the disciple who had betrayed his old mentor and had him executed after the war.

This forgotten story comes to light when Claudio Castillejo's son, Florencio, returns from his teaching position in the US to work in the university his father founded. Florencio eventually kills himself after failing in his quest to clear the Castillejo name and to recover the memory of his father by exposing the lies constructed by Desmoines. Upon his own return to Spain, Cifuentes fills the teaching vacancy left by Florencio and embarks on a quest to discover the true identity of his old professor. He contacts his old friend Orejudo the narrator in the hopes that Orejudo will help him write a book exposing Desmoines as a fraud and manipulator. Cifuentes already has a title for the work, *The Great Pretender*, as well as all of the necessary documentation: '[n]aturalmente no hablaba de oídas; tenía toda la documentación. La tenía en casa, me la enseñaba cuando yo quisiera. Sólo necesitaba mi talento narrativo' (Orejudo: 108).

Augusto Desmoines's story and his legacy are cemented thanks to the political work of his son, Virgilio, who becomes the rector of the university where his father taught before retirement. A mediocre student, he was unable to finish any of the specialisations he tried until he followed in his father's footsteps and joined his department as a '*penene*—PNN—, es decir de Profesor No Numerario' (Orejudo: 103). After joining the PSOE in the 1970s, Virgilio was made a civil servant by the new governing party after the Socialist victory in 1982: '[a]quellos jóvenes de la Transición comprendieron muy pronto que los partidos políticos además de expresar el pluralismo ideológico en una sociedad democrática, son también una manera de ayudarse los unos a los otros, una garantía de que en su seno, como dice el himno de Liverpool, nadie camina solo' (Orejudo: 104).[17]

17 The perceived corruption of the Spanish university system was recently covered in the Spanish press, following the revelation that Íñigo Errejón, the campaign

The Spanish university in Orejudo's novel is portrayed not as a place of learning, but as a space where political supporters receive their rewards and the privileged perpetuate a corrupt system. In describing this situation, the narrator draws not only on his characterisation of the fictional Desmoines, but also on real academic research done on Spanish universities. For instance, Orejudo the narrator reads Jaume Claret Miranda's *El atroz desmoche* to try to understand why the state of Spanish universities is so poor. The conclusion he arrives at expresses clear criticism of the treatment of the legacy of the Spanish Civil War and dictatorship during the transition:

> Nuestro raquitismo cultural, intelectual y científico no obedecía a un ciego y fatal designio, sino al dictado consciente de quienes ganaron la guerra y a la incompetencia coadyutoria de los políticos que vinieron después.
>
> Al perderse en los primeros años de la Transición la oportunidad de corregir drásticamente esta situación, los jóvenes políticos de la democracia facilitaron al franquismo una de sus últimas victorias: garantizaron que los efectos de ese atroz desmoche llevado a cabo por el Régimen en la universidad perdurarían durante siglos. (Orejudo: 203)

In his reading of Claret's study and a book by Mercedes del Amo Hernández, the narrator provides factual information that is hard to dispute. Yet the stories he pieces together are quickly challenged when he meets one of Cifuentes's ex-colleagues and discovers that the story Cifuentes told about his dismissal from his job in the US was a lie. At this point, the narrator starts to doubt everything; comparing Cifuentes's motivation to write a book about Desmoines with the motivations of the other academic publications he had just read, he begins to suspect his friend: 'su afán no sería más prosaico y elemental: conseguir una plaza de catedrático y mejorar su posición económica y laboral' (Orejudo: 209). Unable to distinguish fact from fiction (despite his altered consciousness), the narrator questions the power of the imagination but also the validity of understanding reality: '¿Quién mentía,

manager of Pablo Iglesias (the candidate for the new political party Podemos), has continued to draw a stipend from his university position while participating in politics. Writers like Félix de Azúa have written about the privileged position of academics, which has been widely criticised given the fact that Spanish institutions have suffered under the budgetary cuts caused by the financial crisis ('Un partido de profesores', http://elpais.com/elpais/2014/11/28/opinion/1417202506_176244.html). More recently, in *El cura y los mandarines*, Gregorio Morán criticised the co-opting of intellectuals by political and business institutions. His chapter on the Real Academia Española was deemed unpublishable by Planeta (Morán: 763–76). Eventually, Akal published the text in its entirety at the end of 2014.

Magdalena o él? Imposible saberlo. Dejarse llevar por la imaginación, aunque fuera controlada, no me pareció entonces la mejor manera de entenderlo. Pero ceñirse escrupulosamente a lo que percibía con los órganos socialmente aceptados para captar la "realidad" tampoco garantizaba nada' (Orejudo: 209).

Distinguishing truth from deceit is a continuing obstacle for the narrator as he strives to tell a logical story about the past. Ultimately, his wavering between contradictory accounts offers too messy a standpoint from which to grasp the significance of the memory narrated in Orejudo's novel. As in the other novels analysed in this chapter, ultimately it is the narrator who needs to mediate this memory about the past—a task that Orejudo's narrator-self accomplishes by connecting all of the different stories to his own experience. Although the narrator is unable to fully solve the novel's central mystery, his physical experience of the memories recounted (through his altered consciousness, for instance) helps us to forge a closer connection between the past and the present. It is not until Orejudo, refusing to accept his friend's tales, embarks on a research project of his own that the story being recounted acquires meaning and truthfulness.

This personal involvement is crucial, as the 'secret' Cifuentes wants to reveal to the world is part of Orejudo's own story and is intimately tied to his own sense of identity. The narrator's search for Desmoines's story thus also becomes a story about the search for his own past. Orejudo alludes to this when he reminds us of his reunion with Cifuentes after many years: '[d]ice uhhh, uhhh, soy un fantasma del pasado que viene a perturbar el presente' (Orejudo: 13). This past remains relevant not only to the characters' current lives, but also to Cifuentes's future.

Cifuentes and the narrator are complicit in this forged past, albeit through no real fault of their own: '[l]e debíamos la vida. Y él, Cifuentes, por partida doble. Sin Desmoines nos hubiéramos muerto de asco en España y él se hubiera hundido definitivamente en Missouri. Pero eso no quitaba que Desmoines, nuestro padrino, fuera un falso y un cabrón' (Orejudo: 150). The two men's inability to reject this past is made clear by Cifuentes's decision not to tell the story of Desmoines after he is offered a permanent position at the university by Desmoines's son, Virgilio. By accepting this job, Cifuentes tacitly condones the forged history he has uncovered; ultimately, he himself participates in perpetuating the system he was once so eager to denounce. Cifuentes describes his decision as a choice to 'take a break from his own self', so as to be able to join in the happiness and the complacency of others. It is at this point that the narrator decides to betray his friend, to 'take a break' from the promise he made to Cifuentes to keep his secret and share his story.[18]

---

18 The title of the novel refers to this break.

The decisions of both Cifuentes and the narrator to break with their principles are indicative of a situation in which nothing ever changes. At the point of making his decision, Cifuentes has joined an institutional structure he has resolved no longer to question, while the narrator is resigned to continue telling these stories about the past and revealing their connections to an unchanging present. The affective work of memory that we see in this novel is one of the forces that shapes our understanding of our present. As Berlant writes: 'memory and the past emerge in mediated zones of visceral presence distributed across scenes of epistemological and bodily activity. You forget when you learned to *use your inside voice*—it just seems like the default mode, even to write in it' (2011: 52). The physical experience that both Cifuentes and the narrator go through to bring back the memory of the past reflects this mediated process, in which each of them ends up following his default mode of existence: Cifuentes joins the university and Orejudo the narrator remains at its margins. But, as Berlant points out, examining these affective practices also makes us aware of the orthodoxies of institutions and practices and 'provide[s] a way to assess the disciplines of normativity' (2011: 53). In *Un momento*, this exercise in memory forces the narrator to acknowledge why he has failed in his project to write a Spanish campus novel. He reflects on the words of Raquel Medina, a scholar working in England who was committed to an asylum after serving on a search committee for a Spanish university:

> ¿Nunca se ha parado a pensar por qué apenas se han escrito novelas de campus en español? Yo se lo voy a decir: porque es imposible escribir una novela sobre la universidad española, que sea elegante y además verosímil. *Lucky Jim*, de Kingsley Amis, o *Small World*, de David Lodge, son tan buenas porque la universidad que toman de referencia, la anglosajona, conserva todavía unas formas impecables, aunque por dentro esté consumida por las mismas corruptelas que la de aquí. En la universidad española por el contrario la grosería aparece tal cual, sin los ropajes de la buena educación. Una novela realista, cualquier libro sobre la universidad española, aunque sea un libro de investigación sobre el suyo, está condenado a convertirse en una astracanada. Los que no conocen el mundillo académico pensarán además que es inverosímil. Haga la prueba. (Orejudo: 175)[19]

---

19 Antonio Muñoz Molina's *Carlota Feinberg* (1999) could be considered a Spanish campus novel despite the fact that it pertains to the academic world of the US. Unfortunately, Muñoz Molina's unfamiliarity with American academia and his stereotyped discussion of literary theory and feminist studies offers a limited view

Finally, the narrator realises the truth of Medina's words for 'cualquier intento de novelar la universidad española acaba en sainete' (Orejudo: 240). Instead, he is able to offer the reader *un momento de descanso*, allowing us to get closer to what Berlant would call 'the encounter of what is sensed with what is known and what has impact in a new but also recognisable way' (2011: 53). This new perspective is yet another example of how a troubled past continues indefinitely to shape an equally conflictive present.

Rafael Reig's crime novel *Todo está perdonado* offers a retelling of the years of the *Transición* through a convergence of several stories within a dystopian Madrid, an urban space first introduced in Reig's previous novels *Sangre a borbotones* (2002) and *Guapa de cara* (2003). Reig explores Spain's recent political memory through a blend of different literary genres and plotlines set in an alternate history in which the logic of neoliberal capitalism has been followed to its extreme. The path towards this development is first established during the *Transición*; as a result, the recounting of that period is crucial for an understanding of the present of the novel.[20]

Todo está perdonado sees the return of an ailing Carlos Clot, the detective from Reig's earlier novels, who sets out to solve the murder of a woman named Laura, the daughter of entrepreneur Perico Gamazo. The novel also tells the story of the Gamazo family from the days of the 1868 Revolution to the present, tracing the patriarch's ascent in Spanish society and the financial success of his descendants. This 'tale of winners' is countered by the story of Rosario, the daughter of an anarchist mother, killed next to her lover during a robbery. In addition to these plots, the novel functions as the memoir of the narrator, Antonio Menéndez Vigil, or Toñín, whose story shadows that of the Gamazo family. His services to the family span two generations; his own father worked for Perico's father, Gonzalo Gamazo, the Marquis of Morcuera, and perished alongside him in a car accident.

In Toñín's Madrid, a mysterious galleon arrives out of nowhere at the port of Atocha, the entire crew dead except for two beautiful mad women whose laughter can be heard from a distance. This ship, which runs aground before entering the port, haunts the narrator throughout the novel. A separate,

---

of the academic environment, missing an important opportunity to address some of academia's relevant shortcomings.

20 Analysing this dystopian Madrid in *Sangre a borbotones*, David Knutson imagines this space as part of a dark future, while considering that it might also refer to the present (56). *Todo está perdonado* makes it clear that this alternate history *does* take place in our present, as the novel develops alongside the key matches of the 2008 European Cup.

parallel narrative details the matches played by the Spanish national soccer team during the UEFA Euro Cup of 2008—a contest that, after many decades of disappointment, Spain finally won.[21] Tracing the narrative thread of these games allows the author to draw an extended parallel between the team's most significant failures and Spain's political discourse.[22]

These layered stories are interleaved with ten separate texts—culled from newspapers, speeches, Reig's own blog, and works of fiction—that sustain the plotline of the novel.[23] The mix of factual and fictional texts, as in the other novels analysed in this chapter, challenges the reader's understanding of the past. Finally, *Todo* reveals its affiliation with the narrative genre of science fiction, as the author offers his telling of a profound personal and political crisis through the lens of a different universe and an alternate history.[24] The multiple stories and literary styles utilised in this book intersect and revolve around a central account of what the narrator refers to as the 'Immaculada Transición' (Reig: 20).

A prolific writer, Rafael Reig has published more than ten books and won a number of prominent literary awards. *Todo está perdonado* won the VI Premio Tusquets Editores de Novela, while his earlier *Sangre a borbotones* won the Premio de la Crítica de Asturias. His other novels are *Esa oscura gente* (1990), *Autobiografía de Marilyn Monroe* (1992), *La fórmula Omega* (1998), *Guapa de cara* (2004), *Hazañas del capitán Carpeto* (2005), and, most recently, *Lo que no está escrito* (2012). Reig is also an academic currently teaching at Hotel Kafka, a creative writing school established by a group of authors and artists. He has also worked as a journalist, writing columns for newspapers like *El Mundo*, *Público*, and *Abc Cultural*.

Reig's writing has been critical of the Spanish transition and the missed opportunities this period represented for Spain. In an interview with *Europa Press* after the publication of *Todo está perdonado*, he declared that Spain could have had a revolution like Portugal but that, instead, the Spanish

21 The chapters of the novel follow the structure of the competition. The book is divided into four parts: 'Fase eliminatoria: Examen de conciencia', 'Cuartos de final: El dolor de los pecados', 'Semifinales: El propósito de la enmienda', and 'Final: La penitencia' (Reig: 7).

22 The relationship between nationalism and soccer has been widely studied. Julián Sanz Hoya has examined the nationalistic role of soccer under Francoism, tracing how the game was controlled and utilised by the dictatorship (280–84). Regarding the nationalistic discourse behind the *furia española* and its more recent performance in the 2010 World Cup, see Luisa Elena Delgado (2010).

23 The initial text signed by the narrator of the novel, Antonio Menéndez Vigil, was first used in 2008 in the blog Reig wrote for *Público*.

24 Susan Divine makes an excellent case for Reig's use of science fiction as a valuable genre for narrating a time of crisis (239–40).

transition was aimed at avoiding conflict and disenfranchising people. It is for this reason, according to Reig, that 'ahora a la gente no les interesa ningún proyecto colectivo de transformación social, sino que le importa que pongan en la tele fútbol, a Belén Esteban o que en Zara o Milano [*sic*] halla trajes a cien euros'.[25] In the same interview, Reig points to the dictatorship as the origin of Spain's present economic situation: 'la sociedad "low cost" la empezó Franco, con el 600, las minifaldas y los ye-yé, y dura hasta ahora con los muebles de Ikea, la ropa de Zara y el derecho a Internet' (*europapress.es*). While this generalisation is far from unusual, I highlight this quote because it reflects two of Reig's main literary themes: the direct connection between Spain's current financial and political problems and its past (especially regarding the missed opportunities to enact true financial and political structural change during the *Transición*) and the dubious economic forces that have shaped Spain's reality since the dictatorship. As Susan Divine explains, Reig's novels 'redirect national memory away from strictly political arguments and toward the process of neoliberal capitalism as the real motor of change' (236). The dystopian Madrid in Reig's fiction imagines a society in which this neoliberal drive has been mistakenly identified with progress and the future. The transformation of the capital and its urban reorganisation are, as Divine smartly analyses in her discussion of *Sangre a borbotones*, the consequence of neoliberal policies in which the market has replaced the government as the agent for environmental and social change (241, 245–47).

In the alternate historical scenario created by Reig in his latest novels, *Guapa de cara*, *Sangre a borbotones*, and *Todo está perdonado*, the author experiments with different variations of the political events that occurred following the end of the dictatorship; in Reig's world, these events end up creating a surreal Madrid flooded to help with transportation after an oil shortage. In place of a government, ruthless private companies rule the city, driven by the sole purpose of maximising their profits. In *Sangre*, this political scenario is depicted as the result of a different outcome in the elections of the 1980s, in which the ousting of the communists causes a disastrous chain of events. As Divine describes it, '[f]rom here, the real Cold War anticommunist interventionism of the United States makes a plausible, but fictional, leap from Latin America to Spain after the elections, takes over the government, outlaws the speaking of Spanish, and renames the country the US-Iberian Federation' (246). In *Todo*, the US colonisation of Spain remains visible in Madrid's flooded arteries, but the true focus of

25 Interview available at http://www.europapress.es/andalucia/sevilla-00357/ noticia-escritor-rafael-reig-cree-transicion-espanola-puso-limites-muy-estrechos-democracia-nada-real-20110317175424.html.

the political narrative pushes backwards, extending past the *Transición* to a period many decades before the dictatorship to trace the idea of a search for a 'national project', the haunting notion that an '[o]tra España era posible'. As becomes clear over the course of the novel, this dream was always driven by the economic interests of the ruling elite (Reig: 61).

Present throughout this history and shadowing the country's political shifts since the Revolution of 1868, we find the private fortunes of the four patriarchs of the Gamazo family. *Todo* begins as the prospect of preserving the family's wealth into the future is truncated by the death of Laura, the sole remaining heir to the Gamazo financial empire. Perico Gamazo, Laura's father and the last Gamazo patriarch, has already suffered the loss of his son (killed in an altercation by police) and his wife (dead by suicide after her son's death) before the story opens.

In the alternate Madrid of *Todo está perdonado*, blessed Communion wafers from the Vatican are sold in vending machines called HTMs, 'conveniently packaged' in vacuum-sealed containers. As Spaniards have a special dispensation from the Pope to receive the blessed wafers in their hands instead of directly into their mouths, the possibility of taking Communion without a priest becomes a reality in this surreal world,[26] although priests remain available, a toll-free call away, for quick visits as needed and are found roaming near the machines in case someone does not want to touch the blessed host.[27] The merging of religious demands and capitalism is perfectly captured in this venture, developed by Perico Gamazo, whose company provides the containers for the wafers.

When Laura Gamazo is found dead, poisoned by a vending-machine Communion wafer on the day of her wedding, Inspector Carlos Clot initiates his investigation by trying to figure out who could be ideologically motivated to introduce poison into these sealed packages. This storyline grants us entry into the world of an ongoing spiritual war among a number

---

26 This dispensation is real, as documented in one of the factual texts included in the novel: 'En España se podrá distribuir la comunión en la mano' (Reig: 190). This text is excerpted from an article that appeared on page 24 of the newspaper *Abc* on 19 March 1976; the full text is available online at http://hemeroteca.abc.es/nav/Navigate.exe/hemeroteca/madrid/abc/1976/03/19/036.html.

27 The number is 900-VATICAN, '[l]lamada sin cargo, gratis total. O envíe CURA al 3927. Siempre a su servicio, noche y día, 7 por 24' (Reig: 191). As one of the priests explains to Clot: 'Morir recién comulgado es el mayor premio en esta vida. Cuanto más a menudo, más papeletas tiene para que le toque el Gordo' (Reig: 191). The direct parallel drawn between taking Communion and the chance of winning the lottery drives home the equivalence of spiritual and financial salvation in a world ruled by wild capitalism.

of Latin-speaking urban tribes including ex-terrorists from GRAPO. In this new turf war, religion represents another form of power, and its followers are as driven by greed as the other political groups. As Micawber, Clot's friend and informant, tells him, '[l]a teología es contabilidad. El misticismo es una garantía de liquidez, como un aval en el First National Bank' (Reig: 91).

Clot's investigation of Laura's murder and his descent into the underground religious war takes place on the margins of the novel; the main narrative of the book centres on narrator Antonio Menéndez de Vigil's (Toñín) recounting of the past. While monitoring Clot's sleuthing, Toñín reveals an almost omniscient knowledge of everything that is going on in Madrid. He is connected to each of the characters and their stories, and reveals himself to be particularly obsessed with explaining the past. In tandem with a detailed account of the Euro 2008 matches, Toñín recounts a number of significant political events that he believes help to explain the present. Most of his retelling of the past is based on his personal experience; it is Toñín's physical presence at each event that renders him capable of mediating this knowledge about the past. This is how Toñín sums up his own story:

> Nací en 1940 y crecí en la España una, grande y libre del Caudillo, tuve un Seiscientos y otros muchos coches, hasta que se acabó el petróleo, viví la II Restauración borbónica, la Inmaculada Transición, el golpe del 23-F, la ayuda norteamericana para consolidar la democracia (y para la ejecución de las obras del Canal Castellana), el entusiasmo institucional con el referéndum de 1984 ('De entrada no', decían los del PSOE con calculada ambigüedad), que nos convirtió en Estado Asociado a los USA, con el inglés como lengua cooficial (a partir del segundo referéndum, el del 86) y una monarquía tributaria del Imperio de Washington. (Reig: 20)

While the narrator observes that his life is one that can be told in 'dos patadas', his knowledge and experience is vast, deeply connected to the shadow world of the power structures of both the dictatorship and the Socialist government of Felipe González. Toñín has worked in the Guardia Civil and the intelligence services of the SECED, CESID, CNI, and many other secretive organisations, always under the protection of Perico Gamazo. He justifies his work by paraphrasing a well-known statement made by González: '"El Estado de Derecho también se defiende desde las cloacas." Alguien tiene que hacer el trabajo sucio' (Reig: 20).[28] Here, again, we have a

---

28 González's original statement about the murders of GAL, the state-sponsored death squads, is 'El Estado de Derecho se defiende también en las alcantarillas'.

narrator who acts as mediator, capable of transmitting his knowledge of the past through the vehicle of his own personal and intimate experience. A key phrase employed by Toñín as he recounts political events, soccer matches, and situations in the characters' lives is the categorical 'yo estuve allí'—a statement that precludes any contestation of his first-hand knowledge of what took place.

The narrator's account of Spanish history goes back to the Revolution of 1868 and touches on moments of political opposition during the dictatorship, including the student rebellion of the 1950s, in which Perico Gamazo was involved and consequently thrown into jail. Perico's worried father visits his politician friend Montovio, who tells him to relax: '[e]l que no es comunista a los veinte años no tiene corazón' (Reig: 56). Montovio is clear about where people like him and the Gamazos stand in the changing times of the dictatorship, preparing in case 'algún día pueda dar la vuelta la tortilla' (Reig: 52). One thing is for sure, the narrator reminds us—the generation of Perico's father had a duty, and they fulfilled it: 'Para eso habían ganado una guerra: para dejarnos a sus hijos un país a la medida: "España a su medida", como todavía declara la prensa casi cincuenta años después' (Reig: 35). As Montovio explains to Gonzalo Gamazo, the Marquis of Morcuera, '[t]ú y yo ya hemos ganado una guerra, camarada. Ahora les toca a ellos, a los muchachos ganar una paz. ¿O vamos a dejar que la paz nos la ganen los rojos?' (Reig: 52). Montovio reveals that those who have worked for the dictatorship have a strategy in place to make sure they end up on top when the change arrives:

> Déjate de bolcheviques. El comunismo no es ninguna conjura: nos es más que el hambre. Contra el comunismo, la mejor arma es el nivel de vida. Tú dale al obrero un automóvil y ya verás como entra en razón. Esa es la consigna. Desarrollo. El plan de Estabilización. Los Americanos. Y el desarrollo, tarde o temprano, significa democracia, Morcuera, desengáñate. No hay por qué asustarse: lo que hay que hacer es ir tomando posiciones. Ojo: una democracia administrada por nosotros, no te confundas. (Reig: 52–53)

After his sojourn in prison, Perico is sent abroad to figure out a strategy for bringing democracy and change to Spain while guaranteeing his family's position. This mission becomes especially important after Morcuera and Montovio decide to combine their transport and packaging businesses and marry their children, further uniting the two families. During his time abroad, Perico meets a woman and at one point even decides to break off his existing engagement with Montovio's daughter; however, his will is weaker than that of his family, and he ends up following Morcuero and Montovio's wishes at the expense of his own. In the end, as the narrator explains, his personal and political fate was clear:

> Tanto Pepe Montovio como el papá de Perico, don Gonzalo, marqués de Morcuera, habían hecho dinero en los cincuenta y sesenta, porque para eso habían ganado una guerra. Perico Gamazo multiplicó la fortuna familiar en los ochenta, gracias al acuerdo con el Vaticano para fabricar envases eucarísticos, porque para eso ellos habían ganado una paz. (Reig: 47)

The generational story of the *Transición* told by the narrator is a story of the winning of peace. The political change that comes about after the dictatorship teaches Perico and his kind that '[l]a paz no se gana con obuses ni a tiro limpio como la guerra. Ahora les toca a ellos y sus armas con otras, pero todo queda en casa' (Reig: 55).

The *Transición*, as told through the story of this family's business, both personal and financial, represents an extreme privatisation of history. Susan Divine makes this connection in her analysis of Reig's criticism of neoliberalism, which she describes as not only a political position but also a mental framework. In her words, '[t]he movement from public to private maintains its economic and political hegemony by promoting a cultural attitude that simultaneously shifts the responsibility for a safe and just society to the individual as expressed through the patriarchal family structure, an institution that then must be maintained at all costs' (242).

The focus on the Gamazo family reflects this shift, but in *Todo* we also witness (with the narrator's help) how this private sphere enters a crisis. Toñín, like the detective Clot, is a marginalised subject, wandering through different social classes and connecting their multiple stories.[29] If a detective is an outsider because of the work he does, the narrator is also made an outcast by his secretive work, shadowing the private and public domains, closely following both political and personal events, keeping tabs and harbouring secrets that grant him infinite insight into the time in which he is living. In *Todo*, the secret to keep is Toñín's own: his sexual relationship with Perico's then-12-year-old daughter, Laurita. The girl's murder means that this story will be safely guarded, but the narrator is unable to hide his

---

29 Manuel Vázquez Montalbán has written about the detective as a marginalised subject, the ultimate urban *flâneur*, 'un merodeador social' able to roam the city in search of clues. He has theorised why detective fiction is the perfect genre for the Spanish society of the 1970s: 'abocada ya al delirio neocapitalista y parademocrático, dependiente de la doble verdad, la doble moral y la doble contabilidad del capitalismo avanzado' (1998: 145).

guilt, wondering about his own complicity in the Gamazo family's crisis. His role in the killing of Perico's son by the police, despite a promise made to protect him, adds to his guilty feelings of betrayal and responsibility towards the Gamazo family. But Toñín's guilt is ambiguous; in his narration of the interests of the elite pitted against the rest of the country, it becomes clear that he could never belong to the first group. How he ends up mediating and condoning their demise is, perhaps, part of the story he is telling.

As Clot nears the completion of his murder investigation, Toñín already knows who is responsible for poisoning the Communion wafers. We realise, in fact, that he has always known, since he mentioned the poisoner's name early in the novel. The daughter of an anarchist and the former housemaid for the Gamazo family, Rosario, also known as Charo or Charito, serves as the face of those who have always remained outside of the frame of change that the narrator describes throughout the novel. She is the one disturbing the chain of programmatic transformation towards an ideal of Spain, a different, possible one, an 'España a su medida' (Reig: 35).

Rosario's involvement in the poisoning is foreshadowed by a story the narrator tells about his own father. Toñín explains how people like his father, a progressive doctor, turn their back on the common people and side with the elite when confronted with the realisation that achieving a different Spain would mean a restructuring of the country's social classes so that, '"los buenos" ya no eran ellos ... sino lo más inesperado y temido: auténticos campesinos y obreros' (Reig: 105). He describes this realisation using a well-known quote from Stendhal: '[e]se disparo que interrumpe el concierto de la orquesta filarmónica', replacing politics with '[e]l denso, el opaco, el impenetrable pueblo' (Reig: 105).[30] This interruption, embodied by Rosario, is what breaks open the private sphere that is used by Toñín to explain the logic of the Gamazos' world: 'Rosario Valverde, tal vez, la inevitable Charo, pisando el parquet encerado con sus zapatillas de suela de goma, esa mujer tan indefensa como peligrosa, esa ráfaga de viento que abrió de golpe la ventana que daba a la calle' (Reig: 106). This 'gust of wind' brings first the poisoned hosts and later a terrorist act that blasts the Plaza Cibeles as throngs of Spaniards, celebrating the Euro 2008 victory, are approaching the statue to deposit the Euro Cup to the mother of the gods. Up to this point, the narrator has presented the soccer matches leading to

30 This explanation of the people is later connected with the consumption of the Communion wafers, for which there should be no need in a democratically transformed Spain: 'La eucaristía de la democracia burguesa no cree—gracias a Dios, hasta ahí podíamos llegar—en la "presencia real" del pueblo: le basta con que la hostia consagrada en las urnas sea solo un símbolo que les llena de gracia' (Reig: 107).

the national team's victory as part of a story of historical redemption for the entire nation. The opportunity to render concrete this feat by symbolically placing the trophy in the Plaza Cibeles is irretrievably lost when the statue of Cybele, and the cup along with it, is blown to pieces at the crucial moment. Toñín describes this terrorist act by its affective significance: '[a]quello era un atentado dirigido al corazón mismo de un pueblo' (Reig: 357).

Rosario, a figure from the past, reappears in this exact moment to shatter the possibility of a new future for the old Spain—a Spain that the narrator has been painstakingly recreating through his personal memories. What is being denied is the logical end to a successful narration of the *Transición*, crowned with a European trophy. It is clear that despite the subjectivity of the narrator's story, the memories he has been recounting were never really his own. At one point, Toñín declares: '[p]ero esta es otra historia y la contaremos en otro lugar quienes la protagonizamos y aquellos a quienes se les impuso. A nosotros y a ellos nos llegará el momento de hablar (y de callar), de escribir (y de leer), de aparecer en pantalla (y de ver lo que pongan por la tele)' (Reig: 79). In the end, the story he tells belongs to the Gamazo family; the moment to tell his own version of history (and those of Rosario and Clot) only arrives when all of the myths of the past are finally shattered along with one of the most important symbols of Madrid.

These stories are yet to come as the ailing Clot and Charo let go of their dreams to run away. Rosario rejects the possibility of forgetting everything and living peacefully and privately alone with her partner: '[n]o quiero morir sola, en la oscuridad, sin que el marinero piense en mí. No quiero morir sola, en la inmensidad, sin que el minero piense en mí. No quiero un cachito de cielo para nosotros dos' (Reig: 365). Her call for solidarity gestures to a future that, while still uncertain, will only be possible once action is taken in the present: '[e]l cielo hay que tomarlo por asalto y para todos' (Reig: 365).

As for the narrator, his story cannot continue, for in truth he never really had one. Toñín acknowledges his usefulness and its end, that he was only a vessel for the narrative we have read. He leaves Madrid and his life as he heads towards the abandoned ship, determined to join the dead and, ultimately, the unknown. Despite the title of the novel, nothing in this story is forgiven, much less forgotten. As Divine observes, Reig's novel 'evinces the difficulty of destroying myths of history and its narration' and finally concludes that 'a true "forgiveness" which could lead to a different future is impossible'.[31]

---

31 Susan Divine, 'Historical Debt and Cultural Capital: Rafael Reig's *Todo está perdonado*'. Unpublished conference paper. I thank the author for kindly allowing me access to a copy of the presentation.

The criticism of neoliberal politics in Reig's novel is part of the spreading precariousness that Laurent Berlant traces in her study of cruel optimism, one that 'provides the dominant *structure* and *experience* of the present moment, cutting across class and localities' (Berlant 2011: 192). The political changes of the *Transición*, described in economic terms, reveal a reality in which, as David Harvey and others have pointed out, the interests of private owners have caused a profound deterioration of the social good that once structured our societies.[32] Berlant describes the logic of this system as a 'neoliberal feedback loop', one that reveals 'its efficiency at distributing and shaping the experience of insecurity throughout the class structure and across the globe' (2011: 193). Ultimately, in Reig's narrative as in the other novels discussed in this chapter, we encounter an exploration of the process by which an underlying rhetoric of crisis negotiates the memory of a troubled past and the perception of its unresolvedness.

My interest in these works, as I have said, stems from their identification as part of a generational response to the experience of the *Transición*. At first sight, the critical stance taken in these novels feels little different from those expressed in earlier novels about the political transition. A close reading of these works, however, reveals not only an act of remembering but a structure of affect that produces a particular relationship with the past. Berlant writes about affect theory being a way to 'bring us back to the encounter of what is sensed with what is known and what has impact in a new but also recognisable way' (2011: 53). The works of Prado, Reig, Martínez de Pisón, and Orejudo demand a new reading of the familiar stories and known critical perspectives on Spain's political transformation and the country's relationship with its troubled past.

As Berlant observes, '[l]aws, norms, and events shape imaginaries, but in the middle of the reproduction of life people make up modes of being and responding to the world that altogether constitute what gets called "visceral response" and intuitive intelligence' (2011: 53). The discussion of the memory of the political transition in Spain in these works reveals a shift in the extent to which these private and familiar responses matter in the public sphere. These memories and experiences have become insistent and necessary, not as ways of making peace with the past, but as a path to thinking about the future. Faced with a present in which the project of political transformation started after Franco's death has finally run aground amid financial and real estate crises, political corruption, and the increasing

---

32 David Harvey explains neoliberalism as a new form of capitalism in which private property rights, free market, and free trade dominate the economic structure (2–3).

loss of social goods, there is a need to reimagine what is next to come. We should pay attention to how these expectations about the future continue to be structured through a generational experience deeply connected with the memory of the *Transición*.

Conclusion

Madrid se ha vuelto una ciudad de supervivientes.
Manuel Vázquez Montalbán,
Un polaco en la corte del Rey Juan Carlos, 37

In 1987, Manuel Vázquez Montalbán published *Historias de política ficción*, three short stories in which detective Pepe Carvalho solves three separate crimes triggered by the failed military uprising of 1981. These crimes all involve elderly men who had not forgotten their experience of the Spanish Civil War, and for whom the 23-F represented an intrusion of the past into the present. What Carvalho learns from investigating these murders is the extent of the younger generation's ignorance about the country's past. The silence that separates those who survived the war and the dictatorship from those who have no recollection of any of those experiences is, for the detective, a generational conflict in need of a resolution. The inability to address this gap, Carvalho predicts, will mean the continuation of the past into the present and, ultimately, the impossibility of a future. More than two decades after the publication of these stories, Carvalho's words acquire new significance amid the recent revisiting of the 23-F, especially now that the question of the past, and the present's failure to overcome it, has been transformed into a generational question that challenges the triumphant narrative of the *Transición*.

Despite the enduring narrative of a successful political transformation of Spain, the overall popular perception of this experience is one of disappointment. A quick read of current newspaper headlines, opinion columns, and digital media emphasises this dissatisfaction; more and more, we see the day-to-day political crises, financial corruption, and social emergencies of contemporary Spain narrated from this perspective. The idea of crisis that underlies recent narratives pits a younger generation against its elders, sometimes as part of a tense filial relationship in which the parents' time has passed and the future of their progeny has yet to arrive. Certainly this is the view expressed by philosopher José Luis Pardo Torío in a recent opinion column for *El País*, in which he describes the transition as an affair between fathers and sons.[1] In 'Padres e hijos: la *Transición* interminable', Pardo Torío points to the feeling of the younger generation that their elders have failed in their political experiment, 'ni liquidaron el franquismo ni establecieron una democracia real', and that they themselves must start from scratch.[2]

This same desire to start over is expressed by historian José Enrique Ruiz-Domènec in an interview in which he, too, draws a generational connection to the present crisis. When the interviewer mentions how the *Transición* is currently being questioned and brings up the emergence of grassroots movements like 15-M or political parties like Podemos, Ruiz-Domènec refers to 'la pérdida del impulso del proyecto de la Transición'. The result, for the historian, is a nation whose weakened state has affected even the significance of the 1978 Constitution, the pillar that heretofore sustained the successful narrative of Spain's political transition.

Taking into account this generational turn in the critical discourse concerning the *Transición*, I close this book with a brief account of three more films that embody this collective perception. The memory of the past as an opportunity for a generational confrontation is the topic of the film *Remake* (Dir. Roger Gual, 2006), in which a group of middle-aged friends gather together in the country house they had run as a hippy commune in the 1970s. Their adult children, who were born in the house and lived there for four years, also join the reunion. When the friends discover the old 8 mm films they made, they watch them together, comparing the peace of their former lives to the frustration and stress of the present. At some point, challenging this idealisation of the past, Víctor (Juan Navarro), a member of the younger generation and an out-of-work bookstore clerk, confronts the older group. Speaking especially to his father, he says:

> Don't give me that sexual revolution crap. That was in other countries, with other people. Besides, that was in the '60s. What were all those values you brought us up on supposed to be good for? In that false

1 While the translation of the title could be a gender-neutral 'parents and children', in the context of a discourse on the nation, I believe the preferred gender is male.

2 Opinion column available at http://elpais.com/elpais/2014/10/01/opinion/1412 165074_715999.html.

freedom to do what we wanted so as to be freer human beings in the future? Come on, man, please! The parallel reality in which we lived, what good was it to us? Why did you think you were better? ... You were not better than them. No better teachers than your own parents. You imposed certain values just like your parents did. What you did was to repeat the model, repeat the model ... Well, maybe I'm an idiot, but can anyone tell me why I'm such an idiot? Why my life's a fuckin' disaster? ... And today you come and start talking about how you lived, with nostalgia and convinced that what you did was right! ... Look, I'm sick of living your failures. I'd have loved to avoid it now and then. But even in that I'm too much like my dad.[3]

Víctor's outburst interrupts the party and pinpoints the moment at which a clear break appears between the adult children and their elders. Even if none of the children have any professional prospects in their own lives, their futures can no longer depend on the stories told by their parents. The rejection of these stories is their first step towards finding their own identities.

In another recent film, *Madrid 1987* (Dir. David Trueba, 2011), a young journalism student and aspiring writer interviews a famous, ageing newspaper columnist and writer. Feeling flattered by the interest of the young and beautiful woman, Miguel (José Sacristán) invites Ángela (María Valverde) back to his friend's workshop, intending to seduce her. In an absurd turn of events, the two become trapped in a tiny bathroom in the studio, in a building that is otherwise empty because of a long holiday. In these close quarters, Miguel and Ángela engage in an intimate conversation in which the distance that separates them temporally, ideologically, and politically is made clear. More importantly, what becomes apparent is the young woman's rejection of the older man's platitudes:

¿Por qué habláis como si hubierais inventado el mundo? ¿Como si antes de vosotros no hubiera habido nadie? ... Una especie de lección de fascículos. Que te tienes que tragar ... De cada cosa. De vida sexual, de vida profesional, de los estudios, delo que tienes que hacer, lo que tienes que pensar. Dejadnos en paz, dejadnos vivir. (Trueba: 99–100)

Ángela challenges Miguel's assumptions about the sexual encounter they end up having in the small bathroom. Her desire for agency and control surprises Miguel who, in the end, acknowledges the failures of his generation: '[p]uede que solo seamos una generación violenta y corrupta, que ha defraudado

---

3 This translation is taken from the subtitles to the DVD.

todas las expectativas. Espero que seáis mejores' (Trueba: 125). While the conversation (and the encounter) takes place in the late 1980s, long before today's criticism of the *Transición*, the narrative of a generational confrontation between the past and the present in the aftermath of this political period resonates amid the current critical perspectives of this time.

Finally, in the experimental film *El futuro* (Dir. Luis López Carrasco, 2013), we see a group of young people talking and drinking at a party. We cannot hear their conversations or what is happening as the camera mimics the quality of the old 8 mm films; the only verbal reference we get is the speech of Felipe González after the PSOE's victory in the 1982 general elections in Spain. As a member of the filmmaking collective Los Hijos, López Carrasco explores the issues of temporality and technology in his work. By recovering (through a digital recreation) the physical aspect of an old film about a nondescript party in 1982, López Carrasco is able to play with our perception of time. Steven Marsh has analysed the generational quality that López Carrasco and Los Hijos bring to their work, pointing out that these artists, born in the early 1980s, grew up navigating a complex national and historical legacy as the children of the cohort that brought democracy, free market economics, and neoliberalism to Spain.[4]

The title *El futuro* captures the feeling of progress and change later identified with the underground movements of la Movida; however, what López Carrasco's film—with no plot, and no narrative beyond improvised action and background music—offers most clearly is an image of a *frozen past*, one that still lingers, even while González proclaims in his victory speech that '[n]ingún ciudadano debe sentirse ajeno a la hermosa labor de modernización, de progreso y de solidaridad que hemos de realizar entre todos'. The lack of context in the film draws these words into question. As Marsh cleverly observes, '[t]he immediacy of film, the particular instantaneity of its form of representation while suggesting presence and a present, in fact always points to a present that is always already past, whose nowness is always other' (352). I suggest that this image also signals a frozen *present*, the product of this lingering past. Whether these young people are gathering together for a victory party or just another weekend evening is never clarified, but the images that remain from these celebratory days still haunt us: scenes of a generation past that remain active in our present imagination.

All three of these films narrate instances of failed communication and missed connections, depicting a world in which the memories and experiences

---

4 From 'Untimely Materialities: Spanish Film and Spectrality', published in a special issue of *Journal of Spanish Cultural Studies* edited by Steven Marsh (2015). I thank Steve for sharing a copy of his essay on López Carrasco before its publication.

of older adults, those who lived through the country's tumultuous past, seem no longer pertinent to the present. I would argue, however, that these memories remain relevant precisely because of their connection to the undefined present of a younger generation who face a future with no clear alternatives.

Ironically, although the members of this younger generation seem incapable of comprehending the past represented by their elders and the memories they harbour, it is in this failure of intergenerational contact that their memory work extends and continues into the future. In other words, the interest in the past and its memories persists precisely *because* the Spanish relationship with the past is one of uncertainty. The perception of the past as a period of inconclusiveness—a perception that permeates the works I have analysed in this book—can be explained by the affective structure built into the relationship between the present and the past. In the preceding chapters, I have discussed the recent memory works produced about the period of the *Transición* both from a generational standpoint and from the viewpoint of the present state of impasse in which Spain finds itself. I have linked the past not just to the present, but to the impossibility of a future, drawing attention to the fact that none of the structures represented in these works, political or affective, offer any vision of a scenario different from the present. The final three works reviewed in this chapter emphasise these ideas and lay bare the clear generational divide that exists in explanations of the present: a confrontation between the old and the new, where the 'new' no longer feels new. The ultimate results of this clash remain to be seen.

Filmography

Principal films, documentaries, and television series discussed in this book

23-F: *El día más difícil del Rey* (TV miniseries, 2009)
Director: Sílvia Quer
Writer: Helena Medina
Executive Producers: Helena Moreno Núñez, Pablo Usón
Producers: Daniel Hernández, Pablo Usón
Music: Alberto Demestres
Cinematography: David Omedes
Editing: Elena Ruiz
Cast:
   Juan Carlos I – Lluís Homar
   Sabino Fernández Campo – Emilio Gutiérrez Caba
   Sofía de Grecia – Mónica López
   Antonio Tejero – Manel Barceló
   Alfonso Armada – Juan Luis Gallardo
   Príncipe Felipe – Lluís Bou

23-F: *Historia de una traición* (TV miniseries, 2009)
Director: Antonio Recio
Writers: Juan Carlos Blázquez, José Luis Martín
Executive Producers: Daniel Cubillo, José Luis Martín, Lola Moreno
Music: Juan Carlos Cuello
Cinematography: José Luis Pecharromán
Editing: Víctor Sáiz
Cast:
   Zárate – Sergio Peris-Mencheta
   Young Zárate – Héctor Colomé
   Leal – Manuel Zarzo
   Young Leal – Pau Cólera
   Pilar – Inés Morales
   Young Pilar – Xenia Tostado
   Arantza – Bárbara Goenaga
   Gonzalo – Rodrigo García

23-F: La película (2011)
Director: Chema de la Peña
Writer: Joaquín Andújar
Executive Producers: Ignacio Salazar-Simpson
Producers: Enrique Bunbury, Gonzalo Salazar-Simpson, Ignasi Estapé, Ignacio Salazar-Simpson
Music: Antonio Fernández, Queti Pazos, Alejandro Román
Cinematography: David Azcano
Editing: Meco Paulogorrán
Cast:
  Antonio – Paco Tous
  Alfonso Armada – Juan Diego
  Juan Carlos I – Fernando Cayo
  Adolfo Suárez – Ginés García Millán
  Juan García Carrés – Juanma Lara
  Santiago Carrillo – Joan Pera

Cuéntame cómo pasó (TV series, 2001–)
Directors: Agustín Crespi (92 episodes), Antonio Cano (64 episodes), Ramón Fernández (26 episodes), Azucena Rodríguez (24 episodes), Sergio Cabrera (19 episodes), Moisés Ramos (19 episodes), Óscar Aibar (9 episodes), Manuel Palacios (7 episodes), Antonio Cuadri (7 episodes), Gracia Querejeta (2 episodes), Miguel Ángel Bernadeau (1 episode), Cecilia Bartolomé (1 episode), José María Caro (1 episode)
Writers: Miguel Ángel Bernardeau (272 episodes), Eduardo Ladrón de Guevara (208 episodes), Alberto Macías (123 episodes), Patrick Buckley (84 episodes), Sonia Sánchez (60 episodes), Jacobo Delgado (59 episodes), Ignacio del Moral (37 episodes), Curro Royo (30 episodes), Laura Pousa (20 episodes), Javier G. Amezúa (14 episodes), Carlos Molinero (12 episodes), Verónica Fernández (11 episodes), Marisol Ferré (11 episodes), Carlos Asorey (6 episodes), Bernardo Sáncehz (5 episodes), Ángeles González Sinde (3 episodes), Moisés Gómez Ramos (3 episodes), Oscar Lirueña (2 episodes), Miguel Ángel Fernández (1 episode), Joaquín Górriz (1 episode), Cecilia Bartolomé (1 episode), Montserrat Fernández (1 episode), Azucena Rodríguez (1 episode), Antonio Onetti (1 episode)
Executive Producer: Miguel Ángel Bernardeau
Producers: Miguel Ángel Bernadeau, Carlos Gazón, Miguel Ángel Forneiro, Manuel Forneiro, Manuel Guijarro, Esperanza Carlón
Music: Mario de Benito (176 episodes), Fernando Ortí Salvador (63 episodes), Bernardo Fuster (8 episodes), Luis Mendo (8 episodes), Álvaro de Cárdenas (3 episodes), Juan José Ortí (3 episodes), Alberto Estébanez (1 episode)
Cinematography: Tote Trenas (254 episodes), José Luis Martínez (57 episodes), Manuel Velasco (51 episodes), Miguel Tejerina (42 episodes), Teo Delgado (20 episodes), Fulgencio Rodríguez (12 episodes), Miguel Ángel Mora (11 episodes), Ángel Villarías (6 episodes), Federico Ribes (3 episodes), Suso Bello (2 episodes), Raúl Mota (1 episode)
Editing: Joaquín Roca (127 episodes), José Ares (124 episodes), Carlos Usillos (109 episodes), Juan Macua (83 episodes), Paco Castaño (68 episodes), Paola Recio (41 episodes), Mario Larrode (39 episodes), José Luis Picado (21 episodes), Ana

Garrido (19 episodes), Javier Cuadrado (19 episodes), Esperanza San Esteban (6 episodes), Felipe Poche (5 episodes), Rafael de la Cueva (1 episode), Jorge Silván (1 episode), Hebrard Ochoa Derek Ivor (1 episode)

Cast:

Antonio Alcántara – Imanol Arias
Mercedes Fernández – Ana Duato
Carlos Alcántara – Ricardo Gómez
Toni Alcántara – Pablo Rivero
Herminia – Caría Galiana
Adult Carlos (voice) – Carlos Hipólito
Inés Alcántara – Irene Visedo, Pilar Puzano (77 episodes, 2010–15)

El futuro (film, 2013)
Director: Luis López Carrasco
Writers: Luís E. Parés, Brays Efe, Luis López Carrasco
Producers: Manuel Calvo, Ion de Sosa, Luis Ferrón, Luis López Carrasco
Cinematography: Ion de Sosa
Editing: Sergio Jiménez
Cast:

Lucía Alonso, Rafael Ayuso Mateo, Marta Bassols, Marina Blanco, Manuel Calvo, Sara Campos, Juan Ceacero, Borja Domínguez, Brays Efe, Susana Ford, Quiet Herrero, Sergio Jiménez, Marta Loza Alonso, Alberto López, Andrea Noceda, Luis E. Parés, Martín Puñal, Aida Páez, Luis Tausia, Francisco Valero

La chica de ayer (TV finiseries, 2009)
Director: Álvaro Ron (3 episodes), Alfonso Arandia (3 episodes), Ignacio Mercero (2 episodes), José Ramos Paino (2 episodes)
Writers: Susan López Rubio (3 episodes), Dario Madrona (3 episodes), Agustín Martínez (2 episodes)
Executive Producers: Ignacio Mercero, Álvaro Ron
Producer: Pablo Alejos
Music: César Benito
Cinematography: Macari Golferichs
Editing: Pepe Abellán (8 episodes), Marta Salas (8 episodes), Imma Salcedo (8 episodes), Agustín Serrano (8 episodes), Antonio Gónez-Escalonilla (4 episodes)
Cast:

Samuel Santos – Ernesto Alterio
Quin Gallardo – Antonio Garrido
Ana Valverde – Manuela Velasco
Raimundo García – Mariano Llorente
José Cristóbal Mateo – Javier Rey
Pilar Juárez – Mamen Duch
José Santos – Biel Durán

Madrid 1987 (film, 2011)
Director: David Trueba
Writer: David Trueba
Producer: Jessica Berman

Cinematography: Leonor Rodríguez
Editing: Marta Velasco
Cast:
    Miguel – José Sacristán
    Ángela – María Valverde

Operación Palace (TV mockumentary, 2014)
Director: Jordi Évole
Writers: Ramon Lara, Juan Luis de Polis, David Picó
Producers: Vanesa Legaspi, Mónica Álvarez
Editing: Jaume Patris
Cast:
    Narrator (voice) – Pedro Tena
    Himself – Fernando Ónega
    Himself – Iñaki Gabilondo
    Himself – Jorge Vestrynge
    Himself – Luis María Ansón

¿Qué he hecho yo para merecer esto? (film, 1984)
Director: Pedro Almodóvar
Writer: Pedro Almodóvar
Executive Producer: Hervé Hachuel
Music: Bernardo Bonezzi
Cinematography: Ángel Luis Fernández
Editing: José Salcedo
Cast:
    Gloria – Carmen
    Antonio – Ángel de Andrés López
    Miguel – Miguel Ángel Herranz
    Toni – Juan Martínez
    Abuela – Chus Lampreave
    Cristal – Verónica Forqué
    Lucas Villalba – Gonzalo Suárez

Remake (film, 2006)
Director: Roger Gual
Writers: Javier Calvo, Roger Gual
Executive Producers: Cecilia Bossi, Quique Camín
Producers: Michel Ruben, Ariel Saúl
Music: Guillermo Scott Herren
Cinematography: Cobi Migliora
Editing: Alberto de Toro
Cast:
    Damián – Juan Diego
    Patricia – Silvia Munt
    Álex – Eusebio Poncela
    Carol – Mercedes Morán
    Max – Mario Paolucci

Ernesto – Gustavo Salmerón
Laura – Marta Etura
Fidel – Àlex Brendemühl
Víctor – Juan Navarro

Works Cited

Aguado Mínguez, Txetxu (2010). *Tiempos de ausencias y vacíos* (Deusto: Universidad de Deusto).

Aguilar, Paloma (2001). 'Justice, Politics, and Memory in the Spanish Transition', in Alexandra de Brito Barahona et al. (eds), *The Politics of Memory and Democratization: Transitional Justice in Democraticizing Societies* (Oxford: Oxford University Press), 92–118.

— (2002). *Memory and Amnesia: The Role of the Spanish Civil War in the Transition to Democracy.* Trans. Mark Oakley (New York and Oxford: Berghahn Books).

Ahmed, Sara (2012). *The Cultural Politics of Emotion* (New York and Oxford: Routledge).

Alonso, Gregorio and Diego Muro (2011). *The Politics and Memory of Democratic Transition: The Spanish Model* (New York and London: Taylor & Francis).

Altares, Guillermo (2014). 'Javier Cercas: "La memoria histórica se ha vuelto una industria"'. *El País Babelia.* 15 November. http://cultura.elpais.com/cultura/2014/11/12/babelia/1415819975_800516.html. Accessed 2 January 2015.

Álvarez Monzoncillo, José María and Juan Menor Sendra (2014). 'La estructura audiovisual en la Transición', in Manuel Palacio (ed.), *Las imágenes del cambio. Medios audiovisuales en las transiciones a la democracia* (Madrid: Biblioteca Nueva), n.pag.

Amago, Samuel (2011). 'On the Archaeological Impulse in Contemporary Spanish Narrative Fiction'. *Bulletin of Spanish Studies* LXXXVIII (7–8): 327–43.

Anderson, Steve (2001) 'History TV and Popular Memory', in Gary R. Edgerton and Peter C. Rollins (eds), *Television Histories: Shaping Collective Memory in the Media Age* (Lexington: University Press of Kentucky).

Barahona, Alexandra de Brito et al. (2001). *The Politics of Memory and Democratization: Transitional Justice in Democratizing Societies* (Oxford: Oxford University Press).

Bermúdez, Silvia (2013). 'Memory and Archive: La Movida, Alaska and Processess of Cultural Archeology', in William J. Nichols and H. Rosi Song (eds), *Toward a Cultural Archive of la Movida: Back to the Future* (Madison and Teaneck, Farleigh Dickinson University Press), 293–306.

Berlant, Lauren (2010). 'Cruel Optimism', in Melissa Gregg and Gregoty Seigworth (eds), *The Affect Theory Reader* (Durham, NC: Duke University Press), 93–117.

— (2011). *Cruel Optimism* (Durham, NC: Duke University Press).

Boym, Svetlana (2001). *The Future of Nostalgia* (New York: Basic Books).

Brinkema, Eugenie (2014). *The Forms of the Affects* (Durham: Duke University Press).

Cameron, Bryan (2015). 'Spain in Crisis: 15-M and the Culture of Indignation', *Journal of Spanish Cultural Studies* 15 (1–2): 1–11.

Carr, Raymond (1982). 'El legado franquista', in John Crispin et al. (eds), *España 1975–1980: Conflictos y logros de la democracia* (Madrid: José Porrúa Turanzas), 129–40.

Casanova, Julián et al. (2004). *Morir, matar, sobrevivir. La violencia en la dictadura de Franco* (Barcelona: Editorial Crítica).

Cascajosa Virino, Concepción (2012). '*La chica de ayer*: memoria y desmemoria televisivas de la transición en España', *Journal of Spanish Cultural Studies* 13 (3): 260–75.

Cercas, Javier (2009). *Anatomía de un instante* (Barcelona: Mondadori).

— (2014). 'Sin El Rey No Habría Democracia'. *El País*, 2 June. http://politica.elpais.com/politica/2014/06/02/actualidad/1401719800_079533.html. Accessed 24 March 2014.

Colmeiro, José F. (2005). *Memoria histórica e identidad cultural. De la postguerra a la postmodernidad* (Barcelona: Anthropos Editorial).

Colomer, Josep M. (1998). *La transición a la democracia: el modelo español* (Madrid: Anagrama).

Corbalán, Ana (2009). 'Reconstrucción del pasado histórico: nostalgia reflexiva en *Cuéntame cómo pasó*'. *Journal of Spanish Cultural Studies* 10 (3): 341–57.

Cruz Suárez, Juan Carlos and Martín Diana González (eds) (2012). *La memoria novelada II: ficcionalización, documentalismo y lugares de memoria en la narrativa memorialista española* (Bern: Peter Lang).

Cruz Suárez, Juan Carlos and Hans Lauge Hansen (eds) (2012). *La memoria novelada: hibridación de géneros y metaficción en la novela española sobre la guerra civil y el franquismo* (Bern: Peter Lang).

de Eusebio, Carmen (2013). 'Javier Cercas: "El pasado no es ajeno al presente, es una dimensión del presente"'. *Cuadernos hispanoamericanos* 753 (March): 105–16.

Delgado, Luisa Elena (2010). 'The Sound and the Red Fury: The Sticking Points of Spanish Nationalism'. *Journal of Spanish Cultural Studies* 11 (3–4): 263–76.

— (2014). *La nación singular. Fantasías de la normalidad democrática española* (Madrid: Siglo XXI).

Derrida, Jacques (1996). *Archive Fever: A Freudian Impression* (Chicago: University of Chicago Press).

Díaz, Susana (2013). 'La transición política como pretexto: *23-F. El día más difícil del Rey*'. *Zer* 18 (35): 165–90.

Díez Puertas, Emeterio (2003). '*Cuéntame cómo pasó* (2001–): la transición política, social y sentimental de los españoles', in Emeterio Díez Puertas (ed.), *Eduardo Ladrón de Guevara. Cuéntame cómo pasó. Querido maestro* (Madrid: Fundamentos), 101–11.

Divine, Susan (2011). '*Sangre a borbotones*: Rafael Reig and a New Understanding of City Future as City Past in Madrid'. *Clio* 40 (2): 235–58.

Edgerton, Gary R. (2001). 'Introduction', in Gary R. Edgerton and Peter C. Rollins (eds), *Television Histories: Shaping Collective Memory in the Media Age* (Lexington: University Press of Kentucky), 1–17.

Elkins, James (2003). 'What Does Peirce's Sign Theory Have to Say to Art History?' *Culture, Theory and Critique* 44 (1): 5–22.

Encarnación, Omar G. (2008). *Spanish Politics: Democracy after Dictatorship* (Cambridge: Polity).

— (2014). *Democracy without Justice in Spain: The Politics of Forgetting* (Philadelphia: University of Pennsylvania Press).

Escobedo, María (2011). 'El pasado nos persigue hasta que logra justar cuentas con nosotros'. *Cuadernos Hispanoamericanos* 731 (May): 89–96.

Estrada, Isabel M. (2013). *El documental cinematográfico y televisivo contemporáneo. Memoria, sujeto y formación de la identidad democrática española* (Woodbridge: Tamesis Books).

Fernández Zaurín, Luis (2008). 'Ignacio Martínez de Pisón: "Cuando uno escribe con claridad es porque ve los hechos con claridad"'. *El Ciervo* 57 (687): 33–35.

Foucault, Michel (2002). *Archaeology of Knowledge* (London: Routledge).

Frosh, Paul (2011). 'Television and the Imagination of Memory: *Life on Mars*', in Motti Neiger et al. (eds), *On Media Memory: Collective Memory in a New Media Age* (New York: Palgrave Macmillan), 117–31.

Fusi, Juan Pablo (1999). 'España: el fin del siglo XX', in Raymond Carr (ed.), *Visiones de fin de siglo* (Madrid: Taurus), 161–88.

Gilbert, Mark (1995). *The Italian Revolution: The End of Politics, Italian Style?* (Boulder: Westview Press).

Gitlin, Todd (2002). *Media Unlimited* (New York: Metropolitan Books).

Gómez-Montero, Javier (2007). *Memoria literaria de la Transición española* (Madrid: Iberoamericana).

Graham, Helen (2012). *The War and its Shadow: Spain's Civil War in Europe's Long Twentieth Century* (Eastbourne: Sussex Academic Press).

Gregg, Melissa and Gregory J. Seigworth (eds) (2010). *The Affect Theory Reader* (Durham: Duke University Press).

Grossberg, Lawrence (1997). *Dancing in Spite of Myself* (Durham, NC: Duke University Press).

Halbwachs, Maurice (1992). *On Collective Memory*. Ed. and trans. Lewis A. Coser (Chicago: University of Chicago Press).

Hart, Patricia (1987). *The Spanish Sleuth: The Detective in Spanish Fiction* (Lanham: Fairleigh Dickinson University Press).

Harvey, David (2007). *A Brief History of Neoliberalism* (Oxford: Oxford University Press).

Hoskins, Andrew (2001). 'New Memory: Mediating History'. *Historical Journal of Film, Radio and Television* 21 (4): 333–46.

Huyssen, Andreas (2000). 'Present Pasts: Media, Politics, Amnesia', *Public Culture* 12 (1): 21–38.

— (2003). *Present Pasts: Urban Palimpsests and the Politics of Memory* (Stanford: Stanford University Press).

Ibáñez Ehrlich, María-Teresa (2010). 'De héroes y realidades: John Dos Passos y Ernest Hemingway en *Enterrar a los muertos* de Ignacio Martínez de Pisón', in Christian von Tschilschke and Dagmar Schmelzer (eds), *Docuficción. Enlaces entre ficción y no ficción en la cultura española actual* (Madrid: Iberoamericana-Vervuert), 265–81.

Junquera, Natalia (2014). 'El Rey ante la muerte de Suárez: "Mi dolor es grande. Mi gratitud, permanente"'. *El País*, 23 March. http://politica.elpais.com/politica/2014/03/23/actualidad/1395588334_429118.html. Accessed 24 March 2014.

Kavka, Misha (2008). *Reality Television, Affect and Intimacy: Reality Matters* (New York: Palgrave Macmillan).

Kitch, C. (2002), 'Anniversary Journalism, Collective Memory and the Cultural Authority to Tell the Story of the American Past', *Journal of Popular Culture* 36 (1): 44–67.

Knutson, David (2006). 'Madrid postglobal: Rafael Reig y *Sangre a borbotones*', in Jorge H. Valdivieso and L. Teresa Valdivieso (eds), *Madrid: En la literatura y las artes* (Phoenix: Orbis), 56–61.

Labanyi, Jo (2000). 'History and Hauntology: Or, What Does One Do with the Ghosts of the Past? Reflections on Spanish Film and Fiction of the Post-Franco Period', in Joan Ramon Resina (ed.), *Disremembering the Dictatorship: The Politics of Memory in the Spanish Transition to Democracy* (Amsterdam: Rodopi), 65–82.

— (2008a). 'Entrevista Con Emilio Silva'. *Journal of Spanish Cultural Studies* 9 (2): 143–55.

— (2008b). 'The Politics of Memory in Contemporary Spain'. *Journal of Spanish Cultural Studies* 9: 119–25.

Labrador Méndez, Germán (2009). *Letras arrebatadas: poesía y química en la transición española* (Madrid: Devenir Ensayo).

Landsberg, Alison (2004). *Prosthetic Memory: The Transformation of American Remembrance in the Age of Mass Culture* (New York: Columbia University Press).

Life on Mars: The Complete Series (2009). ABC Studios.

Lobo, Ramón (2015). 'No podemos ser un país unitario, porque en realidad no lo hemos sido nunca'. Interview with José Enrique Ruiz-Domènec. *Eldiario.es*, 3 January. http://www.eldiario.es/politica/podemos-pais-unitario-realidad_0_341565946. html. Accessed 5 January 2015.

Loureiro, Ángel G (2008). 'Pathetic Arguments'. *Journal of Spanish Cultural Studies* 9 (2): 225–37.

Maginn, Alison (2003). "¿Más allá de la posmodernidad en la novela contemporánea española?: una lectura de *Ventajas de viajar en tren* por Antonio Orejudo Utrilla'. *Bulletin of Hispanic Studies* 80 (4): 537–51.

Marks, Laura U. (2000). 'Signs of the Time: Deleuze, Peirce, and the Documentary Image', in Gregory Flaxman (ed.), *The Brain is the Screen: Deleuze and the Philosophy of Cinema* (Minneapolis and London: University of Minnesota Press), 93–214.

Marsh, Steven (2015). 'Retrospective Future Perfect: History, Black Holes and Time Warps in the Films of Los Hijos and Luis López Carrasco'. *Journal of Spanish Cultures* 15 (3): 351–71.

Martín-Cabrera, Luis (2011). *Radical Justice: Spain and the Southern Cone beyond Market and State* (Lewisburg: Bucknell University Press).

Martin-Jones, David (2006). *Deleuze, Cinema and National Identity: Narrative Time in National Contexts* (Edinburgh: Edinburgh University Press).

Martínez, Guillem et al. (2012). *CT O La Cultura de La Transición. Crítica a 35 Años de Cultura Española* (Barcelona: Debolsillo).

Martinez de Pisón, Ignacio (2011). *El día de mañana* (Barcelona: Seix Barral).

Massumi, Brian (2002). *Parables for the Virtual: Movement, Affect, Sensation* (Durham: Duke University Press).

Medina, Alberto (2001). *Exorcismos de la memoria: políticas y poéticas de la melancolía en la España de la Transición* (Madrid: Ediciones Libertarias).

Merino, Eloy E. and H. Rosi Song (eds) (2005). *Traces of Contamination: Unearthing the Francoist Legacy in Contemporary Spanish Discourse* (Lewisburg, PA: Bucknell University Press).

Molinero, Carme (2010). 'La Transición y la "renuncia" a la recuperación de la "memoria democrática"'. *Journal of Spanish Cultural Studies* 11 (1): 33–52.

Morán, Gregorio (2014). *El cura y los mandarines. Historia no oficial del bosque de los letrados. Cultura y política en España 1962–1996* (Madrid: Akal).

Moreiras Menor, Cristina (2002). *Cultura herida: literatura y cine en la España democrática* (Madrid: Ediciones Libertarias).

Neiger, Motti, Oren Meyers, and Eyal Zanberg (2011). *On Media Memory: Collective Memory in a New Media Age* (London: Palgrave Macmillan).

O'Connor, John E. (1990). *Image as Artifact: The Historical Analysis of Film and Television* (Melbourne, FL: Krieger).

Orejudo, Antonio (2011). *Un momento de descanso* (Barcelona: Tusquets).

Palacio, Manuel (2014). *Las imágenes del cambio. Medios audiovisuales en las transiciones de la democracia* (Madrid: Biblioteca Nueva).

Pardo Torío, José Luis (2014). 'Padres e hijos: la Transición interminable'. *El País*, 2 October. http://elpais.com/elpais/2014/10/01/opinion/1412165074_715999.html. Accessed 1 October 2014.

Peirce, Charles Sanders (1960). *Collected Papers of Charles Sanders Peirce: Principles of Philosophy and Elements of Logic*. Ed. Charles Hartshorne, Paul Weiss, and Arthur Walter Burks (Cambridge, MA: Harvard University Press).

Pisters, Patricia (2012). *The Neuro-Image: A Deleuzian Film-Philosophy of Digital Screen Culture* (Stanford: Stanford University Press).

Prado, Benjamín (2011). *Operación Gladio* (Madrid: Alfaguara).

Prego, Victoria (1996). *Así se hizo la Transición* (Madrid: Plaza & Janés).

— (1999). *Diccionario de La Transición* (Barcelona: Mondadori).

Preston, Paul (1987). *The Triumph of Democracy in Spain* (London: Methuen).

— (2004). 'Las víctimas del franquismo y los historiadores', in Emilio Silva et al. (eds), *La memoria de los olvidados: un debate sobre el silencio de la represión franquista* (Valladolid: Ámbito), 13–21.

— (2012). *The Spanish Holocaust: Inquisition and Extermination in Twentieth-Century Spain* (London: Harper Press).

Reig, Rafael (2011). *Todo está perdonado* (Barcelona: Tusquets).

Resina, Joan Ramon (ed.) (2000). *Disremembering the Dictatorship: The Politics of Memory in the Spanish Transition to Democracy* (Amsterdam: Rodopi).

— (2000b). 'Short of Memory: The Reclamation of the Past since the Spanish Transition to Democracy', in Joan Ramon Resina (ed.), *Disremembering the Dictatorship: The Politics of Memory in the Spanish Transition to Democracy* (Amsterdam: Rodopi), 83–126.

Rosa Camacho, Isaac (2007). *¡Otra maldita novela sobre la guerra civil!* (Barcelona: Seix Barral).

Rosenstone, Robert A. (1994). *Revisioning History: Film and the Construction of a New Past* (Princeton: Princeton University Press).

Rueda Laffond, José Carlos and Carlota Coronado Ruiz (2009). *La mirada televisiva: ficción y representación histórica en España* (Madrid: Fragua).

Saltzman, Lisa (2006). *Making Memory Matter: Strategies of Remembrance in Contemporary Art* (Chicago: University of Chicago Press).

Sánchez-Biosca, Vicente (2006). *Cine de historia, cine de memoria: la representación y sus límites* (Madrid: Cátedra).

Sánchez León, Pablo (2004). 'Estigma y memoria de los jóvenes de la transición', in Emilio Silva et al. (eds), *La memoria de los olvidados: un debate sobre el silencio de la represión franquista* (Valladolid: Ámbito), 163–82.

Santamaría Colmenero, Sara (2012). 'Historia, testigo y nación en *Mala gente que camina* de Benjamín Prado', in Juan Carlos Cruz Suárez and Hans Lauge Hansen (eds), *La memoria novelada. Hibridación de géneros y metaficción en la novela española sobre la guerra civil y el franquismo (2000–2010)* (Bern: Peter Lang), 55–67.

Sanz Hoya, Julián (2013). 'La patria en los estadios. Fútbol, nación y franquismo', in Ferrán Archilés et al. (eds), *Nación y nacionalización. Una perspectiva europea comparada* (Valencia: Universitat de València), 275–301.

Sconce, Jeffrey (2004). 'What If? Charting Television's New Textual Boundaries', in Lynn Spigel and Jan Olsson (eds), *Television after TV: Essays on a Medium in Transition* (Durham, NC: Duke University Press), 93–112.

Serna, Justo (2011). 'Un hombre solo. Historia y virtud en *Anatomía de un instante*, de Javier Cercas'. *Historia Contemporánea* 23: 95–112.

Silverstone, Roger (1994). *Television and Everyday Life* (London: Routledge).

Smith, Paul Julian (2004). 'The Emotional Imperative: Almodóvar's *Hable con ella* and Televisión Española's *Cuéntame cómo pasó*'. *MLN* 119 (2): 363–75.

— (2006). *Spanish Visual Culture: Cinema, Television, Internet* (Manchester: Manchester University Press).

— (2009). *Spanish Screen Fiction: Between Cinema and Television* (Liverpool: Liverpool University Press).

— (2012). 'The Television Mini-Series as Historical Memory: The Case of *23-F, El día más difícil del Rey* (TVE-1, 2009)'. *Hispanic Issues On Line* 11: 52–63.

Sobchack, Vivian (1996). *The Persistence of History: Cinema, Television, and the Modern Event* (New York and London: Routledge).

Song, H. Rosi (2003). 'La producció del patriotisme constitucional', in *Les mentides del PP* (Barcelona: Angle Editorial): 26–41.

— (2005). 'El patriotismo constitucional o la dimensión mnemotécnica de una nación', in Joan Ramon Resina and Ulrich Winter (eds), *Casa encantada: lugares de memoria en la España constitucional (1975–2004)* (Madrid and Amsterdam: Vervuert Iberoamericana), 223–39.

— (2014). 'El intelectual español y el problema de la nación: del franquismo a la Constitución de 1978'. *Hispanic Research Journal* 15 (4): 345–59.

Stewart, Kathleen (2007). *Ordinary Affects* (Durham, NC: Duke University Press).

Sturken, Marita (1997). *Tangled Memories: The Vietnam War, the AIDS Epidemic, and the Politics of Remembering* (Los Angeles: University of California Press).

Subirats, Eduardo (1993). *Después de la lluvia: sobre la ambigua modernidad española* (Madrid: Temas de Hoy).

Trouillot, Michel-Rolph (2012). *Silencing the Past: Power and the Production of History* (Boston, MA: Beacon Press)

Trueba, David (2012). *Madrid 1987* (Barcelona: Anagrama).

Urbano, Pilar (2014). *La gran desmemoria. Lo que Suárez olvidó y el Rey prefiere no recordar* (Madrid: Planeta).

Urioste de, Carmen (2009). *Novela y sociedad en la España contemporánea (1994–2009)* (Madrid: Editorial Fundamentos).

Valenzuela, Alfredo (1998). 'El arte de la gamberrada'. *Renacimiento* 19–20 (Spring): 84–85.

Valis, Noël Maureen (ed.) (2007). *Teaching Representations of the Spanish Civil War* (New York: The Modern Language Association of America).

Van Dijck, José (2007). *Mediated Memories in the Digital Age* (Stanford: Stanford University Press).

Vázquez Montalbán, Manuel [1985] (2005). *Crónica sentimental de la transición* (Barcelona: Debolsillo).

— (1989). *Historias de política ficción* (Barcelona: Planeta).

— (1996). *Un polaco en la corte del Rey Juan Carlos* (Barcelona: Alfaguara).

— (1998). *La literatura en la construcción de la ciudad democrática* (Barcelona: Letras de Crítica).

Von Tschilschke, Christian and Dagmar Schmelzer (eds) (2010). *Docuficción: enlaces entre ficción y no-ficción en la cultura española actual* (Madrid: Vervuert).

Vilarós, Teresa M. (1998). *El mono del desencanto. Una crítica cultural de la transición española, 1973–1993* (Barcelona: Siglo Veintiuno).

Wetherell, Margaret (2012). *Affect and Emotion: A New Social Science Understanding* (London: SAGE Publications).

Williams, Linda (2011). 'Ethnographic Imaginary: The Genesis and Genius of *The Wire*'. *Critical Inquiry* 38 (Autumn): 208–26.

Williams, Raymond (1977). *Marxism and Literature* (Oxford: Oxford University Press).

Winter, Ulrich (2010). 'De la memoria recuperada a la memoria performativa. Hacia una nueva semántica cultural de la memoria histórica en España a comienzos del siglo XXI', in Christian von Tschilschke and Dagmar Schmelzer (eds), *Docuficción. Enlaces entre ficción y no ficción en la cultura española actual* (Madrid: Iberoamericana-Vervuert), 249–64.

Yelo, Antonio (2013). 'Gregorio Morán: "Los padres de la transición eran absolutamente impresentables"'. *Jot Down Cultural Magazine*, December. http://www.jotdown.es/2013/12/gregorio-moran-los-padres-de-la-transicion-eran-absolutamente-impresentables/. Accessed 1 August 2014.

Zelizer, B. (1995). 'Reading the Past against the Grain: The Shape of Memory Studies', *Critical Studies in Mass Communication* 12: 214–39.

Index